Transnational Advocacy Networks and Human Rights Law

This book asks the fundamental question of how new human rights issues emerge in the human rights debate. To answer this, the book focuses on nongovernmental organizations (NGOs) and on the case study of LGBTI (lesbian, gay, bisexual, transgender and intersex) rights.

The work argues that the way in which NGOs decide their advocacy, conceptualise human rights violations and strategically present legal analysis to advance LGBTI human rights shapes the human rights debate. To demonstrate this, the book analyses three data sets: NGO written statements submitted to the United Nations Human Rights Council, NGO oral statements delivered during the Universal Periodic Review and 36 semi-structured interviews with NGO staff. Data are analysed with a combination of quantitative and qualitative approaches to discover what issues are most important for LGBTI networks (issue emergence) and how these issues are framed (issue framing). Along with NGO efficiency in lobbying for the emergence of new human rights standards, the book inevitably discusses important questions related to NGOs' accountability and democratic legitimacy. The book thus asks whether the right to marry is important for LGBTI advocates working transnationally, because this right is particularly controversial among activists and LGBTI communities, especially in non-Western contexts.

Giulia Dondoli obtained her PhD in Human Rights Law from Te Piringa, Faculty of Law, University of Waikato, New Zealand.

Transnational Advocacy Networks and Human Rights Law

Emergence and Framing of Gender Identity and Sexual Orientation

Giulia Dondoli

Routledge
Taylor & Francis Group

LONDON AND NEW YORK

First published 2019
by Routledge
2 Park Square, Milton Park, Abingdon, Oxon OX14 4RN

and by Routledge
52 Vanderbilt Avenue, New York, NY 10017

First issued in paperback 2020

Routledge is an imprint of the Taylor & Francis Group, an informa business

British Library Cataloguing-in-Publication Data
A catalogue record for this book is available from the British Library

Library of Congress Cataloging-in-Publication Data
Names: Dondoli, Giulia, author.
Title: Transnational Advocacy Networks and Human Rights
    Law: Emergence and Framing of Gender Identity and Sexual
    Orientation/By Giulia Dondoli.
Description: New York, NY: Routledge, 2019. | Includes
    bibliographical references and index.
Identifiers: LCCN 2018044937 | ISBN 9781138387508 (hbk)
Subjects: LCSH: Gender identity—Law and legislation. | Human
    rights—International cooperation. | Non-Governmental
    Organizations. | Sexual minorities—Civil rights.
Classification: LCC K3243. D66 2019 | DDC 342.08/7—dc23
LC record available at https://lccn.loc.gov/2018044937

ISBN 13: 978-0-367-66206-6 (pbk)
ISBN 13: 978-1-138-38750-8 (hbk)

Typeset in Galliard
by Apex CoVantage, LLC

Contents

Detailed Contents

Documents

United Nations Human Rights Council

Nongovernmental organizations' written statements

Other United Nations' documents

United Nations Human Rights Committee

Domestic and international case law

European Union

Domestic legislation

Treaties and protocols

Figures

Acknowledgements

I have conducted most of the research for this book, during my PhD programme at the University of Waikato. I want to thank the chief supervisor of my PhD thesis, Dr Claire Breen, who mentored me to become a skilled and professional researcher. I also want to thank my second supervisor, Dr Andrew Erueti, and all the academic staff of the University of Waikato who read and commented upon my work, in particular, Dr Lynda Johnson, whose advice in the later stage of my PhD has been precious. I am thankful to the examiners of my PhD thesis, Dr Miriam Smith and Dr Kelly Kollman, for carefully reading my works and providing insightful comments and feedback.

I thank the University of Waikato and Te Piringa – Faculty of Law for their financial support. I was awarded the University of Waikato Doctoral Scholarship and Doctoral Completions Scholarship which allowed me to focus on my research. Te Piringa has also awarded me three travel grants to attend conferences abroad, where I could share my research with a wider audience and connect with scholars working in my field. Participating in these conferences was crucial for me to refine my thinking and to test my arguments. I would also like to thank all the administrative staff of the university and the faculty for their kindness and help.

I met some amazing individuals during my studies at the University of Waikato. I want to thank the law postgraduate students – in particular Dee Holmes and Dr Rogena Sterling, who kindly read my manuscript – the members of the Rainbow Staff and Student Alliance, and the members of the Postgraduate Student Association for their friendship and camaraderie. Moreover, I want to thank the human rights advocates who I interviewed for this research. Without them, this book would not have been possible.

Finally, I want to thank my family and friends, in Italy and in New Zealand, whose support and love have been unmatched. To my parents, my brother and my closest friends in Italy, thank you for tolerating the emotional burden of this great physical distance. I know that my choice to move to New Zealand was harder on you than on me. A special thank you to my partner, you believed in me more than anybody else has ever done, and part of who I am today is thanks to your unconditional trust in my abilities.

Abbreviations

ACPD	Action Canada for Population and Development
ALMA	Australian Lesbian Medical Association
ARC	Allied Rainbow Communities International
ASEAN	Association of South East Asia Nation
CAL	Coalition of African Lesbians
CAT	Committee against Torture
CESCR	Committee on Economic, Social and Cultural Rights
C-Fam	Catholic Family and Human Rights Institute
CHLN	Canadian HIV/AIDS Legal Network
COC	Cultural and Recreational Centre
ECOSOC	Economic and Social Council
EEG	Eastern European Group
EU	European Union
FELGTB	Federación Estatal de Lesbianas, Gais, Transexuales y Bisexuales
FIDH	International Federation for Human Rights
FLHR	Finnish League for Human Rights
GRULAC	Latin America and Caribbean Group
HR	Human Rights
HR Comm	United Nations Human Rights Committee
HR Council	United Nations Human Rights Council
HRW	Human Rights Watch
ICCPR	International Covenant on Civil and Political Rights
ICJ	International Commission of Jurists
ICSE	International Committee for Sexual Equality
IGLHRC	International Gay and Lesbian Human Rights Committee
ILGA	International Lesbian, Gay, Bisexual, Trans and Intersex Association
INGOs	International Nongovernmental Organizations
J4S	Justice for Sisters
JOH	Jerusalem Open Society
LGBTI	Lesbian, Gay, Bisexual, Transgender, Intersex
MDGs	Millennium Development Goals
NAMBLA	North American Man Boy Love Association
NGO	Nongovernmental organization

OHCHR	Office of the High Commissioner for Human Rights
OIC	Organization of Islamic Conference
RFSL	Swedish Federation for Lesbian, Gay, Bisexual, Transgender and Queer Rights
SDGs	Sustainable Development Goals
SOGIE	Sexual orientation, gender identity and expression
SOGII	Sexual orientation, gender identity and intersex status
TAN	Transnational Advocacy Network
TRP	Transnational Radical Party
UNDP	United Nations Development Program
UNESCO	United Nations Educational, Scientific and Cultural Organization
UNICEF	United Nations Children's Fund
UPR	Universal Periodic Review
UUA	Unitarian Universalist Association
WEOG	Western European and Others Group
WHO	World Health Organization
WLSR	World League for Sexual Reform
YIFoS	Youth Interfaith Forum on Sexuality
YPs	Yogyakarta Principles
YPs+10	Yogyakarta Principle plus Ten

1 Introduction

Introduction: *Joslin v New Zealand*

In the 1990s, a group of activists from New Zealand mobilised to ask domestic courts to recognise the right of a person to marry a same-sex spouse as a consequence of the recognition of their "full and equal treatment before the law".[1] In 1998, the New Zealand Court of Appeal decided in *Quilter v Attorney-General* that the exclusion of same-sex couples from marriage was not an unlawful discrimination because the then Marriage Act 1955 forbade same-sex marriage.[2]

The following year, applicants in the domestic case – Juliet Joslin and Jennifer Rowan – and their legal advisor brought their claims before the United Nations Human Rights Committee (HR Comm), in *Joslin and Others v New Zealand* ('*Joslin*').[3] Joslin, Rowan and their legal advisor planned to form an NGO (non-governmental organization). The three of them involved a few more lesbian, gay and bisexual (LGB) people, and they set their first meeting. I interviewed the legal advisor for *Joslin* and they remember that, during that first meeting, it was suggested they consult with New Zealand LGB communities to see if the right to marry was what they wanted. A concern was that some LGB people might see the marriage institution as an archaic, conservative and heteronormative institution.[4] However, consulting with LGB communities would have been costly, while the core group wanted to focus on what they believed was right: marriage equality.

---

1   Nigel Christie "The New Zealand Same-Sex Marriage Case: From Aotearoa to the United Nations" in Robert Wintemute and Mads Tønnesson Andenæs (eds) *Legal Recognition of Same-Sex Partnerships: A Study of National, European, and International Law* (Hart Pub, Oxford, Portland, 2001) 317 at 320. See also, Olivia Rundle "Following the Legislative Leaders: Judicial Recognition of Same Sex Couples in Australia and New Zealand" in Pietro Pustorino, Luca Paladini, and Daniele Gallo (eds) *Same-Sex Couples before National, Supranational and International Jurisdictions* (Springer, Heidelberg, 2014) 127 at 145.

2   *Quilter v Attorney General* 1 NZLR 323, 1998.

3   *Joslin and Others v New Zealand* HR Comm 902/99, A/57/40 at 214, 17 July 2002.

4   See for example, Verta A Taylor and Mary Bernstein "Marital Discord: Understanding the Contested Place of Marriage in the Lesbian and Gay Movement" in Verta A Taylor and Mary Bernstein (eds) *Marrying Kind? Debating Same-Sex Marriage within the Lesbian and Gay Movement* (University of Minnesota Press, Minneapolis, 2013) 1.

Therefore, Joslin, Rowan and their legal advisor dropped the idea of creating an official NGO, yet continue their advocacy work as a small informal group with some people occasionally involved for fundraising purposes. In the interviewee's opinion, a small group helped them to set their vision, goals and standards.[5]

Before the HR Council, the applicants and their legal advisor argued that the expression "men and women" in Article 23(2) of the International Covenant on Civil and Political Rights (ICCPR) means that men as a group and women as a group have the right to marry, not necessarily that a man may marry a woman and vice versa.[6] The HR Comm did not accept such a view and said that the wording of "men and women" means different sex couples,[7] therefore confirming that the right to marry, as enshrined in Article 23, refers only to different sex couples.[8]

The interviewee reports that even though they were uncertain as to whether the *Joslin* communication would have been a success, the group still engaged in such strategic litigation at the HR Comm to raise political awareness on marriage equality on the national level.[9] As one NGO scholar, Hodson, argues, activists "will not necessarily perceive a lost case as a failure if, for example, it contributes to social change through public debate or if it highlights 'how ridiculous the law is' ".[10] The advocacy around *Joslin* is a good example of domestic activists reaching out to an international organization to keep the momentum of the marriage equality debate. Despite the legal defeats, the use of the national courts and the HR Comm created a broader frame of advocacy that eventually led to the legalisation of marriage equality in New Zealand. Civil unions were legalised in 2004,[11] then marriage equality in 2013.[12]

I chose to start with this brief story of the battle for marriage and family equality in New Zealand because it raises two important themes for this book. First, when activists and NGOs work at the local level, and when they feel they have exhausted the channel to lobby their governments, they reach out to international allies, in this case, the HR Comm, to pressure their government from above and from below.[13] Such international advocacy action can produce consequences

---

5 Interview with an independent activist in New Zealand (Face-to-face, 20 March 2015).

6 *Joslin and Others v New Zealand*, above n 3, at [3.8]. See also, Nigel Christie "Access to Marriage for Same-Sex Couples in New Zealand: A Matter of Human Rights" (PhD, The University of Waikato, 2009) at 374–384.

7 Luca Paladini "Same-Sex Couples before Quasi-Jurisdictional Bodies: The Case of the UN Human Rights Committee" in Daniele Gallo, Pietro Pustorino, and Luca Paladini (eds) *Same-Sex Couples before National, Supranational and International Jurisdictions* (Springer, Heidelberg, 2014) 533 at 545.

8 *Joslin and Others v New Zealand*, above n 3, at [8.2].

9 Independent activist in New Zealand, above n 5.

10 Loveday Hodson *NGOs and the Struggle for Human Rights in Europe* (Hart Publishing, Oxford, Portland, 2011) at 138.

11 Civil Union Act 2004 (2004) (New Zealand).

12 Marriage (Definition of Marriage) Act 2013 (2013) (New Zealand).

13 See especially, Margaret E Keck and Kathryn Sikkink *Activists beyond Borders: Advocacy Networks in International Politics* (Cornell University Press, Ithaca, 1998).

both in the domestic arena and in international human rights law. In the New Zealand case, the activists did not set up an NGO because they believed that maintaining a small decision-making core group would have been beneficial for setting their goals. This leads to the second theme.

The second theme raised by this account is that activists might have different views on issues and different advocacy agendas. Because activists and NGOs can shape human rights discourse with their advocacy actions, it is important to understand how these NGOs choose advocacy issues and how they decide how to strategically frame such issues as human rights claims.[14] Understanding which issues to advocate for, however, is not always straightforward. The *Joslin* example highlights that marriage and family equality are controversial topics, and lesbian, gay, bisexual, transgender and intersex (LGBTI) activists do not always agree on these matters. Sometimes a compromise can be found, yet as seen in *Joslin*, sometimes it cannot.

This book develops the themes of transnational advocacy and issue emergence and framing. The book researches the way in which the NGOs, as part of transnational advocacy networks (TANs), create meaning, shape ideas, conceptualise human rights violations and present their legal analysis to advance LGBTI people's rights. Understanding what issues are advocated by NGOs, and how these issues are framed, helps clarify why some issues emerge and consolidate in the international human rights law debate, and subsequently they become human rights standards. Before formulating the research questions and laying down the arguments of this research, the next section provides some context and definitions for the key topics addressed in the book.

Context, definitions and caveat

This book investigates LGBTI TANs advocacy at the UN, and to do so it analyses three bodies of data: (i) NGOs' written statements submitted to the HR Council, (ii) NGOs' oral statements delivered during the Universal Periodic Review (UPR) process and (iii) interviews with NGO staff members. While a much broader discussion of the methodology and the limitations of this study is presented in the appendix of this book,[15] this section provides a brief legal, historical and contextual background for the analysis. Many scholars discuss same-sex sexual attraction, transgenderism and transvestitism, and intersexuality in history,[16]

---

14 See especially, Clifford Bob *The International Struggle for New Human Rights* (University of Pennsylvania Press, Philadelphia, 2009).

15 See Appendix 1.

16 Some examples are William N Eskridge "A History of Same-Sex Marriage" (1993) 79 *Virginia Law Review* 1419; Colin Spencer *Homosexuality: A History* (Fourth Estate, London, 1996); Eva Cantarella *Bisexuality in the Ancient World* (2nd ed, Yale University Press, New Haven, 2002); Leila J Rupp *Sapphistries a Global History of Love between Women* (New York University Press, New York, 2009); Robert Aldrich *Gay Life and Culture: A World History* (Thames and Hudson, London, 2010); Charles Hupperts "Homosexuality in Greece and

in religion,[17] and in the law.[18] This section does not aim to compete with such works; instead, it aims to present the key concepts for the book.

Intersex status and a note on the use of acronyms

The language about gender and sexuality varies over time, across places and among cultures. Moreover, there is a plethora of acronyms used by both scholars and activists, sometimes referred to as the alphabet soup.[19] Because this book focuses on international human rights law, I use the acronyms LGBTI and SOGII (as in sexual orientation, gender identity and intersex status), whose uses are consolidated within the work of the UN and in transnational advocacy.

However, some NGOs addressed in this study, such as International Gay and Lesbian Human Rights Commission (ILGHRC – now OutRight Action International, hereafter 'OutRight'), give minimal attention to intersex issues,[20] and some intersex activists do not feel part of the LGBT movement and believe that alliance with the disability movement better serves their cause.[21] Moreover, intersex is a rising issue at the UN and many documents analysed in this book, especially the older ones, do not mention intersexuality. Therefore, when I analyse NGO and UN documents, I sometimes use 'SOGI' and 'LGBT', therefore lacking the 'I' because I follow what terminology NGOs and the UN use, which occasionally does not mention intersex people.

Human rights: between hard- and soft-law

SOGII are not mentioned in the Universal Declaration of Human Rights, in the ICCPR or other UN covenants and conventions. LGBTI human rights have evolved through resolutions, recommendations, international adjudications and concluding observations. Many states question that LGBTI rights provisions are even human rights law. For example, in February 2016, at the occasion of

Rome" in Robert Aldrich (ed) *Gay Life and Culture: A World History* (Thames and Hudson, London, 2010) 29 at 35.

17 Jeffrey S Siker *Homosexuality and Religion: An Encyclopaedia* (Greenwood Press, Westport, 2007); Paul Johnson and Robert M Vanderbeck *Law, Religion and Homosexuality* (Routledge, Abingdon, New York, 2014); Achim Hildebrandt "Christianity, Islam and Modernity: Explaining Prohibitions on Homosexuality in UN Member States" (2015) 63(4) *Political Studies* 852.

18 Mary Bernstein, Anna-Maria Marshall, and Scott Barclay (eds) *Queer Mobilizations: LGBT Activists Confront the Law* (New York University Press, New York, 2009); Paul Johnson *Homosexuality and the European Court of Human Rights* (Routledge, Abingdon, 2013).

19 Susan Stryker *Transgender History* (Seal Press, Berkeley, 2008), at 21. One example is LGBTIQQA, where QQA stands for queers questioning and allies.

20 Ryan R Thoreson *Transnational LGBT Activism: Working for Sexual Rights Worldwide* (University of Minnesota Press, Minneapolis, 2014) at 88.

21 Julie Greenberg and Robert Stam *Intersexuality and the Law: Why Sex Matters* (New York University Press, New York, 2012) at 5.

unveiling new stamps at the UN to promote the Free & Equal campaign,[22] the chairman of the African Group wrote a letter to the Secretary General of the UN asking for the event to be cancelled because the African Group "strongly rejected any attempt to undermine the international human rights system by seeking to impose concepts . . . that falls outside the internationally agreed human rights legal framework".[23]

One of the reasons for this resistance is because the documents that enshrine LGBTI human rights protection are 'soft-law' instruments. Soft-law is often considered non-law, or less than hard-law because states are less inclined to comply with them. Indeed, hard-law norms, like international treaties and international custom, are binding norms,[24] while soft-law is defined as "nonbinding norms that set forth non-obligatory but highly recommended standards of state conduct",[25] such as HR Council resolutions; and as "those nonbinding rules or instruments that interpret or inform our understanding of binding legal rules",[26] such as HR Comm's views and general comments.

Some authors question the effectiveness of the human rights treaties (hard-law) because states are highly internationally pressured to ratify human rights treaties, but since the violation of such treaties has little consequences, they do not have strong incentives to actually make domestic changes to comply.[27] The impact of soft-law can be considered even lower as states might have fewer incentives to internalise soft-law because of its 'softness'. Still, LGBTI NGOs can benefit from advocating for soft-law provisions because soft-law can produce some legal and political consequences.

First, regarding the legal consequences, non-binding documents, for example General Assembly resolutions, can accelerate the process of consolidation of international custom,[28] and international courts and quasi-judicial bodies' views

---

22 United Nations News Service Section "New Stamps Promoting LGBT Equality Worldwide Unveiled at UN" (4 February 2016) UN News Centre <https://news.un.org/en/story/2016/02/521612-new-stamps-promoting-lgbt-equality-worldwide-unveiled-un> (Retrieved 26 July 2018).

23 A/70/738 *Letter Dated 3 February 2016 from the Permanent Representative of Swaziland to the United Nations Addressed to the Secretary-General* (General Assembly, 2016) at 1.

24 Dinah L Shelton *Commitment and Compliance: The Role of Non-Binding Norms in the International Legal System* (Oxford University Press, Oxford, 2000) at 6.

25 H Victor Condé *An Encyclopaedia of Human Rights in the United States* (2nd ed, 2011) Soft-law.

26 Andrew T Guzman and Timothy Meyer "International Soft-law" (2010) 2(1) *The Journal of Legal Analysis* 171 at 174.

27 Oona A Hathaway "Do Human Rights Treaties Make a Difference?" (2002) 111 *The Yale Law Journal* 1935 at 2020; Emilie M Hafner-Burton and Kiyoteru Tsutsui "Human Rights in a Globalizing World: The Paradox of Empty Promises" (2005) 110(5) *American Journal of Sociology* 1373. See in general, Eric Neumayer "Do International Human Rights Treaties Improve Respect for Human Rights?" (2005) 49(6) *The Journal of Conflict Resolution* 925; Wade M Cole "Mind the Gap: State Capacity and the Implementation of Human Rights Treaties" (2015) 69(2) *International Organization* 405.

28 Rosalyn Higgins *Problems and Process: International Law and How We Use It* (Clarendon Press, Oxford, 1994) at 23. See also, Donald R Rothwell "The General Assembly Ban on

on LGBTI issues can produce legal effects also for the states that are not part of the dispute.[29] Second, regarding political consequences, when states enter in a soft-law agreement they promise to maintain a certain conduct, and if they fail to do so, the international community is less likely to believe the state's future promises.[30] NGOs take advantage of this type of political outcome because part of NGOs' advocacy relies on the 'name and shame' strategies, which means that NGOs investigate human rights violation to expose the gap between states' international commitments (soft or hard) and the actual human rights practices at the domestic level.

In other words, Abbott and Snidal explain that NGOs "generally seek hard legal arrangement that reflect their particular interests and values, but these demands often conflict with those of other private actors and governments".[31] In these circumstances, soft-law provisions help find an agreement between competing interests by providing compromises among governments, among non-state actors, and between governments and non-state actors. Therefore, soft-law provisions might be more achievable as a compromise solution. At the same time, NGOs might have interest in promoting soft-law norms by which to hold states accountable, rather than having no provisions at all.[32]

In sum, NGOs can pressure international organizations and states to develop new human rights standards and, in doing so, they contribute to a broader framework of action that leads to legal changes. However, it has to be acknowledged that human rights evolution is a complex and multi-causal phenomenon. It is not possible to pinpoint the exact cause-consequence relation between the NGOs' advocacy and the evolution of human rights standards because NGOs' advocacy is only one of the factors that influence these dynamics. In particular, the study of the drafting processes addressed in this book has proven challenging. It was not always possible to find a clear cause-effect connection between LGBTI TANs' advocacy and the response of the UN. One limitation was due to the fact that NGOs' advocacy often happens informally over numerous conversations between activists and governmental delegates. When possible, and especially thanks to the interviewees' answers, I was able to highlight the correlation between LGBTI and religious/conservative TANs' lobbying actions and LGBTI issues framing. Other times, such connections were less clear.

This book focuses on two keys human rights issues: the right to non-discrimination and the right to marry. These rights are addressed next, in turn.

Driftnet Fishing" in Dinah L Shelton (ed) *Commitment and Compliance: The Role of Non-Binding Norms in the International Legal System* (Oxford University Press, Oxford, 2000) 121 at 121.

29 Andrew T Guzman and Timothy Meyer, above n 26, at 212; Laurence R Helfer and Erik Voeten "International Courts as Agents of Legal Change: Evidence from LGBT Rights in Europe" (2014) 68(1) *International Organization* 77 at 105.

30 Andrew T Guzman and Timothy Meyer, above n 26, at 195–196.

31 Kenneth W Abbott and Duncan Snidal "Hard and Soft Law in International Governance" (2000) 54(3) *International Organization* 421 at 455.

32 At 452.

Prohibition of discrimination

Article 26 of the ICCPR reads:[33]

> All persons are equal before the law and are entitled without any discrimination to the equal protection of the law. In this respect, the law shall prohibit any discrimination and guarantee to all persons equal and effective protection against discrimination on any ground such as race, colour, sex, language, religion, political or other opinion, national or social origin, property, birth or other status.

Therefore, Article 26 of the ICCPR is a standalone equality principle that goes beyond the scope of the ICCPR,[34] and it includes both the prohibition of discrimination and an obligation for states to actively take measures against discrimination. This means that states shall not only avoid discrimination, but they also must take positive measures to protect vulnerable groups from discrimination.

In addition, Article 2(1) of the ICCPR urges the state parties to recognise the rights enclosed in the ICCPR to all individuals "without distinction of any kind, such as race, colour, sex, language, religion, political or other opinion, national or social origin, property, birth or other status".[35] In other words, Article 2(1) is an accessory prohibition of discrimination to ensure that all the rights enclosed in the ICCPR are enjoyed by all individuals, without discrimination. Indeed, the prohibition of discrimination is a fundamental principle of international human rights law because it is the 'key' to interpreting all other international human rights principles. Without the prohibition of discrimination on the grounds of SOGII, any other human rights norm could be discretionally denied to LGBTI people.[36]

As notable, neither Article 26 nor Article 2(1) explicitly mentions SOGII as prohibited ground of discrimination. The prohibition of discrimination on the grounds of SOGII has been developed by interpretation and through soft-law instruments.

In the 1980s and 1990s, the prohibition of discrimination on the grounds of SOGII has been treated inconsistently among UN organs. In 1983, the Economic and Social Council (ECOSOC) promoted a report titled *The Legal and Social Problems of Sexual Minorities*, debated within the Sub-Committee on Prevention of Discrimination and Protection of Minorities. NGOs, such as Minority

---

33 International Covenant on Civil and Political Rights, United Nations (opened for signature 16 December 1966, entered into force 23 March 1976) Article 26.

34 Manfred Nowak *UN Covenant on Civil and Political Rights: CCPR Commentary* (2nd ed, NP Engel, Kehl, Arlington, 2005) at 605.

35 International Covenant on Civil and Political Rights, United Nations (opened for signature 16 December 1966, entered into force 23 March 1976) Article 2(1).

36 Debra L DeLaet "Don't Ask, Don't Tell: Where Is the Protection Against Sexual Orientation Discrimination in International Human Rights Law" (1997) 7 *Law & Sexuality: Rev Lesbian, Gay, Bisexual & Transgender Legal Issues* 31 at 53.

Rights Group, submitted information on sexual minorities, but the ECOSOC's report was rather superficial and "failed to reflect the concerns identified by advocates of equality for sexual minorities".[37] In 1989, the UN missed another opportunity to take a position on SOGII discrimination, when the HR Comm released General Comment 18 on non-discrimination, without mentioning SOGII discrimination.[38]

In 1993, during the World Conference on Human Rights held in Vienna, some states' delegates, Australia, Austria, Canada, Germany and the Netherlands, made positive references to sexual orientation issues. Canada proposed adding "sexual orientation" to the list of grounds for prohibition of discrimination in the final statement of the Vienna Declaration and Programme of Action.[39] As is a recurring theme in the book, a number of states brought up concerns regarding marriage and family equality to block any reference to the prohibition of discrimination on the grounds of sexual orientation. Indeed, Singapore responded that same-sex sexual relationships are a matter of lifestyle choice and that right to marry is only for different sex couples. Eventually, because the delegates were not able to find agreement on the matter, the prohibition of discrimination statement was redrafted without mentioning any listed ground of prohibited discrimination.[40]

One year later, in 1994, the HR Comm stated in *Toonen v Australia* ('*Toonen*') that in Articles 2(1) (prohibition of discrimination) and 26 (equality before the law) of the ICCPR, the word "sex" is to be read as also encompassing the expression "sexual orientation".[41] Subsequently, the HR Comm repeated in *Joslin* that the prohibition of discrimination on the grounds of "sex" in Article 26 also encompasses "sexual orientation".[42] On the other hand, other UN committees locate "sexual orientation" within "other status".[43] The most prominent example being the 2009 Committee on Economic, Social and Cultural Rights General Comment 20 on non-discrimination, which clarifies that the expression "other status" includes sexual orientation and gender identity.[44] This inconsistency between the HR Comm and other UN committees "may potentially

---

37 Nicole LaViolette and Sandra Whitworth "No Safe Haven: Sexuality as a Universal Human Right and Lesbian and Gay Activism in International Politics" (1994) 23(3) *Millennium: Journal of International Studies* 563 at 572; E/CN.4/Sub.2/1988/31 *The Legal and Social Problems of Sexual Minorities* (Comm on HR, 1987).

38 HRI/GEN/1/Rev.9 (Vol I) *General Comment No 18: Non-discrimination* (1989).

39 A/CONF.157/23 *Vienna Declaration and Programme of Action* (General Assembly, 1993).

40 Douglas Sanders "Getting Lesbian and Gay Issues on the International Human Rights Agenda" (1996) 18 *Human Rights Quarterly* 67 at 90.

41 *Toonen v Australia* HR Comm CCPR/C/50/D/488/1992, 31 March 1994, at [8.7].

42 *Joslin and Others v New Zealand* above 3, at Appendix.

43 Michael O'Flaherty and John Fisher "Sexual Orientation, Gender Identity and International Human Rights Law: Contextualising the Yogyakarta Principles" (2008) 8(2) *Human Rights Law Review* 207 at 215.

44 E/C.12/GC/20 *General Comment No 20 Non-discrimination in Economic, Social and Cultural Rights (Art 2, para 2, of the International Covenant on Economic, Social and Cultural Rights)* (CESCR, 2009) at [32].

generate misunderstanding about the nature of the discrimination".[45] Finally, the HR Council expressed grave concerns and strongly deplored acts of violence and discrimination against individuals because of their SOGI in 2011,[46] 2014[47] and 2016,[48] concerns echoed by the Special Rapporteur on LGBT issues in 2017.[49]

The prohibition of discrimination of LGBTI individuals is a politically controversial issue.[50] Even more controversial is the prohibition of discrimination on grounds of SOGII in connection with the right to marry. LGBTI people's right to marry and its controversial nature are addressed next.

Marriage equality debate: pro, against and neither

This book discusses marriage equality and, to a lesser extent, family equality. The legal definitions of both 'marriage' and 'family' are challenging because international human rights treaties and conventions do not provide any useful definition of marriage and family, and they are also heteronormative.[51] For this book I refer to "[m]arriage, for civil purposes, [as] the lawful union of two persons to the exclusion of all others",[52] "regardless of their sex, sexual orientation, or gender identity"[53] and intersex status. Moreover, I define the members of the family as the spouse; the civil partner; the direct descendant, dependent of the spouse or the civil partner; and the direct ascendant, dependent of the spouse or the civil partner.[54]

---

45 Elena Abrusci "A Tale of Convergence? Discrimination Based on Sexual Orientation in Regional Human Rights Bodies and the Human Rights Committee" (2017) 35(3) *Nordic Journal of Human Rights* 240 at 255.

46 A/HRC/RES/17/19 *Human Rights, Sexual Orientation and Gender Identity* (HR Council, 2011).

47 A/HRC/RES/27/32 *Human Rights, Sexual Orientation and Gender Identity* (HR Council, 2014).

48 A/HRC/RES/32/2 *Protection Against Violence and Discrimination Based on Sexual Orientation and Gender Identity* (HR Council, 2016).

49 A/HRC/35/36 *Report of the Independent Expert on Protection Against Violence and Discrimination Based on Sexual Orientation and Gender Identity* (HR Council, 2017) at [66(a)].

50 Frederick Cowell and Angelina Milon "Decriminalisation of Sexual Orientation through the Universal Periodic Review" (2012) 12(2) *Human Rights Law Review* 341 at 344; Joel Voss "Contesting Sexual Orientation and Gender Identity at the UN Human Rights Council" (2018) 19 *Human Rights Review* 1.

51 Stevi Jackson "Interchanges: Gender, Sexuality and Heterosexuality: The Complexity (and Limits) of Heteronormativity" (2006) 7(1) *Feminist Theory* 105 at 107; Paul Johnson "Challenging the Heteronormativity of Marriage: The Role of Judicial Interpretation and Authority" (2011) 20(3) *Social & Legal Studies* 349 at 350.

52 Civil Marriage Act 2005 (Canada) at [2].

53 Marriage Act 1955 (2013) (New Zealand) at [2.1].

54 European Union Directive 2004/38/EC on the Right of Citizens of the Union and Their Family Members to Move and Reside Freely within the Territory of the Member States (2004), Article 2.

Marriage equality is a highly debated topic, as it is at the same time too radical and too conservative.[55] For religious/conservative scholars and activists, LGBTI couples' marriages would disrupt the 'traditional' heterosexual family,[56] while some queer/feminist scholars and activists criticise LGBTI couples' marriage institutions for still being based on heteronormative and patriarchal understanding of couples and sexual monogamy.[57]

Even though the international law is slowly moving towards weakening the linkage between marriage and family,[58] in many states' domestic legislation family rights are still deeply connected with the marriage status. Some opponents of marriage and family equality aim to speak for the wellbeing of children raised in LGBTI households, who are deemed to be disadvantaged, as opposed to children raised in heterosexual households, and "less traditionally gender-typed".[59] At the same time, some LGBTI rights advocates and scholars argue that the SOGII of the parents does not hurt the children's wellbeing[60] and that children are better off when their relationships with their LGBTI parents are legally recognised.[61] In claiming so, they attract the disapproval of some queer and feminist scholars, who criticise LGBTI activists' focus on marriage and family equality, at the expense of an advocacy agenda addressed towards more progressive family reform.[62]

Despite the strong connection between marriage and family rights, this book focuses on LGBTI people's right to marry as an aspect of the equality principle.

---

55 William N Eskridge "The Ideological Structure of the Same-Sex Marriage Debate (and Some Postmodern Arguments for Same-Sex Marriage)" in Robert Wintemute, Mads Tønnesson Andenæs (eds) *Legal Recognition of Same-Sex Partnerships: A Study of National, European, and International Law* (Hart Pub, Oxford, Portland, 2001) at 113.

56 See for example, Sherif Girgis, Ryan T Anderson, and Robert P George *What Is Marriage? Man and Woman: A Defense* (Encounter Books, New York, London, 2012).

57 Verta A Taylor and Mary Bernstein "Marital Discord: Understanding the Contested Place of Marriage in the Lesbian and Gay Movement" in Verta A Taylor and Mary Bernstein (eds) *Marrying Kind? Debating Same-Sex Marriage within the Lesbian and Gay Movement* (University of Minnesota Press, Minneapolis, 2013) 1.

58 For example, it is now accepted that procreation does not constitute an essential part of marriage and that children should not be discriminated against because they are born from unmarried (heterosexual) partners. See, *Schalk and Kopf v Austria* (30141/04) First Section, ECtHR 24 June 2010 at [11]; Sarah Joseph and Melissa Castan *The International Covenant on Civil and Political Rights* (3rd ed, Oxford University Press, Oxford, 2013) at 709.

59 Judith Stacey and Timothy J Biblarz "(How) Does the Sexual Orientation of Parents Matter?" (2001) 66 *American Sociological Review* 159 at 176.

60 Carlos A Ball *Same-Sex Marriage and Children: A Tale of History, Social Science, and Law* (Oxford University Press, New York, 2014) at 84.

61 Robert Wintemute, *App No 25951/07, Gas and Dubois v France, ECtHR, Fifth Section: Written Comments of FIDH, ICJ, ILGA-Europe, BAAF and NELFA* (ILGA-Europe, Online, 2011).

62 Nancy D Polikoff "For the Sake of All Children: Opponents and Supporters of Same-Sex Marriage Both Miss the Mark" (2005) 8 *New York City Law Review* 573; Karen Zivi, "Performing the Nation: Contesting Same-Sex Marriage Rights in the United States" (2014) 13(3) *Journal of Human Rights* 290; Laurie Shrage "Decoupling Marriage and Parenting" (2018) 35(3) *Journal of Applied Philosophy* 496.

Indeed, religious opponents of marriage and family equality and LGBTI supporters of marriage and family equality advance their positions by using prohibition of discrimination arguments and the principle of equality.

Marriage rights and the anti-discrimination principle

For some scholars, the right to marry for LGBTI people brings about important symbolic meanings, as it represents the legal recognition of the equality between sexually and gender diverse people and heterosexual and cisgender people. For example, Nigel Christie argues that when LGBTI couples are allowed to access civil partnership agreements rather than marriage, they are still discriminated against because they are entitled to lesser rights and benefits compared to heterosexual married couples.[63] At least in Western societies, many LGBTI people support the right to marry as a matter of equality.[64] Other scholars say that queer people are better off without marriage equality or other forms of LGBTI couples' recognitions[65] because these are based on patriarchal-heterosexual marriage models.[66]

Strikingly, conservative/religious coalitions also use anti-discrimination arguments to support marriage inequality. Indeed, a line of argument against marriage equality portrays LGBTI people as the oppressors of religious liberty.[67] For example, religious rights advocates claim that marriage equality acts force churches to recognise LGBTI couples' marriages.[68] The religious/conservative activists' focus on marriage inequality is used as a pretext. This is because the marriage inequality rhetoric serves to bar any form of public manifestation of sexual and gender diversity,[69] or, as shown in this book, to continue justifying SOGII discrimination. There is, indeed, a strong connection between LGBTI couple rights and the anti-discrimination principle. The next section explores to what extent the international human rights law protects LGBTI couples from discrimination.

---

63 Nigel Christie "The New Zealand Same-Sex Marriage Case: From Aotearoa to the United Nations" in Robert Wintemute and Mads Tønnesson Andenæs (eds) *Legal Recognition of Same-Sex Partnerships: A Study of National, European, and International Law* (Hart Pub, Oxford, Portland, 2001) 317 at 320.

64 Kathleen E Hull "The Cultural Power of Law and the Cultural Enactment of Legality: The Case of Same-Sex Marriage" (2003) 28(3) *Law & Social Inquiry* 629

65 See for example, Darren Rosenblum "Queer Legal Victories: Intersectionality Revised" in Mary Bernstein, Anna-Maria Marshall, and Scott Barclay (eds) *Queer Mobilizations: LGBT Activists Confront the Law* (New York University Press, New York, 2009) 38.

66 Nicola Barker *Not the Marrying Kind: A Feminist Critique of Same-Sex Marriage* (Palgrave Macmillan, London, 2012).

67 Douglas NeJaime "Marriage Inequality: Same-Sex Relationships, Religious Exemptions, and the Production of Sexual Orientation Discrimination" (2012) *California Law Review* 1169.

68 Scot M Peterson and Iain McLean *Legally Married: Love and Law in the UK and the US* (Edinburgh University Press, Edinburgh, 2013) 9.

69 Douglas NeJaime, above n 67, at 1176.

International law protections for LGBTI couples

To discuss how the principle of non-discrimination applies to LGBTI couples it is useful to briefly turn to regional human rights organizations, which developed an extended jurisprudence on the matter. The European Court of Human Rights ('European Court') developed the analogous situations and the significantly different situations approaches. The first one serves to identify direct discrimination, and it asks whether individuals can compare themselves with another group of people who are treated more favourably. The second approach is used to identify indirect discrimination. Indirect discrimination happens when states fail to treat differently persons whose situations are significantly different. Therefore, the European Court said that, on the one hand, unmarried LGBTI couples suffer direct discrimination when they are not allowed to enjoy rights and benefits that unmarried different sex couples would enjoy.[70] And on the other hand, unmarried same-sex couples suffer indirect discrimination when they are not allowed to access rights and benefit attached to marriage because for them marriage is an insurmountable obstacle.[71]

Such a doctrine based on the indirect discrimination principle has the potential to be used by same-sex couples to acquire more family rights, such as the right to adopt a child or to access assisted reproductive treatment, which are often the privilege of married (heterosexual) couples in many Council of Europe member states.[72] Still, the European Court maintained that the right to marry (Article 12 of the European Convention on Human Rights) enshrined the meaning of marriage as being between a man and a woman.[73]

The Inter-American Court of Human Rights ('Inter-American Court') moved even further from the European Court to say that excluding same-sex couples from marriage amounts to discrimination. Indeed, in 2018, the Inter-American Court issued Advisory Opinion 12 on gender identity, equality and non-discrimination for same-sex couples. Advisory Opinion 12 declares that the existence of two separate institutions – civil union for LGBTI couples, and marriage for heterosexual couples – was not admissible because this separation creates a discrimination on the grounds of sexual orientation, and therefore it is incompatible with the Inter-American Convention on Human Rights.[74] This is a recent evolution of the Inter-American Court, and it would be interesting to see if the European Court will follow suit.

Conversely, the UN jurisprudence on marriage and family equality is limited. The UN position on LGBTI people's right to marry and to form a family is held upon two pillars. First, as laid down in *Joslin*, the right to marry and to

---

70 *Karner v Austria* (40016/98) First Section, ECtHR 24 July 2003.
71 *Taddeucci and McCall v Italy* (51362/09) First Section, ECtHR 30 June 2016 at [83].
72 Elsewhere I expand on the European Court's jurisprudence and I discuss the European NGOs' advocacy. See, Giulia Dondoli "An Overnight Success a Decade in the Making: Indirect Discrimination on the Grounds of Sexual Orientation" *International Journal of Discrimination and the Law* (2018) 18(1) 5.
73 *Schalk and Kopf v Austria*, above n 58, at [53].
74 Corte Interamericana De Derechos Humanos *Opinión Consultiva Oc-24/17 De 24 De Noviembre De 2017 Solicitada Por La República De Costa Rica Identidad De Género, E Igualdad Y No Discriminación A Parejas Del Mismo Sexo* (2018, Inter-American Court), [224].

form a family (Article 23 of the ICCPR) is to be understood as only referring to heterosexual couples.[75] Second, unmarried same-sex couples are discriminated against when they are not allowed to access the same rights and benefits available for unmarried different sex couples. This principle was laid down in the HR Comm's views released in *Young v Australia*[76] and *X v Colombia*,[77] when the survived same-sex partners of an Australian and a Colombian war veteran were not allowed to receive the pension of the surviving partners, a benefit otherwise accorded to heterosexual couples in an analogous situation. In both cases, the two states were found to be in violation of Article 26 (equality before the law) of the ICCPR because they denied unmarried same-sex couples the same rights and benefits accessible by unmarried heterosexual couples.[78] The principle of unmarried same-sex couple discrimination was consolidated by the Office of the High Commission for Human Rights (OHCHR), which recommended that when governments provide marriage-like benefits to unmarried heterosexual couples, these should be available also for unmarried LGBTI couples.[79]

Finally, regarding family rights, the OHCHR recognised that the lack of legal recognition of LGBTI couples can result in discriminatory behaviour towards their children.[80] Although states maintain a margin of appreciation in defining the concept of family,[81] such a concept must be understood in a wide sense in encompassing various forms of families.[82] Therefore, in 2015, the OHCHR recommended that UN member states provide some form of legal recognition of LGBTI couples[83] and ensure that children born in de facto unions and in LGBTI parent-families have equal rights to those born from married and heterosexual couples.[84]

In sum, the debate on marriage equality and family equality are very controversial, and even though some states understand the principle of non-discrimination as a requirement to enforce LGBTI couples' legal recognition, or marriage equality,[85] most states resist marriage equality claims and even the SOGII anti-discrimination principle more in general. The topic of marriage equality is even more complicated to address when discussed from a transnational advocacy

---

75 See also, A/HRC/19/41, *Discriminatory Laws and Practices and Acts of Violence Against Individuals Based on Their Sexual Orientation and Gender Identity* (OHCHR, 2011), at [68]; A/HRC/29/23, *Discrimination and Violence Against Individuals Based on Their Sexual Orientation and Gender Identity: Report of the Office of the United Nations High Commissioner for Human Rights* (HR Council, 2015), at [67].

76 *Young v Australia* HR Comm 941/00, CCPR/C/78/D/941/2000 (2003), 8 August 2000.

77 *X v Colombia* HR Comm 1361/2005, CCPR/C/89/D/1361/2005, 30 March 2007.

78 Sarah Joseph and Melissa Castan, above 58, at [784–786].

79 A/HRC/29/23, above n 75, at [67].

80 At [68].

81 A/HRC/31/37 *Protection of the Family: Contribution of the Family to the Realization of the Right to an Adequate Standard of Living for Its Members, Particularly through Its Role in Poverty Eradication and Achieving Sustainable Development* (HR Council, 2016) at [26].

82 At [24].

83 A/HRC/29/23, above n 75, at [79(h)].

84 A/HRC/31/37, above n 81, at [42]. See also, A/HRC/29/23, above n 75, at [79(h)].

85 Kelly Kollman *The Same-Sex Unions Revolution in Western Democracies: International Norms and Domestic Policy Change* (Manchester University Press, Manchester, New York, 2013) at 48.

perspective. This is because it is often claimed that marriage is at the centre of the Western LGBTI advocacy, and that Western NGOs impose marriage equality advocacy upon the global LGBTI network. Transnational advocacy and network dynamics are at the core of this book and, therefore, the definitions of key terms, such as TANs and gatekeeper NGOs, are addressed next.

Transnational advocacy networks and gatekeeper NGOs

TANs are groups of people or individuals who mobilise domestically or internationally "to advance claims on behalf of external actors, against external opponents, or in favour of goals they hold in common with transnational allies".[86] In practice, the actors of the TANs are social movements and NGOs,[87] activists, academics, media,[88] corporations and domestic interest groups.[89] TANs are a form of organization where the node of the network has voluntary and reciprocal "patterns of communication and exchange".[90] TANs are hierarchical, with a few international NGOs working as central nodes – acting as 'gatekeepers' – and many peripheral NGOs.[91]

Gatekeeper NGOs are major human rights NGOs functioning as gatekeepers because they have a considerable influence in the standard setting of new human rights norms.[92] They are powerful, well-recognised NGOs[93] with large budgets and professional staff.[94] They are usually located in Western states because human rights NGOs with headquarters in Western democracies are facilitated to develop to the point of becoming gatekeeper NGOs, as they are not under strong state restrictions.[95] Because of their central position in the network, gatekeeper NGOs

---

86 Sidney G Tarrow *The New Transnational Activism* (Cambridge University Press, New York, 2005) at 43.

87 Sanjeev Khagram, James Riker, and Kathryn Sikkink "From Santiago to Seattle: Transnational Advocacy Groups Reconstructing World Politics" in Sanjeev Khagram, James Riker, and Kathryn Sikkink (eds) *Reconstructing World Politics: Transnational Social Movements and Norms* (University of Minnesota Press, Minneapolis, 2001) 3 at 9.

88 Clifford Bob *The Marketing of Rebellion: Insurgents, Media, and International Activism* (Cambridge University Press, Cambridge, New York, 2005).

89 Sanjeev Khagram, James Riker, and Kathryn Sikkink, above n 87, at 9; Eduard Grebe "The Treatment Action Campaign's Struggle for AIDS Treatment in South Africa: Coalition-Building through Networks" (2011) 37(4) *Journal of Southern African Studies* 849 at 855.

90 Margaret E Keck and Kathryn Sikkink, above n 13, at 8.

91 Clifford Bob, above 14; Charli Carpenter "Governing the Global Agenda 'Gatekeepers' and 'Issue Adoption' in Transnational Advocacy Networks" in Deborah D Avant, Martha Finnemore, and Susan K Sell (eds) *Who Governs the Globe?* (Cambridge University Press, Washington DC, 2010) 202.

92 Clifford Bob, above n 14, at 4.

93 Charli Carpenter "Studying Issue (Non)-Adoption in Transnational Advocacy Networks" (2007) 61(3) *International Organization* 643 at 467.

94 Clifford Bob, above n 14, at 6.

95 Bonny Ibhawoh "Human Rights INGOs and the North-South Gap: The Challenge of Normative and Empirical Learning" in Daniel A Bell (ed) *Ethics in Action: The Ethical Challenges of International Human Rights Nongovernmental Organizations* (Cambridge University Press, Cambridge, 2007) 79 at 82.

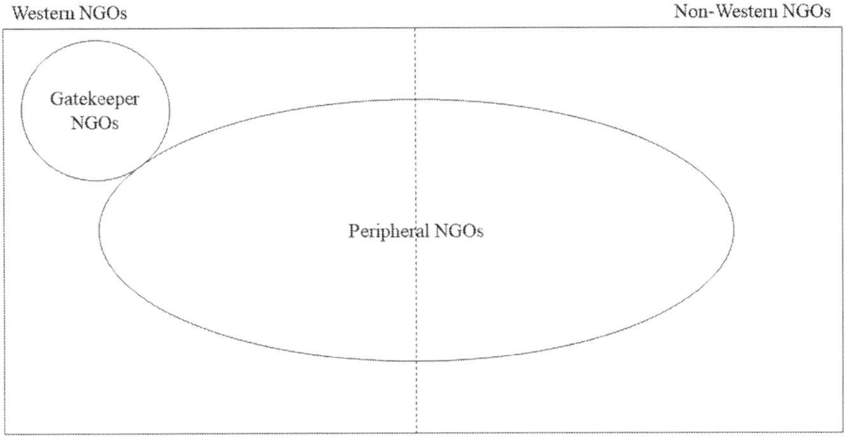

Western NGOs   Non-Western NGOs

Figure 1.1 Distribution of gatekeeper NGOs and peripheral NGOs along the Western/non-Western divide

are more visible to governments and international organizations. They are better placed to gather information and, in general, they are more likely to be perceived as legitimate actors.[96] Finally, gatekeeper NGOs have more experience, more resources and better "technical expertise on human rights law",[97] and they have more knowledge of how the UN functions.[98] At the same time, gatekeeper NGOs need the help of NGOs that are active locally.[99] To distinguish the latter from gatekeeper NGOs, I use the term 'peripheral' NGOs. Although the term 'peripheral' is not as well consolidated as 'gatekeeper' in the TAN literature, it has already been used to refer to LGBTI activists in non-Western states, and it helps to create a distinction.[100] Figure 1.1 shows in a diagram the relationships between Western/non-Western NGOs and gatekeeper/peripheral NGOs.

---

96 Charli Carpenter "Vetting the Advocacy Agenda: Network Centrality and the Paradox of Weapons Norms" (2011) 65(1) *International Organization* 69 at 74.

97 Kiyoteru Tsutsui, Claire Whitlinger, and Alwyn Lim "International Human Rights Law and Social Movements: States' Resistance and Civil Society's Insistence" (2012) 8 *Annual Review of Law and Social Science* 367 at 379.

98 See for example, IGLHRC (now OutRight) *Equal and Indivisible: Crafting Inclusive Shadow Reports for CEDAW* (OutRight, Online, 2009); Aengus Carroll, Beth Fernandez, and ILGA-Europe *Make It Work: Six Steps to Effective LGBT Human Rights Advocacy* (ILGA-Europe, Online, 2010); ARC *The UN Human Rights Council: A Guide for Advocates Working on Human Rights Relating to Sexual Orientation and Gender Identity* (ARC, Online, 2015); Amnesty International *The Human Rights of Lesbian, Gay, Bisexual and Transgender People: A Primer to Working with the United Nations Treaty Monitoring Bodies and the Special Procedures of the United Nations Commission on Human Rights* (IOR 40/004/2005, 2005).

99 Ryan R Thoreson, above n 20, at 180.

100 See for example, Manuela Lavinas Picq "Peripheral Prides: Amazon Perspectives on LGBT Politics" in Manuela Lavinas Picq and Markus Thiel (eds) *Sexualities in World Politics: How LGBTQ Claims Shape International Relations* (Routledge, London, New York, 2015) 108.

Nongovernmental organizations

The term 'NGO' was first used in international law with the drafting of the UN Charter.[101] In 1945, the UN mentioned 'nongovernmental organizations' in Article 71 of the UN Charter, in saying that the Economic and Social Council (ECOSOC) may make arrangement for consultation with NGOs.[102] Nevertheless, the UN did not give any definition of NGOs until 1950, when the ECOSOC reviewed the consultation agreement and stated that, "[a]ny international organization which is not established by intergovernmental agreement shall be considered as a non-governmental organization".[103] Lindblom criticises this definition because it only says what an NGO is not,[104] and she defines NGOs as civil society's organizations, non-profit, without criminal connections, with a formal statute and often enjoying legal personality in the domestic law.[105] NGOs can focus on human rights law, like Amnesty International ('Amnesty') and Human Rights Watch (HRW), or on the provision of humanitarian aid, such as Oxfam. There are identity-based NGOs, of which LGBTI NGOs are an example, and general human rights-based organizations.[106]

The NGOs analysed in this book can serve the cause of promoting the rights of LGBTI people with a mixture of non-legal and legal actions. Some examples of non-legal actions are organising campaigns and manifestations supporting information and education programmes, and supporting individuals with practical aid.[107] Otherwise, some examples of legal actions are supporting individual applications before international human rights courts and committees; collecting information on human rights violations and submitting reports; participating in intergovernmental meetings; lobbying governments to ratify human rights treaties and optional protocols; following-up on states' compliance with international recommendations; or lobbying governmental delegates to sponsor human rights resolutions.[108]

---

101 Anna-Karin Lindblom *Non-Governmental Organizations in International Law* (Cambridge University Press, Cambridge, 2005) at 37.
102 Charter of the United Nations, United Nations (signed 26 June 1945, entered into force 24 October 1945) Article 71.
103 288(X) *Decision Regarding Review of Organizations in Consultative Status* (1950) at B(8). Collected in E/1661 *Resolutions: Economic and Social Council Official Records, 5th Year, 10th Session* (ECOSOC, 1950) at 25.
104 Anna-Karin Lindblom, above n 101, at 38.
105 At 52.
106 Peter J Spiro "NGOs and Human Rights: Channels of Power" in Sarah Joseph and Adam McBeth (eds) *Research Handbook on International Human Rights Law* (Edward Elgar, Cheltenham, Northampton, 2010) 115 at 118–119. See also, Debor Spar and James Dail "Of Measurement and Mission: Accounting for Performance in Non-Governmental Organizations" (2002) 3 *Chicago Journal of International Law* 171 at 175.
107 See especially, Ashley Currier "Deferral of Legal Theory, a Global LGBT Social Movement Organization's Perspective" in Mary Bernstein, Scott Barclay, and Anna-Maria Marshall (eds) *Queer Mobilizations: LGBT Activists Confront the Law* (New York University Press, New York, 2009) 21.
108 See for example, Antonio Cassese "How Could Nongovernmental Organizations Use UN Bodies More Effectively?" (1979) 1(4) *Universal Human Rights* 73; William Korey *NGOs*

This book focuses especially on legal advocacy actions undertaken by contemporary LGBTI NGOs, but LGBTI social movements are not a new phenomenon. The next section provides some description of different waves of LGBTI social movements in history, highlighting their similarity with the current LGBTI global movement.

Sexually and gender diverse people's movements: a history

This section focuses on pointing out the roots of homosexual, homophile and gay liberation movements and their similarities with contemporary LGBTI TANs. Two aspects of similarity are highlighted. First, homosexual, homophile and gay liberation movements have networked and cooperated transnationally since the first groups mobilised at the end of the 19th century. Second, homophile organizations have lobbied the UN and framed sexuality and gender diverse issues as human rights claims since at least 1951.

The roots of homosexual pressure groups

Sexually and gender diverse behaviours have been criminalised on and off for centuries; however, LGBTI pressure groups started to mobilise only towards the end of the 19th century. This is because, until the late 19th century, homosexuality was considered a behaviour rather than an identity and "[t]here was no concept of the homosexual in law".[109] Foucault explains that in the 19th century there was a shift in the medical discourse on sexuality, from perceiving same-sex sexual attraction as a mere behaviour, to a personal characteristic. In Foucault's words:[110]

> This new persecution of the peripheral sexualities entitled . . . a new *specification of individuals*. . . . Homosexuality appeared as one of the forms of sexuality when it was transposed from the practice of sodomy onto a kind of interior androgyny, a hermaphrodism of the soul. The sodomite had been a temporary aberration; the homosexual was now a species.

On a similar note, D'Emilio explains that in the second half of the 19th century, with the development of capitalism, individuals could work for a wage and emancipate themselves from the nuclear family. In this way, "it was possible for homosexual desire to coalesce into a personal identity".[111] Building upon D'Emilio's

---

and the Universal Declaration of Human Rights (Palgrave, New York, 2001); Tullio Treves "Introduction" in Tullio Treves and others (eds) *Civil Society, International Courts, and Compliance Bodies* (TMC Asser Press, The Hague, New York, 2005) 1 at 5–6; Loveday Hodson, above n 10.

109 Jeffrey Weeks *Coming Out: Homosexual Politics in Britain from the Nineteenth Century to the Present* (Quartet Books, London, New York, 1977) at 12.

110 Michel Foucault *The History of Sexuality: The Will to Knowledge* (Vintage Books, New York, 1988) I at 42–43.

111 John D'Emilio "Capitalism and Gay Identity" in Ann Snitow, Christine Stansel, and Sharon Thompson (eds) *Powers of Desire the Politics of Sexuality* (Monthly Review Press, New York, 1983) 100 at 105.

views, Stryker comments that transgender people's identities developed as a consequence of urbanisation because individuals were able to move to cities and express their gender identities, away from their families of origin.[112]

Therefore, even though same-sex sexual behaviours, and sometimes transvestitism, were criminalised on and off for centuries, homosexual movements did not begin until the late 19th century because only "[o]nce homosexuality is transformed into a people, the idea of a gay movement finds its place".[113] Sexually and gender diverse advocates mobilise when sexually and gender diverse identities are formed and visible.[114]

In 1897, one of the first homosexual organizations, Scientific Humanitarian Committee, was founded in Germany to petition the recall of Paragraph 175 of the Imperial Penal Code, criminalising same-sex sexual acts,[115] however, without success.[116] This and other pioneering homosexual organizations, such as the British Society for the Study of Sex Psychology (1914) and the Institute for Sexual Science (1919), used to have some degrees of transnational advocacy.[117] However, the first actual transnational organization on sexual and homosexual issues was founded in the 1920s.

In 1921, the First International Congress for Sexual Reform on the Basis of Sexual Science was held in Berlin; its participants set the basis for the foundation of the World League for Sexual Reform (WLSR),[118] which was an umbrella organization with 190,000 members coming from organizations active nationally.[119] The initial programme of action of WLSR included various issues related to sexuality, such as birth control, marriage reform, abortion, eugenics, sexual education, prostitution and homosexuality. However, the Second World War was a barrier to the development of homosexual activism because thousands of sexually and gender diverse individuals were imprisoned in concentration camps.[120]

---

112 Susan Stryker, above n 19, at 34.
113 Barry D Adam *The Rise of a Gay and Lesbian Movement* (Twayne Publishers, Boston, 1987) at 2.
114 Barry D Adam, Jan Willem Duyvendak, and André Krouwel *The Global Emergence of Gay and Lesbian Politics: National Imprints of a Worldwide Movement* (Temple University Press, Philadelphia, 1999) at 350.
115 Florance Tamagne "The Homosexual Age, 1870–1940" in Robert Aldrich (ed) *Gay Life and Culture a World History* (Thames and Hudson, London, 2010) 167 at 176.
116 Ronald J Hunt *Historical Dictionary of the Gay Liberation Movement: Gay Men and the Quest for Social Justice* (Scarecrow Press, Lanham, 1999), at 6.
117 Leila J Rupp "The European Origins of Transnational Organizing: The International Committee for Sexual Equality" in Phillip Ayoub and David Paternotte (eds) *LGBT Activism and the Making of Europe: A Rainbow Europe* (Palgrave Macmillan, Basingstoke, 2014) 29 at 30.
118 Leila J Rupp "The Persistence of Transnational Organizing: The Case of the Homophile Movement" (2011) 116(4) *The American Historical Review* 1014, at 1014.
119 Pamela Eve Selwyn and Ralf Dose "The World League for Sexual Reform: Some Possible Approaches" (2003) 12(1) *Journal of the History of Sexuality* 1 at 3.
120 Ronald J Hunt, above n 108, at 75. For a history of gay men and lesbian women during the Second World War see, Allan Bérubé, John D'Emilio, and Estelle B Freedman *Coming Out under Fire: The History of Gay Men and Women in World War II* (20th anniversary ed, University of North Carolina Press, Chapel Hill, 1990).

The Holocaust wiped out the first homosexual movements "through systematic extermination and ideological control",[121] and the WLSR and its branches were disbanded during that period.[122]

A new wave of homophile and gay liberation pressure groups after the Second World War

Rupp notes that "[d]espite post-war crackdown on homosexual men in many countries and lingering wartime enemies, organizations and individuals joined across national borders".[123] At the end of the Second World War, the former members of the Dutch Scientific Humanitarian Committee organised a new group, first called the Shakespeare Club, and from 1946 called the Cultural and Recreational Centre (COC),[124] which is still an important NGO in the LGBTI TAN. COC started advocating transnationally in 1951,[125] when it organised the first International Congress on Sexual Equality, held in Amsterdam with representatives of homophile groups from many European countries. At this time, the International Committee on Sexual Equality (ICSE) was founded, and it was a transnational homophile umbrella organization.[126]

The participants of the International Congress on Sexual Equality sent a telegram to the UN to "request the United Nations Organization to initiate steps towards granting [the] status of human, social and legal equality to homosexuel [sic] minorities throughout the world".[127] This signals the first documented example of sexually diverse people's issues framed as a human right claim before the UN and, in particular, framed as an equality matter. ICSE members saw in the UN the highest human rights authority, and they targeted international organizations to achieve the recognition of "same-sex love as a human right".[128] In the following years, ICSE petitioned the UN; the United Nations Educational, Scientific and Cultural Organization; the World Health Organization; and the International Federation for Mental Health, asking for decriminalisation of homosexual sexual conduct, for sexual freedom and for revoking the classification of homosexuality as a disease. Moreover, ICSE lobbied the UN to obtain consultative status at the ECOSOC. For nearly ten years, ICSE financed congresses and international meetings, and issued publications and newsletters on same-sex sexuality matters but eventually ceased its activities in the early 1960s.[129]

---

121 Barry D Adam, above n 113, at 54.
122 Ronald J Hunt, above n 116, at 75.
123 Leila J Rupp, above n 118, at 1037.
124 Leila J Rupp, above n 117, at 30.
125 Juliana Jackson "The Homophile Movement" in David Paternotte and Manon Tremblay (eds) *The Ashgate Research Companion to Lesbian and Gay Activism* (Ashgate, Burlington, 2015) 31 at 32.
126 Leila J Rupp, above n 118, at 1014.
127 At 1016.
128 At 1030.
129 At 1015–1036.

Similar to their predecessors, ICSE was predominately composed of white men, with little attention on issues of gender equality.[130] Some authors note that the fact that the ICSE's membership was mostly European gay men, and to a lesser extent European lesbian women and North American gay men, has contributed to the consolidation of sexually and gender diverse identities as mostly Western identities.[131] This stereotypical Western 'LGBTI' label can prevent the development of the LGBTI network from below.[132]

During the 1960s, LGBT people were engaged in a number of violent protests and demonstrations, especially in the United States.[133] These riots and demonstrations culminated on 28 June 1969, with a police raid on the Stonewall Inn in New York,[134] after which "thousands of people have been galvanised into political action".[135] A few weeks later, some members from the New York branch of the Mattachine Society founded the Gay Liberation Front (GLF), using the word 'gay' to distance themselves from the previous medical discourse on homosexuality and from the moderate political strategies of the homophile groups.[136] GLF's members were mostly students and activists in their teens and 20s,[137] and they aimed for a transformation of the entire society through the promotion of a sexual liberation, and the coming out of sexual and gender diverse individuals.[138] Gay liberation groups focused much of their effort on decriminalisation of same-sex sexual activities in national jurisdictions.[139] Moreover, because of their liberation ideal, these groups rejected marriage on the basis that they viewed it as a form of patriarchal structure.[140]

In 1978, one of the major LGBTI organizations was founded in Europe. NGO delegates from European countries, the United States, Canada and Jamaica participated in the annual conference of the British organization Campaign for Homosexual Equality. During that meeting, the International Gay Association was founded; it is now known as International Lesbian, Gay, Bisexual, Trans and Intersex Association (ILGA).[141] Founded towards the end of the gay liberation

---

130 Pamela Eve Selwyn and Ralf Dose, above n 119.
131 Leila J Rupp, above n 117, at 44; Phillip M Ayoub and David Paternotte "Challenging Borders, Imagining Europe: Transnational LGBT Activism in a New Europe" in Nancy Naples and Jennifer Bickham Mendez (eds) *Border Politics: Social Movements, Collective Identities, and Globalization* (New York University Press, New York, 2014) 230 at 233.
132 See next chapter.
133 Susan Stryker, above n 19, at 82. See also, Barry D Adam, above n 105, at 76; Tina Fetner *How the Religious Right Shaped Lesbian and Gay Activism* (University of Minnesota Press, Minneapolis, 2008) at 15.
134 Marc Stein *Rethinking the Gay and Lesbian Movement* (Routledge, New York, 2012) at 79.
135 Susan Stryker, above n 19, at 85.
136 Marc Stein, above n 134, at 82.
137 Barry D Adam, above n 113, at 76.
138 Marc Stein, above n 134, at 84.
139 Michael J Klarman *From the Closet to the Altar: Courts, Backlash, and the Struggle for Same-Sex Marriage* (Oxford University Press, Oxford, New York, 2013) at 36.
140 William N Eskridge *Equality Practice* (Taylor and Francis, Florence, 2013), at 5.
141 Leila J Rupp, above n 118, at 1036.

period, ILGA was not a gay liberation front type of organization; however, it was influenced by some of the GLF's ideals.[142] ILGA maintained some of the characteristics of its predecessors. For example, ILGA is an umbrella organization as ICSE was, and both ICSE and ILGA targeted the UN, and other international organizations, for their advocacy and called for a consultative status at the ECOSOC.

Historians find various phases in the evolution of the sexually and gender diverse people's movement. But these distinctions are somehow artificial because there is no clear-cut moment between one phase and the next, and different types of groups communicated, collaborated and influenced one another.[143] There are many similarities between contemporary LGBTI TANs and early homosexual, homophile and gay social movements. Current LGBTI NGOs work in continuation with sexually and gender diverse minorities' social movements of the 20th century. As early as 1951, European homophile organizations coordinated transnationally to pressure their governments from above and from below. These are early examples of transnational networking and boomerang patterns of advocacy actions, which are better addressed in the following chapters.

In sum, the way in which contemporary LGBTI TANs organise their cooperation, choose their strategies and name and interpret human rights violations to influence the international human rights law debate did not just happen to be by accident. Contemporary LGBTI NGOs, especially Western/gatekeeper NGOs, have learned from the history of their predecessors, and they are building upon the successes and failures of the activists that came before them. Moving forward from the vast literature on sexuality and gender history, queer mobilisation, and legal analysis of LGBTI rights, briefly summarised above, this book aims to tackle four questions and advance four arguments. These questions and arguments are laid down in the next sections.

Research questions

The book focuses on one fundamental research question: What issues are advocated by LGBTI TANs, and how are these issues framed? To respond to this question, I discuss three sub-questions: (i) How does the way in which gatekeeper and peripheral NGOs work together influence the TANs' advocacy? (ii) How does the broader political context influence the LGBTI TANs' advocacy? (iii) Do LGBTI gatekeeper NGOs impose the advocacy for the right to marry upon their less powerful peripheral partners? This section justifies the rationale for these questions.

---

142 David Paternotte "The International (Lesbian and) Gay Association and the Question of Paedophilia: Tracking the Demise of Gay Liberation Ideals" (2014) 17(1–2) *Sexualities* 121 at 123.

143 Leila J Rupp, above 118, at 1036.

NGOs working in TANs can lobby international organizations and national states to protect the rights of LGBTI people. NGOs can either push governments to comply with existing human rights law, or NGOs can promote the creation of international human rights norms and standards. This book focuses on the second aspect: how LGBTI TANs promote the consolidation of international human rights standards for the protection of LGBTI people.

To do so, the book researches the dynamics of issue emergence and issue framing. Framing is the "conscious strategic efforts by groups of people to fashion shared understandings of the world and of themselves that legitimate and motivate collective action".[144] Indeed, NGOs can draw attention to issues, and 'create' issues by using language that names and interprets problems.[145] Problems are pre-existing injustices, which have not yet been recognised as issues. When activists and NGOs name a problem as a human rights violation, a new issue emerges.[146] It is important to acknowledge that not all the actors of a given TAN have equal ability to decide what problems become issues.

Therefore, I focus on the internetwork relations between LGBTI gatekeeper NGOs and LGBTI peripheral NGOs. Gatekeeper NGOs are powerful actors within the human rights TANs – for example, Amnesty and HRW – whereas peripheral NGOs are smaller, less funded and less professional. LGBTI gatekeeper NGOs have a major role in setting the advocacy agenda of the network, and understanding how gatekeeper NGOs pick which issues to advocate for in the pool of grievances is crucial to understanding how some of these grievances become new human rights standards and others do not.[147] In the book I discuss that the relationships between gatekeeper NGOs and peripheral NGOs shape the outcomes of the TANs' advocacy.

Moreover, LGBTI TANs do not work in a vacuum. Rather their advocacy is facilitated by supportive allies, such as, for example, some Western governments[148] and some international organizations' functionaries, or impaired by opposing TANs and governments (the broader political context). Therefore,

---

144 Doug McAdam, John D McCarthy, and Mayer Zald "Introduction: Opportunities, Mobilizing Structures, and Framing Processes – Toward a Synthetic, Comparative Perspective on Social Movements" in Doug McAdam, John D McCarthy, and Mayer Zald (eds) *Comparative Perspectives on Social Movements: Political Opportunities, Mobilizing Structures, and Cultural Framings* (Cambridge University Press, Cambridge, New York, 1996) 1 at 6.

145 Martha Finnemore and Kathryn Sikkink "International Norm Dynamics and Political Change" (1998) 52(4) *International Organization* 887 at 895. See also, Sanjeev Khagram, James Riker, and Kathryn Sikkink, above n 87, at 12.

146 Charli Carpenter "Setting the Advocacy Agenda: Theorizing Issue Emergence and Non-Emergence in Transnational Advocacy Networks" (2007) 51(1) *International Studies Quarterly* 99 at 102.

147 Charli Carpenter "Studying Issue (Non)-Adoption in Transnational Advocacy Networks" (2007) 61(3) *International Organization* 643.

148 In this book I use the terms 'West' and the 'rest'. I use the classification of the UN Regional Groups, and I refer to West as the Western European and Others Group (WEOG); and the rest to all the other UN Regional Groups, the African Group, the Asian-Pacific Group, the Eastern European Group, the Latin America and Caribbean Group (GRULAC).

along with the internetwork relations approach, the book discusses how these broader opportunities and constrictions influence the issue emergence and the issue framing by LGBTI TANs.

Finally, when discussing NGOs' decision-making, many authors have criticised NGOs and TANs because they lack democratic legitimacy and accountability. In other words, a handful of staff members from gatekeeper NGOs can make decisions for LGBTI communities without anybody formally electing them to do so. A specific criticism that is made against Western LGBTI NGOs regards marriage and family equality. Indeed, some scholars criticise the fact that marriage equality is at the centre of Western LGBTI NGOs' advocacy agenda,[149] and that LGBTI gatekeeper NGOs impose the advocacy for the right to marry for LGBTI people upon the rest of the network.[150] To investigate the democratic legitimacy of the LGBTI network, I specifically research the case study of the transnational advocacy for the right to marry for LGBTI people.

Central arguments of the book

I argue that the way in which TANs decide the advocacy agenda, conceptualise human rights violations and strategically present legal analysis to advance LGBTI rights shapes the human rights debate. I discuss this core argument in three phases.

First, I argue that the way in which NGOs work together in TANs (internetwork relations) influences the advocacy agenda setting. I discuss that the fact that LGBTI gatekeeper NGOs aim to build the network horizontally has consequences in the advocacy decision-making. Second, I argue that political opportunities and constraints provided by international organizations, states and other NGOs outside the network (the broader political context) shape the way in which LGBTI TANs frame LGBTI issues. Specifically, I discuss that LGBTI gatekeeper NGOs frame LGBTI issues in a way that maximises their political opportunities and minimises challenges.

As the third and final aspect, and as a litmus test of my study, I investigate whether Western/gatekeeper NGOs – two categories that often overlap – impose

---

149 David Paternotte and Manon Tremblay "Introduction: Investigating Lesbian and Gay Activism" in David Paternotte and Manon Tremblay (eds) *The Ashgate Research Companion to Lesbian and Gay Activism* (Ashgate, Burlington, 2015) 1 at 3. See also, Verta Taylor and others "Culture and Mobilization: Tactical Repertoires, Same-Sex Weddings, and the Impact on Gay Activism" (2009) 74(6) *American Sociological Review* 865, Michael J Klarman, above n 132. On the contrary see, Mary Bernstein "Same-Sex Marriage and the Future of the LGBT Movement: SWS Presidential Address" (2015) 29(3) *Gender & Society* 1.

150 Timothy Hildebrandt "Development and Division: The Effect of Transnational Linkages and Local Politics on LGBT Activism in China" (2012) 21(77) *Journal of Contemporary China* 845 at 849; Megan Osterbur and Christina Kiel "A Hegemon Fighting for Equal Rights: The Dominant Role of COC Nederland in the LGBT Transnational Advocacy Network" (2017) 17(2) *Global Networks* 234 at 250.

perceived Western priorities, such as the advocacy for the right to marry for LGBTI people, upon the NGOs working in the periphery of the network. If LGBTI gatekeeper NGOs operate democratically, do not impose their views, work to strengthen the network from below and frame LGBTI issues in an unprovocative way, the advocacy for the right to marry would have a low priority in the advocacy agenda of LGBTI TANs.

In general, I aim to rebut the common assumption that Western/gatekeeper NGOs and TANs operate undemocratically. In fact, by investigating the three phases of my core argument I aim to show that, despite some exceptions, gatekeeper NGOs work together with peripheral NGOs to identify and frame LGBTI issues as human rights claim. Therefore, the advocacy that emerges has a more solid basis because it is the outcome of a range of actors.

Overview of the book

The book develops as follows. Chapter 2 represents the theoretical framework of the book and develops a merged use of social movement and transnational advocacy network theories to unfold the central arguments laid down in this introductory chapter. In brief, the way in which gatekeeper NGOs and peripheral NGOs work together, and the broader political context of the international system, determine the way in which LGBTI TANs choose what injustices are to be advocated as human rights issues, and decide how to strategically frame these issues, to influence the international human rights debate on LGBTI people's rights.

Chapter 3 focuses on internetwork relations between LGBTI gatekeeper and peripheral NGOs. The chapter demonstrates that LGBTI gatekeeper NGOs work to build the network horizontally by putting LGBTI peripheral NGOs working in neighbouring states in connection with each other, by training LGBTI activists working in peripheral NGOs to advocate for their rights before international organizations and by putting them in contact with governmental delegates and foreign donors. In this way, LGBTI gatekeeper NGOs decrease their power because they decentralise their position in the LGBTI TAN. Examples from LGBTI advocacy at the HR Council show that gatekeeper NGOs are effective in their advocacy when they empower and coordinate LGBTI peripheral NGOs. Even though LGBTI gatekeeper NGOs partially relinquish their social power and consult with their peripheral partners to set the advocacy agenda, there are some instances in which peripheral NGOs' opinions can be marginalised by gatekeeper NGOs.

Chapter 4 highlights that the LGBTI TANs do not work in a vacuum and their advocacy is influenced by other NGOs and states, for better or for worse. Powerful international allies, for example some governments and some UN agencies, can legitimise and amplify LGBTI claims, but some conservative/religious TANs and states try to prevent the advancement of LGBTI rights. These dynamics inevitably impact on how LGBTI TANs frame their issues. LGBTI TANs and their allies maintain a low profile on LGBTI issues, fearing the backlash of conservative/religious states and TANs. Moreover, despite LGBTI activists' best efforts, religious/conservative states and TANs still use arguments based on religious and traditional understanding of heterosexual marriage to prevent any attempt from advancing LGBTI people's rights protections.

Chapter 5 spells out, in detail, how LGBTI TANs working at the UN frame LGBTI issues. LGBTI TANs frame LGBTI issues mainly, although not exclusively, as anti-discrimination claims. Furthermore, the right to marry has a low priority in the transnational LGBTI advocacy, which is considered a national goal rather than a transnational one. In doing so, Chapter 5 rebuts the common assumption that gatekeeper NGOs act hegemonically, and it demonstrates that gatekeeper NGOs do not misuse their power.

Chapter 6 concludes that LGBTI TANs are lobbying to push the boundaries of international human right law to encompass SOGII as prohibited grounds of discrimination. Moreover, the chapter calls for even more gatekeeper NGO consultations with the periphery of the network, in particular to develop a multilayered understanding of discrimination. Finally, the chapter invites scholars to further research the influence of donors in the advocacy agenda of the LGBTI TANs and the role of religious/progressive NGOs in the advancement of LGBTI people's rights.

Conclusion

The book rebuts the common assumption that gatekeeper NGOs act undemocratically, and it aims to demonstrate that gatekeeper NGOs work to build a stronger and more democratic network from below. To do so, they advocate for rights that enhance the domestic political opportunities of peripheral NGOs. In addition, to be successful in their claims, LGBTI TANs frame LGBTI issues in a way that maximises political opportunities and minimises challenges. The book aims to demonstrate that, as a consequence of these strategic choices, LGBTI TANs use mainly, although not exclusively, the prohibition of discrimination on the grounds of SOGII as a framework to advocate for LGBTI rights. This finding helps to explain that the prohibition of discrimination on the grounds of SOGII is gaining traction in the human rights debate.

As a litmus test to the democratic legitimacy of LGBTI TANs, the book argues that LGBTI gatekeeper NGOs do not impose the advocacy for the right to marry for LGBTI people upon the NGOs working at the periphery of the network and, instead, they listen to the needs and desires of the peripheral NGOs. This is because the right to marry is particularly controversial. It might trigger strong opposition from conservative/religious NGOs and states, and it might not be the ideal advocacy framework for some peripheral NGOs. Therefore, the right to marry has not gained salience in the UN human rights debate.

2 Between friends and foes

Transnational advocacy networks, issue emergence and issue framing

Introduction

In basing their studies on national or cross-national analysis, some social movement theorists provide various interpretations on the agenda priority of LGBTI advocates. For example, transgender movements' priority is deemed to be the elimination of any practices preventing individuals from being treated according to their experienced gender, and the intersex movements' one is eliminating the unnecessary cosmetic surgeries practised on infants born with intersex characteristics.[1] Moreover, some authors argue that marriage equality is at the centre of the Western LGBTI advocacy agenda.[2] However, these studies are often country-focused and cannot properly address transnational and international advocacy. This chapter develops the theoretical model used in the book to study how transnational LGBTI networks decide what problems and injustices are to be advocated as human rights issues, and how these issues are to be strategically framed. To do so, the chapter develops as follows.

First, the pivotal concept of the boomerang pattern of action explains that NGOs can pressure governments internationally and domestically to comply with international human rights law, but since LGBTI rights are still developing concepts in the international human rights law debate, the notions of issue emergence and issue framing are deployed. The two phases of issue emergence and issue framing are distinguished for ease of discussion, as it appears logical to think that an issue first emerges and then it is framed. In practice, however, these phases are not so clearly distinguishable but are intertwined in a continuous process of conversation among activists, UN officials and governments.

Second, gatekeeper NGOs have a crucial role in pushing for some new issues in the international human rights debate, as well as influencing how these issues

---

1 Julie Greenberg and Robert Stam *Intersexuality and the Law: Why Sex Matters* (New York University Press, New York, 2012) at 4. For the intersex movement see also, Sharon E Preves *Intersex and Identity: The Contested Self* (Rutgers University Press, Piscataway, 2003) at 125–158.

2 David Paternotte and Manon Tremblay "Introduction: Investigating Lesbian and Gay Activism" in David Paternotte and Manon Tremblay (eds) *The Ashgate Research Companion to Lesbian and Gay Activism* (Ashgate, Burlington, 2015) 1 at 3.

are framed. Understanding how these gatekeeper NGOs choose what issues are to be advocated contributes to explaining why some human rights violations become important in international law debate. Many factors may influence how gatekeeper NGOs choose how to set their agenda, but this theoretical framework considers only two aspects: the network's structure and the broader political context in which the network works. The first aspect has often been overlooked by TAN theories, and the second is simply too relevant to be omitted.

Third, I set the basis for my arguments by premising that the LGBTI TAN may not develop because of anticipatory countermovement, cultural imperialism, limited opportunities for domestic LGBTI NGOs and unbalanced internetwork relationships. I argue that LGBTI gatekeeper NGOs are aware of the complexity of internetwork relations and they strive to build LGBTI TANs horizontally and empower peripheral NGOs. Such advocacy actions have consequences in the agenda setting of the network that prioritise issues that enhance the domestic political opportunities of peripheral NGOs.

Fourth, the political opportunities and constraints provided by international organizations, states and other NGOs outside the network (broader political context) shape the way in which LGBTI TANs frame LGBTI issues. This means that LGBTI gatekeeper NGOs frame LGBTI issues in a way that maximises their political opportunities and minimises challenges. To do so, LGBTI gatekeeper NGOs mainly use a prohibition of discrimination framework to advocate for the rights of LGBTI people. This is because the prohibition of discrimination framework is well received by many states because it matches existing and well-established human rights principles. However, the prohibition of discrimination framework is sometimes a risky strategy because it is still perceived as provocative by some conservative/religious opponents of LGBTI rights.

Finally, I conclude by analysing the right to marry as an example of possible misuse of power by gatekeeper NGOs. On the one hand, marriage inequality is a strong argument for religious/conservative TANs and states. On the other hand, many scholars are critical of the fact that marriage equality is at the centre of Western LGBTI NGOs' advocacy agenda and that LGBTI gatekeeper NGOs impose marriage equality on the rest of the network. To investigate the democratic legitimacy of the LGBTI network, the chapter researches whether Western/gatekeeper NGOs – two categories that often overlap – impose perceived Western priorities, such as the right to marry for LGBTI people, upon the NGOs working in the periphery of the network.

In sum, because of the internetwork relations among gatekeeper NGOs and peripheral NGOs, and because of the political opportunities and constraints provided by the international system, LGBTI TANs frame LGBTI issues mainly as a prohibition of discrimination claim. These dynamics help to explain that the prohibition of discrimination on the grounds of SOGII is gaining traction in the human rights debate, while other issues, specifically the right to marry, are not. Marriage equality is an aspect of a broader equality debate, but LGBTI transnational advocates do not openly invoke the right to marry for LGBTI people before the UN.

Transnational advocacy networks

People have mobilised in collective actions and groups have developed transnational networks for centuries.[3] The first sexual and gender minorities pressure groups started mobilising in the late 19th century. Early studies of NGOs and transnationalism gained popularity in the United States among young international relations scholars in the 1970s.[4] However, the theoretical interest in NGOs and transnationalism became more relevant at the end of the 1990s, with the NGOs' development "bloom".[5] This is because, since the end of the Cold War, a process of internationalisation provided new opportunities for the transnational advocacy of social movements and NGOs, and thus facilitated the creation of stronger, larger and denser TANs.[6]

In their seminal study on transnational advocacy networks, Keck and Sikkink explain how TANs work in developing the metaphor of the "boomerang pattern of action":[7]

> When channels between the state and its domestic actors are blocked, the boomerang pattern of influence characteristic of transnational networks may occur: domestic NGOs bypass their state and directly search out international allies to try to bring pressure on their states from outside.

The authors explain that TANs can influence issue creation and agenda setting, the public statements of states and international organizations on certain issues, institutional procedures, states and international organizations' policies, and finally state behaviours.[8] TANs can do so by gathering information on human rights violations through testimonies and experts' opinions, creating symbols to

---

3   Steve Charnovitz "Two Centuries of Participation: NGOs and International Governance" (1996) 18 *Michigan Journal of International Law* 183; Margaret E Keck and Kathryn Sikkink "Historical Precursors to Modern Transnational Social Movements and Networks" in John A Guidry, Michael D Kennedy, and Mayer N Zald (eds) *Globalizations and Social Movements: Culture, Power, and the Transnational Public Sphere* (University of Michigan Press, Ann Arbor, 2000) 35; Thomas Richard Davies *NGOs: A New History of Transnational Civil Society* (C Hust and Co, London, 2013).

4   William Emile DeMars *NGOs and Transnational Networks: Wild Cards in World Politics* (Pluto, London, Ann Arbor, 2005) at 35. See for example, Robert O Keohane and Joseph S Nye "Transnational Relations and World Politics: An Introduction" in Robert O Keohane and Joseph S Nye (eds) *Transnational Relations and World Politics* (Harvard University Press, Cambridge, 1972) ix; John W Burton *World Society* (Cambridge University Press, Cambridge, 1972).

5   William Emile DeMars, above n 4, at 34.

6   Sanjeev Khagram, James Riker, and Kathryn Sikkink "From Santiago to Seattle: Transnational Advocacy Groups Reconstructing World Politics" in Sanjeev Khagram, James Riker, and Kathryn Sikkink (eds) *Reconstructing World Politics: Transnational Social Movements and Norms* (University of Minnesota Press, Minneapolis, 2001) 3 at 18; Sidney G Tarrow *Power in Movement Social Movements and Contentious Politics* (3rd ed, Cambridge University Press, Cambridge, New York, 2011) at 246.

7   Margaret E Keck and Kathryn Sikkink *Activists beyond Borders: Advocacy Networks in International Politics* (Cornell University Press, Ithaca, 1998) at 12.

8   At 25.

persuade their audience, by calling the attention of powerful international allies, and finally by exposing the gap between governments' human rights commitments and their actual practices.[9]

A number of scholars use Keck and Sikkink's concept of the boomerang pattern of action to explore how TANs influence norm acceptance and norm internalisation.[10] For example, Sikkink, Risse and Ropp developed the spiral metaphor to identify the dynamic evolution of repeated "boomerang throws",[11] in which states move from violation of norms to non-violation through a spiral process of norms socialisation. Moreover, Holzhacker developed the ricochet model to study the recognition of the right to peaceful assembly for LGBTI groups in Eastern Europe.[12] The military metaphor of the ricochet effect indicates a process by which "information and arguments ricochet rapidly across a set of institutions and civil society that press national governments to protect the right to assembly".[13]

With different nuances, these models illustrate that domestic activists search out international allies to pressure their states, from above and below, to comply with the existing international human rights law. However, Holzhacker points out that he focuses on the right to peaceful assembly, rather than discrimination on the grounds of SOGII because the right to assembly is a consolidated principle in international human rights treaties, while the prohibition of discrimination on the grounds of SOGII is still a developing concept in the international human rights law.[14] Therefore, rather than exploring the states' compliance with not yet consolidated LGBTI human rights principles, a better approach to study LGBTI TANs is through the concept of issue emergence and issue framing. The ensuing paragraphs address the TANs' scholarship on these topics.

Issue emergence and issue framing: a general overview

When activists name a problem as a human rights violation, a new human right issue emerges.[15] How NGOs choose which problems are to be advocated as

---

9 At 16–25.

10 On studies that deal specifically with LGBTI TANs' influence in norm adaptation and norm internalisation see, Phillip M Ayoub "Contested Norms in New-Adopter States: International Determinants of LGBT Rights Legislation" (2015) 21(2) *European Journal of International Relations* 293; Phillip M Ayoub "With Arms Wide Shut: Threat Perception, Norm Reception, and Mobilized Resistance to LGBT Rights" (2014) 13(3) *Journal of Human Rights* 337.

11 Thomas Risse-Kappen, Stephen C Ropp, and Kathryn Sikkink *The Power of Human Rights: International Norms and Domestic Change* (Cambridge University Press, Cambridge, 1999) at 18. See also, Thomas Risse, Stephen C Ropp, and Kathryn Sikkink *The Persistent Power of Human Rights* (Cambridge University Press, Cambridge, 2013).

12 Ronald Holzhacker "State-Sponsored Homophobia and the Denial of the Right of Assembly in Central and Eastern Europe: The 'Boomerang' and the 'Ricochet' between European Organizations and Civil Society to Uphold Human Rights" (2013) 35(1–2) *Law & Policy* 1.

13 At 2.

14 At 8.

15 Charli Carpenter "Setting the Advocacy Agenda: Theorizing Issue Emergence and Non-Emergence in Transnational Advocacy Networks" (2007) 51(1) *International Studies Quarterly* 99 at 102.

human rights issues, and how they frame such problems is to be understood. Keck and Sikkink provide some initial views. They explain that issues regarding "bodily harm", especially in relation to individuals perceived as vulnerable, and issues regarding "legal equality of opportunity" are usually those around which TANs are able to organise more effectively.[16] Moreover, they argue that TANs work better when they are "dense, with many actors, strong connections among groups in the network, and reliable information flows".[17] Bob, and Carpenter and colleagues, expand upon Keck and Sikkink's boomerang model to further develop issues emergence and framing.

Bob elaborates on Keck and Sikkink's work in at least two ways: in unpacking the dynamics of issue emergence and framing in three phases, and by introducing the concept of gatekeeper NGOs. Bob's argument flows as follows. First, politicised groups, activists and domestic NGOs frame "long-felt grievances as normative claims".[18] Second, they pressure gatekeeper NGOs to accept and put such claims on the international agenda. Finally, states and international organizations accept the new norms. Accordingly, Bob advances the argument that gatekeeper NGOs "hold much sway in certifying new rights".[19] Gatekeeper NGOs have a pivotal role in issue emergence because when they decide to advocate for new issues, they can attract the interests of other well-established NGOs and powerful allies, such as donors and UN officials, and ultimately, they can persuade governments and international organizations to accept the new issues as human rights violations.[20]

When commenting upon Bob's work, Carpenter notes that, "[d]espite the evidence that 'gatekeepers' matter, there has been little *systematic* research on how they decide".[21] Therefore, to understand how some grievances become new human rights norms and others do not, it is necessary to study how gatekeeper NGOs pick which issues are to be advocated in the pool of grievances.[22] Contrary to Keck and Sikkink's views on bodily harm and inequality of opportunities, Carpenter demonstrates that approaches merely related to the attribute of the issue itself might not be sufficient to explain how gatekeeper NGOs chose what issues are to be campaigned.[23] And indeed, Carpenter and others explain that in addition to the intrinsic nature of the issues, gatekeeper NGOs' decision-making can

---

16 Margaret E Keck and Kathryn Sikkink, above n 7, at 27.

17 At 28.

18 Clifford Bob *The International Struggle for New Human Rights* (University of Pennsylvania Press, Philadelphia, 2009) at 4.

19 At 4.

20 At 6.

21 Charli Carpenter and others "Explaining the Advocacy Agenda: Insights from the Human Security Network" (2014) 68(2) *International Organization* 449 at 451.

22 Charli Carpenter "Studying Issue (Non)-Adoption in Transnational Advocacy Networks" (2007) 61(3) *International Organization* 643.

23 Charli Carpenter "Setting the Advocacy Agenda: Theorizing Issue Emergence and Non-Emergence in Transnational Advocacy Networks" (2007) 51(1) *International Studies Quarterly* 99 at 100.

be influenced by factors relating to the actors of the network, the environment in which the network operates and the internetwork relations among the actors of the network. These factors are addressed in the ensuing sub-section.

Characteristics for issue emergence and issue framing

Carpenter and others identify four factors to determine issue emergence and issue framing: the peripheral NGOs' attributes, the gatekeeper NGOs' attributes, the broader political context and internetwork relations.[24] These factors are addressed in turn.

First, Carpenter and others explain that if a local NGO is perceived as a credible actor, the chances are higher that gatekeeper NGOs will take on board its claims.[25] Similarly, Bob argues that peripheral NGOs can enhance their credibility by engaging in strategic framing in order to match gatekeeper NGOs' expectations.[26] Insurgent groups are more likely to make their claims heard in the international arena "by framing parochial demands, provincial conflicts and particularistic identities to match the interest and the agenda of distant audiences".[27]

Second, Carpenter and others explain that the preference in campaigning for certain issues rather than others might depend on the attributes of the gatekeeper NGOs themselves. On the one hand, gatekeeper NGOs take on board new issues only if they perceive that these can help them to advance the agenda they already have because gatekeeper NGOs do not want to take on more issues, they actually want to "push them [new issues] out".[28] On the other hand, the desire to maintain their legitimacy as gatekeeper NGOs can also mean that gatekeeper NGOs are pressured to accept new actors and new ideas to remain relevant.[29]

Third, the broader political context is similar to what social movement theorists call political opportunity structures,[30] and refers to all those factors, such as the influence of donors,[31] geographical position[32] and the pressure to adopt a

---

24 Charli Carpenter and others, above n 21, at 452–453.

25 At 452.

26 Clifford Bob *The Marketing of Rebellion: Insurgents, Media, and International Activism* (Cambridge University Press, Cambridge, New York, 2005) at 26.

27 At 4. See also, Christina Kiel "How Transnational Advocacy Networks Mobilize: Applying the Literature on Interest Groups to International Action" (2011) 3 *Josef Korbel Journal of Advanced International Studies* 77 at 79.

28 Charli Carpenter and others, above n 21, at 465.

29 Robyn Linde "Gatekeeper Persuasion and Issue Adoption: Amnesty International and the Transnational LGBTQ Network" (2017) 17(2) *Journal of Human Rights* 245.

30 Charli Carpenter and others, above n 21, at 453.

31 Nitza Berkovitch and Neve Gordon "The Political Economy of Transnational Regimes: The Case of Human Rights" (2008) 52(4) *International Studies Quarterly* 881 at 891. See in general, Alexander Cooley and James Ron "The NGO Scramble: Organizational Insecurity and the Political Economy of Transnational Action" (2002) 27(1) *International Security* 5.

32 Neve Gordon "Human Rights, Social Space and Power: Why Do Some NGOs Exert More Influence Than Others?" (2008) 12(1) *International Journal of Human Rights* 23; J Moreau, A Currier "Queer Dilemmas: LGBT Activism and International Funding" In

neoliberal discourse,[33] that are outside the control of the actors within a TAN. For example, Chua and Hildebrandt comment that LGBTI NGOs in China and Singapore that took state funding to develop HIV/AIDS programmes gradually moved to frame LGBTI issues as primarily HIV/AIDS health concerns.[34] Instead, the NGOs that did not take on HIV/AIDS state funding could be relatively freer to maintain a stronger "gay advocacy" framework.[35]

Finally, internetwork relations show how the relationships between the various actors of a TAN, or the various actors of different TANs, can shape issue emergence.[36] For example, gatekeeper NGOs might not support meritorious issues if such issues are not well accepted by other important actors within the network, and therefore compromise internal alliances with their partners.[37] Also, gatekeeper NGOs can evaluate the credibility of peripheral NGOs in the light of the relations that such peripheral NGOs develop.[38]

Carpenter and others conclude that much of the literature on TAN theories has overlooked the internetwork relations. They criticise Keck and Sikkink's work, as well as the works that followed, because they use the terms 'network' and 'networking' as rather generic metaphors. Therefore, Carpenter and others encourage further research on the aspect of the internetwork relations, to explore how the network structures shape the outcomes of the TANs' advocacy.[39] In embracing Carpenter and others' recommendation, I focus on internetwork relations. However, the result of my empirical work has meant that I was not able to ignore the fact that the broad political context inevitably influences the TANs' ability to frame new issues. Throughout the chapter I use both approaches to develop my arguments; I specify which of the two I am referring to when needed.

Reasons for tensions in internetwork relations: specific challenges to the development of LGBTI transnational advocacy

The analysis of internetwork relations between gatekeeper NGOs and peripheral NGOs develops predominantly, although not exclusively, in the line of division

---

Corinne L Mason (ed) *Routledge Handbook of Queer Development Studies* (Routledge, London, 2018).

33 Jens Lerche "Transnational Advocacy Networks and Affirmative Action for Dalits in India" (2008) 39(2) *Development and Change* 239.

34 Lynette J Chua and Timothy Hildebrandt "From Health Crisis to Rights Advocacy? HIV/AIDS and Gay Activism in China and Singapore" (2014) 25(6) *VOLUNTAS: International Journal of Voluntary and Nonprofit Organizations* 1583 at 1600.

35 At 1601.

36 Charli Carpenter and others, above n 21, at 466. See also, Christina Kiel and Megan E Osterbur, "Pink Links: Visualizing the Global LGBTQ Network", in Marla Brettschneider, Susan Burgess and Christine Keating (eds) *LGBTQ Politics: A Critical Reader* (New York University Press, New York, 2017) 493.

37 Charli Carpenter and others, above n 21, at 465.

38 At 466.

39 At 467.

between the West and the rest. This is because gatekeeper NGOs usually have their headquarters in Western countries. Scholars have already criticised the unbalanced relations between Western and non-Western NGOs,[40] and highlighted how the differences between Western groups and non-Western groups shape the advocacy agenda of other human rights TANs, such as the indigenous peoples' TANs and women's rights TANs.[41]

All human rights networks are challenged on their advocacy, and all human rights networks suffer some specific challenges related to the types of rights they advocate for. LGBTI advocates are no different, and LGBTI networks suffer some specific challenges since LGBTI rights have become an ideological battle between the modern West and the traditional rest.[42] Some authors challenged the ideological division of the West and the non-West in relation to LGBTI rights and homo- and trans-phobia.[43] However, this approach is still relevant for political reasons. For example, some Asian and African political leaders maintain that LGBTI rights are Western issues, even denying that sexually and gender diverse people live in their states.[44]

Consequently, the relationship between Western and non-Western LGBTI activism is complex. Western advocacy can have unexpected and sometimes detrimental consequences in non-Western contexts. Weiss argues that the mere existence of a Western LGBTI TAN seems to produce effects in the non-Western regions. The author finds that a homophobic "anticipatory countermovement"

---

40 Gordon Crawford "Partnership or Power? Deconstructing the 'Partnership for Governance Reform' in Indonesia" (2003) 24(1) *Third World Quarterly* 139 at 155; Thomas Olesen "Globalising the Zapatistas: From Third World Solidarity to Global Solidarity?" (2004) 25 *Third World Quarterly* 255 at 258; Rhoda E Howard-Hassmann *Can Globalization Promote Human Rights?* (Pennsylvania State Press, Philadelphia, 2010) at 109; Magdalena Bexell, Jonas Tallberg, and Anders Uhlin "Democracy in Global Governance: The Promises and Pitfalls of Transnational Actors" (2010) 16(1) *Global Governance: A Review of Multilateralism and International Organization* 81 at 90; Tanja Brühl "Representing the People? NGOs in International Negotiations" in Jens Steffek and Kristina Hahn (eds) *Evaluating Transnational NGOs: Legitimacy, Accountability, Representation* (Palgrave Macmillan, Houndmills, 2010) 181; Helen Meekosha and Karen Soldatic "Human Rights and the Global South: The Case of Disability" (2011) 32(8) *Third World Quarterly* 1383 at 1394.
41 Jutta Joachim "Framing Issues and Seizing Opportunities: The UN, NGOs, and Women's Rights" (2003) 47(2) *International Studies Quarterly* 247; Karen Engle *The Elusive Promise of Indigenous Development: Rights, Culture, Strategy* (Duke University Press, Durham, 2010).
42 Holning Lau "Sexual Orientation: Testing the Universality of International Human Rights Law" (2004) 71(4) *The University of Chicago Law Review* 1689; Neville Wallace Hoad "White Man's Burden, White Man's Disease: Tracking Lesbian and Gay Human Rights" in Neville Wallace Hoad (ed) *African Intimacies: Race, Homosexuality, and Globalization* (University of Minnesota Press, Minneapolis, 2007) 68 at 75.
43 Marc Epprecht *Sexuality and Social Justice in Africa Rethinking Homophobia and Forging Resistance* (Zed Books, London, 2013) at 6; Momin Rahman "Queer Rights and the Triangulation of Western Exceptionalism" (2014) 13(3) *Journal of Human Rights* 274.
44 See for example, Kapya Kaoma *Christianity, Globalization, and Protective Homophobia Democratic Contestation of Sexuality in Sub-Saharan Africa* (Palgrave MacMillan, Basingstoke, 2018) at 1.

mobilised in Southeast Asia, even before any local LGBTI movement developed, because of the achievements of the LGBTI advocates in North America and Western Europe.[45]

Moreover, the direct interference of Western LGBTI NGOs in non-Western LGBTI issues is considered, at times, as being a new layer of cultural and secular imperialism.[46] As Thoreson eloquently explains, in those countries where public opinion is negative towards sexually and gender diverse communities, the classic boomerang models cannot work because the moral, economic or political leverages are lacking. The interference by foreign NGOs can be counterproductive because state authorities gain political power by denying rights to LGBTI people and by resisting external pressures from Western agents.[47]

One major example is the Same-sex Marriage (Prohibition) Bill,[48] discussed by the Nigerian Parliament in 2006. The Bill used to ban same-sex marriage and LGBTI organizations. Local activists voluntarily maintained a low profile, believing that the upcoming political elections in Nigeria would have shifted the attention away from the Bill. They believed the Bill would have lost political importance and ultimately it would have failed. Instead, the Peter Tatchell Foundation and OutRage! (two British NGOs) lobbied the Nigerian government to drop the Bill. Consequently, the Western organizations' intervention caused backlash and the reintroduction of the Bill.[49] Nigerian groups criticised the intervention of the two Western NGOs by saying that it was a form of "neo-colonialism".[50]

In other words, Western LGBTI NGOs and LGBTI gatekeeper NGOs might impair rather than support LGBTI activism in non-Western countries when they are not careful. Dynamics of anticipatory countermovement and the inability to apply the boomerang model in some non-Western contexts limits the growth and the efficiency of the LGBTI TANs. However, the development of LGBTI TANs can also be impaired by the difficulties that peripheral NGOs encounter at the domestic level.

---

45 Meredith L Weiss "Prejudice before Pride: Rise of an Anticipatory Countermovement" in Michael J Bosia and Meredith L Weiss (eds) *Global Homophobia: States, Movements and Politics of Oppression* (University of Illinois Press, Champaign, 2013) 149 at 151.

46 Rhoda E Howard "Gay Rights and the Right to a Family: Conflicts Between Liberal and Illiberal Belief Systems" (2001) 23 *Human Rights Quarterly* 73 at 91. On the contrary see, Baden Offord and Leon Cantrell "Homosexual Rights as Human Rights in Indonesia and Australia" (2001) 40(3–4) *Journal of Homosexuality* 233 at 249.

47 Ryan R Thoreson *Transnational LGBT Activism: Working for Sexual Rights Worldwide* (University of Minnesota Press, Minneapolis, 2014) at 138.

48 Same-sex Marriage (Prohibition) Bill 2006 (Nigeria).

49 Same-sex Marriage (Prohibition) Act 2013 (Nigeria).

50 Michael J Bosia "Strange Fruit: Homophobia, the State, and the Politics of LGBT Rights and Capabilities" (2014) 13(3) *Journal of Human Rights* 256 at 260; Paula Gerber and Joel Gory "The UN Human Rights Committee and LGBT Rights: What is it Doing? What Could it be Doing?" (2014) 14(3) *Human Rights Law Review* 403 at 419. On a similar example, see also Scott Long "Unbearable Witness: How Western Activists (Mis)recognize Sexuality in Iran" (2009) 15(1) *Contemporary Politics* 119 at 119–127.

Weaknesses of peripheral NGOs at the domestic level

The development of internetwork relations and of the transnational LGBTI network itself might be impaired by the fact that many domestic NGOs have limited possibilities to consolidate or to attract transnational cooperation. First, the fact that pioneering homosexual and gay groups had mostly European gay men memberships, and to a lesser extent European lesbian women and North American gay men, has contributed to the consolidation of sexually and gender diverse identities as mostly Western identities.[51] International organizations and social movements are spreading the use of a Western LGBTI label as a comprehensive identity,[52] but sexually and gender diverse identities can vary among and across cultures.[53] Non-Western groups who fail to adopt the 'LGBTI' label might not be able to attract international funding and support.[54] This leads to two possibilities. Either local sexually and gender diverse groups cede to the pressure to adapt to the Western LGBTI label, and therefore trade their identities to be part of the transnational LGBTI network. Or local sexually and gender diverse groups resist this adaption and maintain their identities, but they miss out on all the benefits that come with participating in the LGBTI TANs.

Second, there are problems related to tactics and resources. The typical Western visibility tactics, such as 'coming out' and Pride Parades, do not always apply in non-Western countries.[55] This is because in some repressive states "open and

---

51 Leila J Rupp "The European Origins of Transnational Organizing: The International Committee for Sexual Equality" in Phillip Ayoub and David Paternotte (eds) *LGBT Activism and the Making of Europe: A Rainbow Europe* (Palgrave Macmillan, Basingstoke, New York, 2014) 29 at 44; Phillip M Ayoub and David Paternotte "Challenging Borders, Imagining Europe: Transnational LGBT Activism in a New Europe" in Nancy Naples and Jennifer Bickham Mendez (eds) *Border Politics: Social Movements, Collective Identities, and Globalization* (New York University Press, New York, 2014) 230 at 233.

52 Carl F Stychin "Same-Sex Sexualities and the Globalization of Human Rights Discourse" (2004) 49 *McGill Law Journal* 951 at 954.

53 See, for example, Darren Rosenblum "Queer Legal Victories: Intersectionality Revised" in Mary Bernstein, Anna-Maria Marshall, and Scott Barclay (eds) *Queer Mobilizations: LGBT Activists Confront the Law* (New York University Press, New York, 2009) 38 at 49; Momin Rahman "Sexual Diffusion and Conceptual Confusions: Muslim Homophobia and Muslim Homosexualities in the Context of Modernity" in Manuela Lavinas Picq and Markus Thiel (eds) *Sexualities in World Politics: How LGBTQ Claims Shape International Relations* (Routledge, London, New York, 2015) 92 at 95.

54 Hakan Seckinelgin "Global Activism and Sexualities in the Time of HIV/AIDS" (2009) 15(1) *Contemporary Politics* 103 at 112.

55 Baden Offord "Singapore, Indonesia and Malaysia: Arrested Development!" in Manon Tremblay, David Paternotte, and Carol Johnson (eds) *The Lesbian and Gay Movement and the State Comparative Insights into a Transformed Relationship* (Ashgate, Farnham, Burlington, 2011) 135 at 136; Marc Epprecht "Sexual Minorities, Human Rights and Public Health Strategies in Africa" (2012) 111 *African Affairs* 223 at 230. On Western advocacy tactics, see also Ronald Holzhacker "National and Transnational Strategies of LGBT Civil Society Organizations in Different Political Environments: Modes of Interaction in Western and Eastern Europe for Equality" (2012) 10(1) *Comparative European Politics* 23 at 29–30.

directly confrontational forms of challenges are riskier".[56] As a consequence, some domestic NGOs prefer to adopt discreet or cautious strategies[57] by focusing on health concerns, providing social services for sexually and gender diverse communities, and avoiding legal tactics.[58] But when peripheral NGOs fail to adapt to Western advocacy models, they can find it difficult to attract transnational cooperation.[59]

Finally, domestic political constraints can impair the development of LGBTI NGOs. LGBTI organizations are not able to thrive in some contexts because states limit the freedom of association, assembly and speech of LGBTI advocates, which limits LGBTI activists' ability to mobilise.[60] Also, LGBTI NGOs can have difficulties in obtaining legal status,[61] which is pivotal for engaging with their national government and obtaining funding.[62] Such basic steps are instrumental for the development of the TANs. Although LGBTI NGOs also profit from relations with the international community,[63] they "are highly dependent upon the good will of the state in allowing them to exist in the first place".[64] Transnational advocacy, as described by Keck and Sikkink and by many who follow, is a bottom-up dynamic in which local NGOs seek international allies. Therefore,

---

56 Lynette J Chua "Pragmatic Resistance, Law, and Social Movements in Authoritarian States: The Case of Gay Collective Action in Singapore" (2012) 46(4) *Law & Society Review* 713 at 740.

57 Ashley Currier and Joëlle M Cruz "Civil Society and Sexual Struggles in Africa" in Ebenezer Obadare (ed) *The Handbook of Civil Society in Africa* (Springer New York, 2014) 337 at 344.

58 Ashley Currier "Deferral of Legal Theory, a Global LGBT Social Movement Organization's Perspective" in Mary Bernstein, Scott Barclay, and Anna-Maria Marshall (eds) *Queer Mobilizations: LGBT Activists Confront the Law* (New York University Press, New York, 2009) 21.

59 Clifford Bob, above n 26, at 34–35.

60 Lynette J Chua and David Gilbert "Sexual Orientation and Gender Identity Minorities in Transition: LGBT Rights and Activism in Myanmar" (2015) 37 *Human Rights Quarterly* 1 at 6.

61 A/HRC/19/41 *Discriminatory Laws and Practices and Acts of Violence Against Individuals Based on Their Sexual Orientation and Gender Identity* (OHCHR, 2011) at [63].

62 See in general, Luis Abolafia Anguita "Tackling Corrective Rape in South Africa: The Engagement between the LGBT CSOs and the NHRIs (CGE and SAHRC) and Its Role" (2012) 16(3) *The International Journal of Human Rights* 489 at 506.

63 Barry D Adam, Jan Willem Duyvendak, and André Krouwel "Gay and Lesbian Movements beyond Borders? National Imprints of a Worldwide Movement" in Barry D Adam, Jan Willem Duyvendak, and André Krouwel (eds) *The Global Emergence of Gay and Lesbian Politics: National Imprints of a Worldwide Movement* (Temple University Press, Philadelphia, 1999) 344 at 368; Manon Tremblay and David Paternotte "Conclusion" in Manon Tremblay, David Paternotte, and Carol Johnson (eds) *The Lesbian and Gay Movement and the State Comparative Insights into a Transformed Relationship* (Ashgate, Farnham, Burlington, 2011) 213 at 217.

64 Timothy Hildebrandt "Development and Division: The Effect of Transnational Linkages and Local Politics on LGBT Activism in China" (2012) 21(77) *Journal of Contemporary China* 845 at 864. See also, Akinyi Margareta Ocholla "The Kenyan LGBTI Social Movement – Context, Volunteerism, and Approaches to Campaigning" (2011) 3(1) *Journal of Human Rights Practice* 93 at 95.

when local NGOs are non-existent or limited, this bottom-up dynamic cannot occur. In other words, for the LGBTI TAN to grow, one necessary condition is that domestic activists exist and can enjoy at least some freedom of assembly, speech and organization.[65]

These factors can prevent the LGBTI TANs from effectively advocating for the rights of sexually and gender diverse peoples. However, this book aims to show that NGO staff members working in LGBTI gatekeeper NGOs are aware of the limits, tensions and weakness of the LGBTI TAN that impair the advancement of LGBTI rights; and they work to overcome these obstacles to create a stronger and more democratic network from below.

To address these topics, the next section discusses the democratic legitimacy of TANs and the social power of gatekeeper NGOs. I explain that LGBTI gate-keeper NGOs advocate for eliminating those obstacles to the development of the network and, in doing so, they gradually relinquish their central power, contrib-uting to the creation of a more democratic network. Later in the chapter, I argue that LGBTI gatekeeper NGOs frame LGBTI issues in a way that maximises their political opportunities and minimises resistance. Finally, the last section of the chapter sets the basis of the investigation of whether LGBTI gatekeeper NGOs impose perceived Western priorities, such as marriage equality, upon NGOs working at the periphery of the network. To start the analysis of TANs' demo-cratic legitimacy, the next section provides definitions and highlights common criticisms of the concepts of democracy and accountability in relation to NGOs.

Criticism: lack of democratic legitimacy in the NGOs' networks

NGOs are recognised as legitimate players in the international and domestic spheres because of their effectiveness and their expertise "on the ground".[66] However, some questions on NGOs' legitimacy still remain. In particular: To whom are NGOs accountable? For whom do they speak? More appropriately, whom do they represent?[67] These same questions need to be addressed consider-ing internetwork relations. Given the central role of gatekeeper NGOs, a handful

---

65 See also, Thomas Risse-Kappen *Bringing Transnational Relations Back In: Non-State Actors, Domestic Structures and International Institutions* (Cambridge University Press, Cambridge, New York, 1995) at 25; Susan D Burgerman "Mobilizing Principles: The Role of Transna-tional Activists in Promoting Human Rights Principles" (1998) 20(4) *Human Rights Quar-terly* 905 at 916; Sarah Stroup "National Origin and Transnational Activism" in Thomas Olesen (ed) *Power and Transnational Activism* (Routledge, London, New York, 2010) 151.

66 Sabine Lang *NGOs, Civil Society, and the Public Sphere* (Cambridge University Press, Cam-bridge, New York, 2013) at 2.

67 At 3. See also, Lisa Jordan and Peter Van Tuijl "Political Responsibility in Transnational NGO Advocacy" (2000) 28(12) *World Development* 2051 at 2061; Kathryn Sikkink "Restructur-ing World Politics: The Limits and Asymmetries of Soft Power" in Sanjeev Khagram, James Riker, and Kathryn Sikkink (eds) *Reconstructing World Politics: Transnational Social Move-ments and Norms* (University of Minnesota Press, Minneapolis, 2001) 301 at 306.

of NGO staff members based in New York or in Brussels can make decisions for the LGBTI communities in Asia or in Africa, without anybody formally electing them. I explore TANs' democratic legitimacy by discussing common criticisms about internal accountability and lack of democratic representation.

In general, accountability is defined as the means by which NGOs are held responsible for their actions.[68] NGO accountability can be external or internal. External accountability refers to the process of holding NGOs responsible for their actions before states and international organizations. Even though some systems of external accountability are in place,[69] states and international organizations do not formally recognise NGOs as significant players in international relations.[70] However, investigating the concept of internal accountability is more useful to understand the internetwork relations of the LGBTI TANs, as internal accountability refers to the process of holding actors of an NGO accountable for their work before their members and constituencies.[71]

Internal accountability raises questions of democratic legitimacy and representation, where the common criticism is that NGOs are not elected,[72] and they cannot rightfully represent the interests of the very people they claim they advocate for.[73] Wapner contests such a position in saying that when members of NGOs feel they are not represented by the advocacy agenda, they withdraw their support to the NGO.[74] Nevertheless, Wapner's argument fails for those NGOs that advocate on behalf of vulnerable populations: for example, children and disabled people, whose rights are usually advocated by adult able-bodied NGO staff,[75] and other vulnerable groups who live at the margin of societies, like prostitutes and victims of human trafficking.[76]

---

68 Alnoor Ebrahim "Accountability in Practice: Mechanisms for NGOs" (2003) 31(5) *World Development* 813 at 813.
69 E/RES/1996/31 *Consultative Relationship between the United Nations and Non-Governmental Organizations* (1996). See also Chapter 4.
70 Peter J Spiro "Accounting for NGOs" (2002) 3 *Chicago Journal of International Law* 161 at 166. See also, Marek Havrda and Petr Kutilek "Accountability 20 – In Search for a New Approach to International Non-Governmental Organizations' Accountability" in Jens Steffek and Kristina Hahn (eds) *Evaluating Transnational NGOs: Legitimacy, Accountability, Representation* (Palgrave Macmillan, Houndmills, New York, 2010) 157.
71 L David Brown, Alnoor Ebrahim, and Srilatha Batliwala "Governing International Advocacy NGOs" (2012) 40(6) *World Development* 1098 at 1100.
72 Jens Steffek and Kristina Hahn "Introduction: Transnational NGOs and Legitimacy, Accountability, Representation" in Jens Steffek and Kristina Hahn (eds) *Evaluating Transnational NGOs: Legitimacy, Accountability, Representation* (Palgrave Macmillan, Houndmills, New York, 2010) 1 at 17.
73 Warren Nyamugasira "NGOs and Advocacy: How Well Are the Poor Represented?" (1998) 8(3) *Development in Practice* 297.
74 Paul Wapner "Defending Accountability in NGOs" (2002) 3 *Chicago Journal of International Law* 197 at 201.
75 Anna Holzscheiter "The Representational Power of Civil Society Organizations in Global AIDS Governance: Advocating for Children in Global Health Politics" in Thomas Olesen (ed) *Power and Transnational Activism* (Routledge, London, New York, 2010) 173 at 185.
76 Kristina Hahn "NGOs' Power of Advocacy: The Construction of Identities in UN Counter-Human Trafficking Policies" in Kristina Hahn and Jens Steffek (eds) *Evaluating*

Within a transnational network of NGOs, the question of internal account-ability representativeness is even more problematic. NGOs acting transnation-ally often take decisions 'behind closed doors',[77] and without a "cross-border electoral process".[78] In particular, processes of growing professionalisation of the human rights advocacy increases the distance between NGOs and the communi-ties they represent. This means that NGOs possibly overlook the human aspects of the advocacy, which in turn produces a lack of NGOs' internal accountability towards the very people they claim they advocate for.[79]

In sum, the debate on NGOs' democratic legitimacy has been going on for a long time, without seemingly producing a satisfactory answer. In 2014, a political theorist, Jennifer Rubenstein, revolutionised such a debate by shifting the focus from representation and accountability, and introducing the concept of power. Rubenstein's arguments, and their significance for this study, are explored next.

Transnational advocacy networks are not elected: so what?

Regarding the question of NGOs' democratic legitimacy, Rubenstein suggests a shift in the focus from representation to the concept of misuse of power. Ruben-stein says that NGOs' accountability does not only refer to NGOs being respon-sible of their actions, but also it is defined by NGOs properly using their power. Rubenstein's definition is rather niche and a new approach. Many have writ-ten about NGOs' accountability and democratic legitimacy, and Rubenstein's approach sheds new light on an old debate.

Rubenstein provides some examples to explain how NGOs can misuse their power, which are by hindering the interests of marginalised populations[80] or by interfering with them without ensuring that their actions take into account the interests of the people involved.[81] Then she argues that "[b]eing democratic means minimizing the extent to which INGOs advocates" misuse their pow-er.[82] To adapt Rubenstein's definition to this research, I consider that gatekeeper NGOs misuse their power when (i) they interfere with LGBTI communities and peripheral NGOs; and (ii) they interfere with LGBTI communities and periph-eral NGOs without ensuring that their actions take into account the interests of

---

Transnational NGOs: Legitimacy, Accountability, Representation (Palgrave Macmillan, Houndmills, New York, 2010) 220 at 236.

77 Julie Mertus "From Legal Transplants to Transformative Justice: Human Rights and the Promise of Transnational Civil Society" (1998) 14 *American University of International Law Review* 1335 at 1372.

78 At 1373. For further readings see, Alan Hudson "NGOs' Transnational Advocacy Networks: from 'Legitimacy' to 'Political Responsibility'?" (2001) 1(4) *Global Networks* 331.

79 Loveday Hodson "Activists and Lawyers in the ECtHR: The Struggle for Gay Rights" in Dia Anagnostou (ed) *Rights and Courts in Pursuing of Social Change: Legal Mobilisation in the Multi-Level European System* (Hart Publishing, Oxford, 2014) 181 at 196.

80 Jennifer C Rubenstein "The Misuse of Power, Not Bad Representation: Why It Is beside the Point That No One Elected Oxfam" (2014) 22(2) *Journal of Political Philosophy* 204 at 219.

81 At 222.

82 At 229.

the people involved. If gatekeeper NGOs minimise these misuses of power, they act democratically.

I take on board Rubenstein's comments on power in order to evaluate the LGBTI TANs. Indeed, I argue that both gatekeeper NGOs' efforts to build the network horizontally and to create favourable domestic political opportunities for peripheral NGOs leads to the creation of a more democratic LGBTI TAN in which gatekeeper NGOs work towards, and are motivated by, relinquishing their hegemonic power. In other words, given Rubenstein's definitions of misuse of power and democratic legitimacy, when gatekeeper NGOs decentralise their position in the network and empower peripheral NGOs to conduct their own advocacy, then gatekeeper NGOs minimise their misuse of power because they do not interfere and, instead, they make sure that the populations and the peripheral NGOs are the agents of the advocacy in their local and domestic arenas. Later in the chapter, I propose to look at the marriage equality issue as a litmus test because imposing marriage equality on peripheral LGBTI advocates can be seen as an interference and, therefore, a potential misuse of power. But first, to understand how NGOs can minimise their misuse of power, the next section explains what power means in a network context.

Gatekeeper NGOs: centrality and social power

Network analysis explains that the power of the actors within a network derives not solely from the static attributes of the actors, but also from its position in the network and its relationships with the other actors.[83] Indeed, the nodes of a network possess social power due to their centrality, defined both as the intensities of ties and the exclusivity of ties. First, nodes that have "strong links with many other nodes" may have social power because their central position allows them to easily access information and resources, and to control the flow of such information and resources.[84] Second, nodes that "possess exclusive ties to otherwise marginalized or weakly connected nodes or groups of nodes" gain social power by acting as a bridge between them.[85]

For TANs, social power and centrality means that gatekeeper NGOs are not only influential because they are bigger, and better founded than other NGOs, but also because of their central position within the network.[86] Gatekeeper NGOs can control the flow of information by drafting human rights reports, newsletters, press releases, official written statements and so on. Moreover, gatekeeper NGOs have more organizational resources, such as money and professional expertise, and they can choose with whom they are willing to share their resources. Gatekeeper

---

83 Emilie M Hafner-Burton, Miles Kahler, and Alexander H Montgomery "Network Analysis for International Relations" (2009) 63(3) *International Organization* 559 at 570.
84 At 570.
85 At 571.
86 Charli Carpenter "Vetting the Advocacy Agenda: Network Centrality and the Paradox of Weapons Norms" (2011) 65(1) *International Organization* 69 at 72.

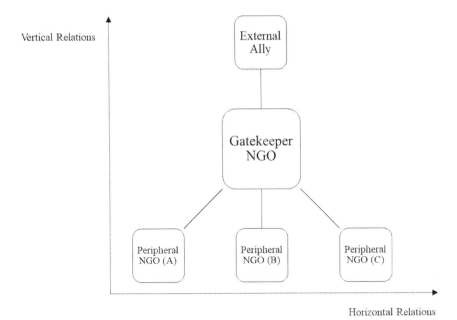

Figure 2.1 Gatekeeper NGOs' social power: intensity and exclusiveness of ties

Note: "External ally" stands for governments' delegates, international organizations and funders.

NGOs have more visibility and greater ties with international organizations and states; ultimately, they have more social power.[87]

Figure 2.1 shows that gatekeeper NGOs have more intense ties and more exclusive ties. It is an example of a simple network, in which the gatekeeper NGO is central and has more social power. Indeed, the gatekeeper NGO has more intense ties because it is the node that has more connections than any other node; and it has exclusive ties with any other node, which is to say that it functions as a bridge in the network. For example, if peripheral NGO (A) needs to get in contact with the external ally, it needs to pass through the gatekeeper NGO.

In sum, gatekeeper NGOs possess social power because they have exclusive or nearly exclusive ties with international organizations and governments. However, with my empirical research I investigate how LGBTI gatekeeper NGOs are decreasing their centrality within the network, redistributing their power and ultimately creating a more democratic network. I develop these arguments in the next sub-paragraphs.

How do LGBTI gatekeeper NGOs respond to the imbalance of power?

Some authors believe that LGBTI gatekeeper NGOs are aware of the limits, the tensions and the imbalance of power of the LGBTI TANs, and they try to minimise

---

87 At 74–75.

them. Thoreson comments on the work of OutRight, which is based in the United States, in explaining that the staff members of the organization were aware that their interference in the domestic affairs of foreign governments could be detrimental for the sexually and gender diverse groups working on the local level.[88] Therefore, instead of openly condemning foreign governments, OutRight prefers to coordinate the work of domestic NGOs and support activists so that they can voice their own concerns, both at the international and domestic levels.[89] I aim to build upon these assumptions to explain how gatekeeper NGOs coordinate peripheral NGOs to develop the network horizontally. This analysis is important because I argue that these dynamics have consequences in the advocacy agenda setting.

LGBTI gatekeeper NGOs work to develop LGBTI TANs horizontally

Tarrow highlights that horizontal relations are developed between actors situated in the same level, i.e. states with other states and domestic NGOs with other domestic NGOs. Vertical relations develop on the links between the subnational, national and international levels – for example, between states and international organizations, or between NGOs and international organizations.[90] In their seminal study on TANs, Keck and Sikkink first point out that the various actors of a transnational network have horizontal relations, as they describe networks as "voluntary, reciprocal, and horizontal patterns of communications and exchange".[91] However, as seen above, Bob, and Carpenter and colleagues rebut the view that transnational networks are flat patterns of relations; instead, they develop the idea that gatekeeper NGOs are hierarchically superior to the peripheral NGOs. Indeed, Carpenter described TANs by saying that "a small numbers of major 'hubs' dominate, and pathways between peripheral nodes are dependents on these hubs".[92] In sum, on the one hand, peripheral NGOs working in neighbour countries have horizontal relationships; and, on the other hand, peripheral NGOs working primarily in the domestic sphere have vertical relations with gatekeeper NGOs that are outside their domestic sphere.

Holzhacker and Thoreson analyse the vertical and horizontal relations between gatekeeper and peripheral NGOs, and they claim that horizontal connections among domestic NGOs can appear because of positive political opportunities, or new internetwork links can be proactively created by the gatekeeper NGOs. First, Holzhacker claims that European Union (EU) clauses on the prohibition of discrimination on grounds of SOGI promoted the mobilisation of European TANs across EU members.[93] This is because domestic NGOs working in EU were

---

88 Ryan R Thoreson, above n 47, at 123.
89 At 210.
90 Sidney G Tarrow *The New Transnational Activism* (Cambridge University Press, New York, 2005) at 7–8.
91 Margaret E Keck and Kathryn Sikkink, above n 7, at 8.
92 Charli Carpenter, above n 86 at 73.
93 Treaty of Amsterdam Amending the Treaty on European Union, The Treaties Establishing the European Communities and Related Acts, European Union (signed 10 November 1997,

facilitated by the new anti-discrimination clauses to create horizontal connections among each other in a process where domestic NGOs "learn and are assisted by" NGOs in other EU states.[94] Second, Thoreson explains that because OutRight relies on peripheral NGOs to gather reliable information on human rights violations, it invests in building partnerships with NGOs and activists working in non-Western countries.[95] In other words, gatekeeper NGOs work to develop vertical relationships between themselves and peripheral NGOs.

I aim to add to Holzhacker and Thoreson's analysis by arguing that the horizontal connections among peripheral NGOs do not only appear to be due to positive circumstances, but they also can be created by gatekeeper NGOs who build these horizontal connections to improve the efficiency of the LGBTI advocacy. The internetwork relations between LGBTI gatekeeper NGOs and the NGOs at the periphery of the network influence the LGBTI advocacy agenda. LGBTI gatekeeper NGOs work to develop the network horizontally, ultimately, with the aim of making the LGBTI TAN stronger and more effective. This strategy has consequences in the advocacy agenda because, to be able to build the network from below, gatekeeper NGOs prioritise and strongly advocate before international organizations for those rights that facilitate the domestic political opportunities of peripheral NGOs.

Issue emergence: gatekeeper NGOs advocate for the rights that enhance domestic political opportunities for peripheral NGOs

To allow a development of the LGBTI network from below, LGBTI gatekeeper NGOs work to enhance the abilities of peripheral NGOs to flourish in their own domestic sphere. Social movement and TAN theories say that political opportunity structures are not fixed. TANs can work to improve political opportunity structures over time;[96] and NGOs can improve the political opportunity structures of their NGO partners.[97] In other words, gatekeeper NGOs can also improve the domestic political opportunity structures of peripheral NGOs to

---

entered into force 1 May 1999), Article 13; Council Directive 2000/78/EC of 27 November 2000 Establishing a General Framework for Equal Treatment in Employment and Occupation (2000).

94 Ronald Holzhacker "Transnational Strategies of Civil Society Organizations Striving for Equality and Nondiscrimination: Exchanging Information on New EU Directives, Coalition Strategies and Strategic Litigation" in Laszlo Bruszt and Ronald Holzhacker (eds) *Transnationalization of Economies, States, and Civil Societies: New Challenges for Governance in Europe* (Springer, New York, London, 2009) 219 at 235.

95 Ryan R Thoreson, above n 47, at 123.

96 Kathryn Sikkink "Patterns of Dynamic Multilevel Governance and the Insider-Outsider Coalition" in Donatella Della Porta and Sidney G Tarrow (eds) *Transnational Protest and Global Activism: People, Passions and Power* (Rowman and Littlefield Publishers, Lanham, 2004) 151 at 154.

97 Sidney G Tarrow "States and Opportunities: The Political Structuring of Social Movements" in Doug McAdam, John D McCarthy, and Mayer Zald (eds) *Comparative Perspectives on Social Movements: Political Opportunities, Mobilizing Structures, and Cultural Framings* (Cambridge University Press, Cambridge, New York, 1996) 41 at 58–61.

develop the overall network. To describe how LGBTI gatekeeper NGOs can do so I turn to a comparative study on LGBTI social movements.

Among numerous country-focused studies on LGBTI social movements,[98] Adam, Duyvendak and Krouwel edit an essay collection that analyses a large number of country-based lesbian and gay social movements and then draws conclusions about the political opportunity structures for lesbian and gay social movements.[99] They claim that lesbian and gay social movements can start developing when social, cultural and economic factors allow public opinion to become more favourable towards sexually and gender diverse peoples,[100] i.e. when sexually and gender diverse identities are formed and can exist in society, and when lesbian and gay people can make their identities visible.[101] Moreover, the development of lesbian and gay social movements can be impaired by the presence of a dominant religious party, while facilitated by urbanisation, industrialisation and individualism.[102]

These factors are necessary, but not sufficient, for lesbian and gay social movements to thrive. Indeed, the development of lesbian and gay social movements is favoured by consensus democracies, states that allow social and political organizations to be formed, states whose political cultures recognise minorities, states with traditionally strong left-wing parties, and finally states where sexual and gender diverse behaviours are legal.[103]

I use Adam, Duyvendak and Krouwel's work to analyse the NGOs' written statements submitted to the UN HR Council and NGOs' oral statements delivered during the Universal Period Review (UPR) process. In other words,

---

98 Stephen M Engel *The Unfinished Revolution: Social Movement Theory and the Gay and Lesbian Movement* (Cambridge University Press, Cambridge, 2001); Mary Bernstein "Nothing Ventured, Nothing Gained? Conceptualizing Social Movement 'Success' in the Lesbian and Gay Movement" (2003) 46(3) *Sociological Perspectives* 353; Melinda D Kane "You've Won, Now What? The Influence of Legal Change on Gay and Lesbian Mobilization, 1974–1999" (2010) 51(2) *Sociological Quarterly* 255; Verta A Taylor and Mary Bernstein *Marrying Kind? Debating Same-Sex Marriage within the Lesbian and Gay Movement* (University of Minnesota Press, Minneapolis, 2013); Ana Cristina Santos *Social Movements and Sexual Citizenship in Southern Europe* (Palgrave Macmillan, Basingstoke, 2013); Robert Rhodes-Kubiak *Activist Citizenship and the LGBT Movement in Serbia: Belonging, Critical Engagement, and Transformation* (Palgrave Macmillan, New York, 2015).

99 Barry D Adam, Jan Willem Duyvendak, and André Krouwel *The Global Emergence of Gay and Lesbian Politics: National Imprints of a Worldwide Movement* (Temple University Press, Philadelphia, 1999). There is also another large case study on LGBTI social movements' structures; however, the authors focus on national structures, which do not help in the advancement of this investigation. See, Manon Tremblay and David Paternotte "Conclusion" in Manon Tremblay, David Paternotte, and Carol Johnson (eds) *The Lesbian and Gay Movement and the State Comparative Insights into a Transformed Relationship* (Ashgate, Farnham, Burlington, 2011) 213 at 214–218.

100 Barry D Adam, Jan Willem Duyvendak, and André Krouwel, above n 99, at 350–360.

101 See also, Phillip M Ayoub *When States Come Out: Europe's Sexual Minorities and Politics of Visibility* (Cambridge University Press, Cambridge, 2016) at 200.

102 See also, John D'Emilio "Capitalism and Gay Identity" in Ann Snitow, Christine Stansel, and Sharon Thompson (eds) *Powers of Desire the Politics of Sexuality* (Monthly Review Press, New York, 1983) 100.

103 Barry D Adam, Jan Willem Duyvendak, and André Krouwel, above n 99, at 361–367.

I research whether NGOs invoke those rights that as Adam, Duyvendak and Krouwel claim, would improve the domestic political opportunities of LGBTI movements and NGOs. It is difficult to analyse some areas, for example, whether and to what extent NGOs can influence the party system of a country, or whether LGBTI NGOs can promote the urbanisation and industrialisation of foreign countries. Investigating these and similar topics would require much deeper country base analysis, outside the scope of this book.[104] Nevertheless, some of the features highlighted by Adam, Duyvendak and Krouwel are easier to analyse and quantify. If gatekeeper NGOs work to strengthen the LGBTI network from below, then the analysis of the NGOs' oral and written statements should find that, first, gatekeeper NGOs advocate for the development of sexual and gender diverse identities and visibility; second, they pressure states to allow LGBTI organizations to be formed and participate in the political system; and, finally, they invoke the decriminalisation of sexual and gender diverse behaviours.

Gatekeeper NGOs are not only influential setting the advocacy agenda, they are also influential in choosing how these issues are framed. In the ensuing paragraphs, I explore how LGBTI issues are framed and what the consequences of these choices are.

Framing LGBTI issues as human rights claims

Having identified the rationale by which gatekeeper NGOs choose what issues are to be advocated, this sub-section addresses more specifically the issue framing process. Traditional arguments to protect sexually and gender diverse individuals claimed that criminal laws condemn the act (same-sex sexual behaviours) rather than homosexuality as an identity. This framework became redundant in the late 1950s when the decriminalisation of same-sex sexual activities was connected with the protection of the right to privacy of consenting adults engaging in same-sex sexual acts.[105] However, this second framework can also be considered to be outdated. Nowadays, there is a general agreement that LGBTI NGOs use human rights frameworks to advance their issues in international fora. Still, the macro category of human rights has many meanings, and there is the need for further investigation of how LGBTI NGOs frame SOGII issues before international organizations.

Tsutsui, Whitlinger and Lim stress that international human rights agreements provide NGOs with powerful external symbols that help them frame their grievances more cogently. However, not all human rights NGOs can benefit from these external symbols because the UN has the potential to encourage some types

---

104 See for example, Sarah L Henderson "Selling Civil Society: Western Aid and the Nongovernmental Organization Sector in Russia" (2002) 35(2) *Comparative Political Studies* 139.

105 Douglas Sanders "Constructing Lesbian and Gay Rights" (1994) 9(2) *Canadian Journal of Law and Society* 99 at 102. See for example, *Dudgeon v the United Kingdom* (7525/76) ECtHR (ser A) 45 22 October 1981; *Toonen v Australia* HR Comm CCPR/C/50/D/488/1992, 31 March 1994.

of NGOs and discourage others.[106] In particular, LGBTI NGOs have difficulties in bringing SOGII claims before the UN because they lose the support of governmental delegates and international organizations when they advocate for issues that "go beyond what other social actors deem reasonable".[107]

Tsutsui, Whitlinger and Lim's analysis suggests that LGBTI TANs experience difficulties in advancing SOGII issues before international organizations, but their research does not reveal much about how LGBTI gatekeeper NGOs can improve the way they frame SOGII issues to overcome these obstacles. To provide a valid account of how the broader political context of international organizations influence the NGOs' issue framing, the following sub-paragraphs analyse three elements of political opportunity structures: access, alliance and political alignment. The three elements are addressed in turn below.

Broader political context and issue framing: access, alliance and political alignment

First, access refers to the openness or closure of the political system. International organizations provide NGOs with many new venues of contestation,[108] and the ability of NGOs to access these avenues is vital for their work. Indeed, when NGOs have limited or no access to the work of international organizations, their ability to provide their input and to shape the issue framing process is restricted.[109] It is hard for NGOs to influence the international human rights system when they are not even allowed to take part in the "game".[110]

Second, political allies, such as powerful governments and UN agencies, are strategic for the development of human rights NGOs' advocacy.[111] In adopting and repeating NGOs' frameworks, allies can "amplify and legitimize" them,[112] but influential allies can be disadvantageous for NGOs when the support of some allies "result in undesired or unintended issue advocacy".[113]

Finally, with regard to the third element, social movements can profit from instability in political alignment.[114] NGOs can benefit from such conflicts among countries' blocs if activists are able to create frames that provide a bridge to

106 Kiyoteru Tsutsui, Claire Whitlinger, and Alwyn Lim "International Human Rights Law and Social Movements: States' Resistance and Civil Society's Insistence" (2012) 8 *Annual Review of Law and Social Science* 367 at 378.
107 At 385.
108 At 376.
109 Jutta Joachim *Agenda Setting, the UN, and NGOs: Gender Violence and Reproductive Rights* (Georgetown University Press, Washington, 2007) at 24.
110 Joke Swiebel "Lesbian, Gay, Bisexual and Transgender Human Rights: The Search for an International Strategy" (2009) 15(1) *Contemporary Politics* 19 at 30.
111 Kiyoteru Tsutsui, Claire Whitlinger, and Alwyn Lim, above n 106, at 376; Margaret E Keck and Kathryn Sikkink, above n 7, at 12.
112 Jutta Joachim "Framing Issues and Seizing Opportunities: The UN, NGOs, and Women's Rights" (2003) 47(2) *International Studies Quarterly* 247 at 251.
113 Jutta Joachim, above n 109, at 30.
114 Kiyoteru Tsutsui, Claire Whitlinger, and Alwyn Lim, above n 106, at 377.

promote consensus among countries.[115] However, the divisions among blocs are detrimental if the tensions are so harsh that they produce a deadlock; in particular, "if issues proposed or supported by one bloc are continuously opposed and voted against by others".[116]

Indeed, the political divisions among pro-LGBTI rights blocs and anti-LGBTI rights blocs are so severe that it has produced an impasse in which LGBTI rights struggle to emerge. Thoreson explains that LGBTI TANs try to overcome this impasse by maintaining a low profile as they try to advance LGBTI rights. Even though gatekeeper NGOs' staff members have a rich understanding of the variegated LGBTI issues, they are also conscious of the global sensitivities around themes such as marriage and family, and therefore they prefer to speak out more forcefully on "fundamental protections".[117]

Following on from the comments immediately above, I would expect to find that LGBTI networks frame LGBTI issues as fundamental human rights for LGBTI people, rather than a more variegated set of LGBTI rights. I continue to investigate how the broader political context contributes to frame LGBTI rights in the ensuing sub-section.

The prohibition of discrimination principle

Activists have a major role in promoting the development of new human rights issues by strategically framing pre-existing problems. However, in order to be successful in influencing the international human rights agenda, activists need to pay "a great deal of attention to framing the issue in terms the organization might swallow".[118] Swiebel comments upon the work of LGBTI advocates in the 1990s, and she maintains that European LGBTI activists framed LGBTI issues as a question of human rights, and more specifically as an anti-discrimination issue. At that time, the EU was adopting measures against racial discrimination, and LGBTI NGOs lobbied the EU to encompass sexual orientation in such anti-discrimination policies.[119]

Similar to Swiebel, I argue that, to enhance their ability to be heard by international human rights organs, LGBTI gatekeeper NGOs frame LGBTI issues using a principle that matches existing human rights values, i.e. the prohibition of discrimination. This is because the prohibition of discrimination is a fundamental principle of international human rights law and because there is an "emerging consensus that all forms of arbitrary distinction are prohibited by international human rights law".[120] Indeed, international human rights law is premised on the

---

115 Jutta Joachim, above n 109, at 30.
116 At 31.
117 Ryan R Thoreson, above n 47, at 218.
118 Joke Swiebel, above n 110, at 28.
119 At 30. See also, Joshua W Busby *Moral Movements and Foreign Policy* (Cambridge University Press, Cambridge, 2010).
120 David Brown "Making Room for Sexual Orientation and Gender Identity in the International Human Rights Law: An Introduction to the Yogyakarta Principles" (2010) 31 *Michigan Journal of International Law* 821 at 849.

principle that all human rights apply without discrimination,[121] and the prohibition of discrimination on the ground of SOGII is the means to promote human rights for LGBTI people.[122] Therefore, I argue that the LGBTI TANs working at the UN predominantly use the prohibition of discrimination on the grounds of SOGII to advocate for the rights of LGBTI people because this framework resonates with the existing international human rights treaties and it enhances LGBTI gatekeeper NGOs to make their message heard and be accepted by international organizations and states.

However, the prohibition of discrimination framework might not always work for TANs. Some authors contend that human rights frameworks and the anti-discrimination frameworks might not be sufficient to ensure the protection of LGBTI individuals[123] and suggest the use of concepts like justice, liberation or self-determination.[124] For example, Saiz argues that the principle of the prohibition of discrimination is inadequate to really tackle the "structural bias" of international human rights law and suggests that the concept of sexual rights would better serve the cause of LGBTI advocates.[125] Moreover, Roseman and Miller argue that the prohibition of discrimination as "compartmentali[sed]" in various grounds fails to address the intersectional essence of discrimination.[126] Finally, McIntosh Sundstrom highlights that foreign NGOs are more successful in mobilising Russian civil society around women issues when they use a prohibition of violence against women framework, as opposed to the prohibition of discrimination on the grounds of gender. This is because the first is welcomed as a universally accepted norm, while the second is perceived as a foreign value.[127] The ensuing sub-paragraphs describe how SOGII anti-discrimination advocacy can trigger backlash from some conservative/religious states and NGOs that juxtapose the prohibition of discrimination with the right to marry.

---

121 Debra L DeLaet "Don't Ask, Don't Tell: Where is the Protection Against Sexual Orientation Discrimination in International Human Rights Law" (1997) 7 *Law & Sexuality: Rev Lesbian, Gay, Bisexual & Transgender Legal Issues* 31 at 32.

122 At 51.

123 Julie Mertus "The Rejection of Human Rights Framings: The Case of LGBT Advocacy in the US" (2007) 29 *Human Rights Quarterly* 1036 at 1039; Kay Lalor "Constituting Sexuality: Rights, Politics and Power in the Gay Rights Movement" (2011) 15(5) *The International Journal of Human Rights* 683 at 691. See in general, Kay Lalor, Arturo Sánchez García, and Elizabeth Mills "How Useful is the Law for Attaining Sexual and Gender Justice" in Kay Lalor and others (eds) *Gender, Sexuality and Social Justice: What's Law Got to Do with It?* (Institute for Development Studies, Brighton, 2016) 16.

124 Matthew Waites "Critique of 'Sexual Orientation' and 'Gender Identity' in Human Rights Discourse: Global Queer Politics beyond the Yogyakarta Principles" (2009) 15(1) *Contemporary Politics* 137 at 138.

125 Ignacio Saiz "Bracketing Sexuality: Human Rights and Sexual Orientation: A Decade of Development and Denial at the UN" (2004) 7 *Health and Human Rights* 48 at 63.

126 Mindy Jane Roseman and Alice M Miller "Normalizing Sex and Its Discontents: Establishing Sexual Rights in International Law" (2011) 34 *Harvard Journal of Law and Gender* 313 at 353.

127 Lisa McIntosh Sundstrom "Foreign Assistance, International Norms, and NGO Development: Lessons from the Russian Campaign" (2005) 59(2) *International Organization* 419 at 421.

The slippery slope argument: marriage inequality to mobilise supporters

When conflicting activists try to advance their own agenda, they can also impact on one another's tactics, agenda setting and outcomes[128] in a "dynamic set of relations".[129] Bob comments that conservative/religious states working in coalition with conservative/religious NGOs to oppose LGBTI rights shape the issue framing of the LGBTI TAN. Indeed, the LGBTI TANs working at the UN fear that the opposition would prevent them from promoting their issues before international organizations, and they "camouflage" the issues they promote in a less threatening way,[130] by framing "their problems in narrow terms, with a focus on discrimination and violence".[131]

Moreover, Fetner studied the LGBTI and the anti-LGBTI networks in the United States and discovered that, in the 1970s and 1980s, the American LGBTI movement gave a low priority to advocating for the right to marry for same-sex couples, seen as a patriarchal and obsolete institution, preferring other issues like discrimination and violence. The religious movements, meanwhile, focused on opposing same-sex marriage because they recognised that the institution of marriage had "strong cultural resonance and popular support",[132] and they considered that fighting the right to marry for same-sex couples would have attracted conservatives who had not yet joined the movement. Therefore, Fetner argues that the American LGBTI movement felt the need to advocate for the right to marry as a response to the religious movement's campaign.[133]

In other words, LGBTI activists frame their issues as fundamental protections and anti-discrimination to match consolidated human rights principles and at the same time avoid controversial issues, such as the right to marry. On the contrary, conservative/religious activists see in the marriage inequality battle the potential to mobilise more supporters. This is because of the strong cultural resonance of heterosexual marriage in many societies.[134] The religious/conservative TANs and states use a sort of 'slippery slope' argument to justify discrimination on the grounds of SOGII, which goes as follows. Some religious/conservative TANs and states want to prevent the development of a SOGII anti-discrimination human rights standard because it could lead to the interpretation of a genderless right to marry and to form a family.[135] They fear that with the consolidation of

128 Clifford Bob *The Global Right Wing and the Clash of World Politics* (Cambridge University Press, New York, 2012) at 5.

129 Tina Fetner *How the Religious Right Shaped Lesbian and Gay Activism* (University of Minnesota Press, Minneapolis, 2008) at xvii.

130 Clifford Bob, above n 128, at 22.

131 At 40.

132 Tina Fetner, above n 129 at 111.

133 At 113.

134 Kelly Kollman "Same-Sex Partnership and Marriage: The Success and Costs of Transnational Activism" in David Paternotte and Manon Tremblay (eds) *The Ashgate Research Companion to Lesbian and Gay Activism* (Ashgate, Burlington, 2015) 307 at 316–319.

135 Françoise Girard "Negotiating Sexual Rights and Sexual Orientation at the UN" in Richard Parker, Rosalind Petchesky, and Robert Sember (eds) *Sex Politics: Reports from the Front Lines* (Sexuality Policy Watch, Rio de Janeiro, 2008) 311 at 346.

a SOGII anti-discrimination standard, the phrase "men and women" have the right to marry and to form a family of international human rights law would become "everyone" has this right.

That is to say that the LGBTI TAN might have in mind fundamental rights when they advocate for the prohibition of discrimination on grounds of SOGII – the right to be free from violence and harassment, the right to be free from unjust and unlawful imprisonment. However, religious/conservative NGOs and states understand the prohibition of discrimination on the grounds of SOGII as leading to marriage and family equality. As McGoldrick explains, some countries might agree that individuals cannot be denied their basic human rights because of their SOGII but, at the same time, they continue to refuse to accept a norm that prohibits SOGII discrimination because of the consequences that such a norm could have on their domestic family law.[136]

It is clear that the conservative/religious TANs oppose marriage and family equality, and often use marriage inequality as an argument to mobilise support and to stop any recommendations and resolutions on SOGII issues. However, the right to marry is more complex than that. As one might expect, religious/ conservative TANs oppose the right to marry for LGBTI people, but how do the LGBTI TANs deal with marriage rights? These issues are controversial among activists and academics, and these topics trigger endless academic debates.[137] I discuss the importance of the right to marry in the advocacy agenda of LGBTI TANs to investigate democratic legitimacy of gatekeeper NGOs.

Power relations and marriage equality: the collaborative decision-making process

Some authors argue that marriage equality is at the centre of the Western LGBTI advocacy agenda.[138] Indeed, some authors highlight that European LGBTI NGOs

---

136 Dominic McGoldrick "The Development and Status of Sexual Orientation Discrimination under International Human Rights Law" (2016) 16(4) *Human Rights Law Review* 613 at 660.

137 Bruce MacDougall "The Celebration of Same-Sex Marriage" (2000) 32 *Ottawa Law Review* 235; Jeffrey Weeks "Regulation, Resistance, Recognition" (2008) 11 *Sexualities* 787; Monte Neil Stewart "Marriage Facts" (2008) 31 *Harvard Journal of Law & Public Policy* 313; Man Yee Karen Lee *Equality, Dignity, and Same-Sex Marriage: A Rights Disagreement in Democratic Societies* (Martinus Nijhoff Publishers, Leiden, Boston, 2010); Paul Johnson "Challenging the Heteronormativity of Marriage: The Role of Judicial Interpretation and Authority" (2011) 20(3) *Social & Legal Studies* 349; Sherif Girgis, Ryan T Anderson, and Robert P George *What Is Marriage? Man and Woman: A Defense* (Encounter Books, New York, London, 2012); William N Eskridge *Equality Practice* (Taylor and Francis, Florence, 2013); Scot M Peterson and Iain McLean *Legally Married: Love and Law in the UK and the US* (Edinburgh University Press, Edinburgh, 2013); Angelia R Wilson *Why Europe Is Lesbian and Gay Friendly (and Why America Never Will Be)* (State University New York Press, Albany, 2013); Bronwyn Winter Maxime Forest Réjane Sénac (eds) *Global Perspectives on Same-Sex Marriage: A Neo-Institutional Approach* (Palgrave Macmillan, Basingstoke, 2018).

138 David Paternotte and Manon Tremblay, above n 2.

have exaggerated the symbolic importance of marriage equality to promote LGBTI rights in Europe,[139] which has attracted a backlash from conservative/religious NGOs and states.

The right to marry can produce a source of tension within the internetwork relations between peripheral NGOs and gatekeeper NGOs, and it can be seen as an interference and, therefore, a misuse of power. Hildebrandt studies the relations between the Chinese LGBTI activists and international NGOs and finds that one of the reasons that there are weak relationships between the two is because of the marriage equality debate. Indeed, Chinese activists place a low priority on marriage equality, but they feel pressured to comply with "a globalized notion of what it means to be gay"[140] as mostly signifying advocating for same-sex marriage. Therefore, they prefer to limit their interactions with international NGOs and donors.

Considering these premises, I use the advocacy for the right to marry for LGBTI people as a litmus test to demonstrate that gatekeeper NGOs partially relinquish their power and frame LGBTI issues in a way that maximises their advocacy. Other authors have used a similar test, however, reaching opposite conclusions. Osterbur and Kiel study the European LGBTI TAN starting from similar premises to those in this chapter. LGBTI gatekeeper NGOs have a position of power in the network because they can choose which issues the network will advocate for and how these issues are framed.[141] Therefore, the authors expect to find "nodes with a large number of ties and gatekeeper power to be able to dominate a TAN's issue frames".[142] To explore their hypotheses, the authors identify COC as the central and hegemonic node within the LGBTI network in Europe, and focus on the specific issue of same-sex couple recognition. They try to predict the hegemony effect of the centrality of COC in the following way:[143]

> Having taken up the issue and subsequently pursuing it, COC will not be satisfied with supporting advocacy campaigns that are demanding low-level equality rights like unregistered partnerships. Instead, it will push for full marriage rights. A rise of full marriage equality as an agenda item beyond the Western European context, particularly in Eastern European countries, would thus reflect COC's influence on issue framing, as we expect less powerful organizations with ties to COC to demand full marriage rights from their governments.

---

139 Francesca Romana Ammaturo "The Right to a Privilege? Homonormativity and the Recognition of Same-Sex Couples in Europe" (2014) 23(2) *Social & Legal Studies* 175 at 191. See also, Kelly Kollman, above n 134, at 319; Scott Long, above n 50, at 128.
140 Timothy Hildebrandt, above n 64, at 850.
141 Megan Osterbur and Christina Kiel "A Hegemon Fighting for Equal Rights: The Dominant Role of COC Nederland in the LGBT Transnational Advocacy Network" (2016) 17(2) *Global Networks* 234 at 238.
142 At 238.
143 At 239.

Consequently, the authors compare how NGOs connected with COC frame issues on same-sex couples' recognition with NGOs that are not as strongly connected with COC. They conclude that "organizations with direct linkages to COC will be more likely to demand stronger forms of partnership recognition than those organizations without such ties".[144]

On the contrary, because I argue that LGBTI gatekeeper NGOs work to develop a democratic network and they avoid misusing their power, I would expect that they do not impose the advocacy of the right to marry upon the peripheral NGOs. Instead, I expect to find that LGBTI gatekeeper NGOs, to be successful in their advocacy action, try to adjust their advocacy agenda in a way that accommodates the various political, social and cultural contexts.[145]

In sum, LGBTI gatekeeper NGOs understand that some peripheral NGOs want to support same-sex marriage, and others do not; gatekeeper NGOs are willing to support the peripheral NGOs either way. The book investigates whether LGBTI gatekeeper NGOs engage in consultation with peripheral NGOs with the aim of adopting a more collaborative decision-making system, while maintaining a significant influence in international human rights law debate. Such participative decision-making is crucial so as to enhance the democratic legitimacy of transnational networks.[146] If my hypotheses are true, I would expect to find that the advocacy for the right to marry has low importance in the LGBTI TANs. Ultimately, I want to demonstrate that LGBTI gatekeeper NGOs partially renounce their power of imposing perceived Western issues priorities upon peripheral NGOs.

Conclusion

This chapter spells out the theoretical framework that underpins the book. To better understand the complex and multifaceted nature of LGBTI activism, the chapter develops a syncretic use of TANs' theories and social movements' theories, to capture domestic and international dynamics at the same time. The chapter provides a brief overview of TANs' models, the boomerang, spiral and ricochet models, which describe how NGOs pressure countries from above and from below to comply with existing human rights norms. But, because LGBTI human rights norms are not well consolidated in the international human rights debate, this chapter, and in general this book, looks specifically to the theme of issue emergence and issue framing. Therefore, I argue that the way in which TANs decide the advocacy agenda, name human rights violations and strategically present legal analysis to advance LGBTI rights shapes their advocacy agenda and subsequently the human rights debate.

---

144 At 249.
145 Wendy H Wong *Internal Affairs: How the Structure of NGOs Transforms Human Rights* (Cornell University Press, Ithaca, 2012) at 192.
146 See especially, David J Norman "Building Democratic Public Spheres? Transnational Advocacy Networks and the Social Forum Process" (2017) 17(2) *Global Networks* 300 at 13.

Among the many factors that determine gatekeepers' decisions, this book focuses on two: the internetwork relations among the actors of a TAN and the broader political context in which the TAN operates. Therefore, I argue that, first, the way in which NGOs work together (internetwork relations), and second, the political opportunities and constraints provided by international organizations, states and other NGOs outside the network (the broader political context), shape the way in which LGBTI TANs prioritise and frame LGBTI issues.

Starting from the internetwork relations, I discuss first that LGBTI gatekeeper NGOs understand that, because of phenomena such as anticipatory counter-movement and cultural imperialism, and domestic constraints to the development of peripheral LGBTI NGOs, LGBTI TANs find it difficult to flourish. Therefore, gatekeeper NGOs work to build the network horizontally. Following network analysis on gatekeeper NGOs' social power, I claim that by building the network horizontally, LGBTI gatekeeper NGOs are decentralising their position in the network and they are relinquishing part of their social power. Moreover, following Rubenstein's interpretation that NGOs are democratically legitimate when they minimise the misuse of their power, I claim that LGBTI gatekeeper NGOs strive to build a stronger, more efficient and more democratic network from below.

Second, I discuss that LGBTI gatekeeper NGOs' strategy of building the network from below has consequences in the advocacy agenda decision-making. Using Adam, Duyvendak and Krouwel's analysis of LGB social movements and domestic political opportunities, I make the hypothesis that, if LGBTI gatekeeper NGOs aim to improve the domestic political opportunities of LGBTI peripheral NGOs, they need to advocate for the development of sexual and gender diverse identities and visibility, for states to allow LGBTI organizations to be formed and participate in the political system, for the decriminalisation of sexual and gender diverse behaviours.

Moving to discuss the broader political context approach, I discuss that LGBTI gatekeeper NGOs try to minimise challenges by maintaining a low profile, and they try to maximise their ability to influence the international human rights debate by framing LGBTI issues in a way that international organizations and states might "swallow".[147] In other words, they strategically present their legal analysis of LGBTI human rights violation as prohibition of discrimination on the grounds of SOGII at the UN. Nonetheless, the prohibition of discrimination on the grounds of SOGII is still perceived as provocative by some conservative/religious TANs and states. This is because some conservative/religious states and NGOs claim that the right to equality for LGBTI people would potentially erode the heteronormative privileges of married different sex couples. The UN has clearly said that the prohibition of discrimination on the grounds of SOGII does not cover the right to marry of LGBTI couples.[148] But such a slippery slope argument

---

147 Joke Swiebel, above n 110, at 28.
148 *Joslin and Others v New Zealand* HR Comm 902/99, A/57/40 at 214, 17 July 2002.

appeals to conservative/religious supporters because of the strong cultural and religious resonance of marriage.

Finally, I corroborate my claim on the democratic legitimacy of LGBTI gate-keeper NGOs by discussing the right to marry in the advocacy of LGBTI TANs. Similar to Ostebur and Kiel, I investigate whether LGBTI gatekeeper NGOs impose perceived Western priorities, such as the advocacy for the right to marry, upon NGOs working in the periphery of the network. However, I aim to reach an opposite conclusion to Ostebur and Kiel because I want to show that LGBTI gatekeeper NGOs do not impose the right to marry in the advocacy of peripheral NGOs, and therefore they do not interfere with peripheral NGOs and they do not misuse their power.

In conclusion, the strategy choices of LGBTI TANs, and LGBTI gatekeeper NGOs in particular, have consequences in the way in which new issues emerge and are framed in the TANs' agenda, and ultimately in the international human rights debate. The ensuing chapters investigate the way in which LGBTI TANs strategically present their legal analysis and name LGBTI people human rights violations at the UN.

3 LGBTI transnational advocacy networks

Internetwork relations and horizontal networking

Introduction

This chapter focuses on the internetwork relations, and it demonstrates that LGBTI gatekeeper NGOs operate democratically by building LGBTI TANs from below. This is because they strive to build the LGBTI network horizontally, to decentralise their position in the network, and to partially relinquish their social power. In doing so, LGBTI gatekeeper NGOs improve their democratic accountability and they enhance the efficiency of their advocacy.

These strategic choices, which are apt to develop the LGBTI network horizontally, have consequences in the advocacy agenda decided by LGBTI gatekeeper NGOs. On the one hand, stronger and empowered peripheral NGOs that work in consultation with gatekeeper NGOs can influence the advocacy agenda decision-making with their specific peripheral perspectives. On the other hand, LGBTI gatekeeper NGOs strongly advocate for rights that enhance the domestic political opportunities of peripheral NGOs, using mainly a prohibition of discrimination framework and avoiding controversial issues, such as the right to marry. The consequences of these strategic choices in the advocacy agenda are better addressed later in the book This chapter develops as follows.

First, the chapter analyses the result of the interviews I conducted with NGO staff members, and it highlights that gatekeeper NGOs work to build the network horizontally. It emerges from the interviews that peripheral NGOs working in neighbouring states can benefit from the collaboration with neighbours because they share common struggles and they can coordinate a common strategy. Consequently, gatekeeper NGOs strive to put neighbouring NGOs in connection with one another. In doing so, gatekeeper NGOs decentralise their relative position in the network because they retain relatively less intense ties. Moreover, LGBTI gatekeeper NGOs build the network by training LGBTI activists working in peripheral NGOs to advocate for their rights before international organizations, and by putting them in contact with governments' delegates and foreign donors. In this way, LGBTI gatekeeper NGOs decrease the exclusivity of their ties with these influential agents. In following network analysis theories, both dynamics contribute to challenging the social power of gatekeeper NGOs and therefore contribute to building a more democratic network.

Second, the chapter examines the LGBTI TAN's advocacy at the Commission on HR, the General Assembly and the HR Council. The finding of this analysis correlates with what I have discovered with the interviews. Shortly after the failed Brazilian resolution, LGBTI gatekeeper NGOs decided to develop the capacity of NGOs in non-Western states, and to promote the visibility of LGBTI issues at the UN. Examples from the drafting group of the Yogyakarta Principles (YPs) and of the so-called 'Argentinian statement' delivered at the General Assembly continue to demonstrate that the LGBTI TAN aims to de-centralise and de-Westernise the LGBTI advocacy.

Third, to further demonstrate that a strong horizontal advocacy contributes to the efficiency of the LGBTI TAN, the chapter describes the lobbying process around the three HR Council resolutions on human rights and SOGI. It is highlighted that LGBTI gatekeeper NGOs ensured the success of these resolutions by mobilising and coordinating the advocacy from hundreds of NGOs from all the regions of the world. The chapter concludes by explaining that, although gatekeeper NGOs attempt to promote a collaborative advocacy, occasionally the NGOs working in the periphery of the network can be dissatisfied with the advocacy agenda. In general, I aim to rebut that gatekeeper NGOs work hegemonically, but they still maintain the central position within LGBTI TANs and, ultimately, they decide the advocacy agenda.

Internetwork relations

TANs' theories claim that gatekeeper NGOs operate as central hubs of advocacy networks and that there are vertical relationships between gatekeeper NGOs and NGOs working at the periphery of the network. The interviewees' answers confirm these theoretical assumptions. The interviewees working in peripheral NGOs highlighted that their main link with international organizations is through LGBTI gatekeeper NGOs. For example, interviewees from peripheral NGOs in Liberia, Malaysia, Nepal and Mongolia stated that they are supported by ILGA[1] and OutRight to prepare the documentations for the UPR process, and by COC and ILGA to fund their travels to Geneva.[2]

At the European level, some interviewees from peripheral NGOs stated that ILGA-Europe is their only point of contact to work with European regional organizations, such as the Council of Europe and the European Union.[3] ILGA-Europe has good relations with the European institutions; for example, they have good relationships with some state diplomats sitting at the Parliamentary Assembly of the Council of Europe and therefore they can negotiate with them

---

1   Interview Stop AIDS Liberia (Questionnaire, 30 May 2016); interview Justice for Sisters (Skype call, 16 May 2016); interview Blue Diamond Society (Skype call, 1 March 2016).
2   Interview LGBT Centre Mongolia (Skype call, 9 March 2016).
3   Interview Hungarian LGBT Alliance (Skype call, 29 April 2016); interview Malta LGBT Movement (Skype call, 5 May 2016).

on recommendations or part of recommendations for the protection of LGBTI people's rights.[4] Thus, peripheral NGOs use ILGA-Europe as a bridge to make their voices heard in these avenues.[5]

Some interviewees confirm that ILGA needs grassroots knowledge; in other words, the knowledge coming from the NGOs working on the local and national levels. Therefore, consultations and information sharing between gatekeeper NGOs and the periphery is of primary importance.[6] Indeed, nine of the interviewees from peripheral NGOs said that they consider reporting, researching and monitoring of LGBTI people's human rights violations at the domestic and local levels to be important aspects of their work.[7]

This book argues that the way in which TANs decide the advocacy agenda and strategically frame human rights violation to advance LGBTI people's rights influences the international human rights discourse on SOGII. In this chapter I discuss that understanding the structure of a TAN, analysing the way in which gatekeeper NGOs and peripheral NGOs work together, and in general investigating the internetwork relations between the various NGOs that are part of a TAN, help clarify how LGBTI TANs strategically frame LGBTI issues to influence the international human rights debate. The ensuing sub-paragraphs show that LGBTI gatekeeper NGOs strive to build the network horizontally. In doing so, they are decreasing their centrality within the network, they are redistributing their power and, ultimately, they are contributing to create a more democratic network.

Building stronger and more democratic LGBTI networks: horizontal links between peripherals NGOs

The importance of sharing information and of creating partnerships among NGOs which are part of the same network is not a new concept.[8] However,

---

4   Interview ILGA-Europe (Skype call, 15 July 2015); interview ILGA-Europe (Skype call, 21 August 2015).

5   Interview Pink Armenia (Skype call, 21 April 2016).

6   ILGA-Europe (Skype call, 21 August 2015), above n 4; interview anonymous NGO (Skype call, 1 April 2016).

7   Stop AIDS Liberia, above n 1; interview Bilitis Resource Center (Questionnaire, 14 May 2016); interview Campaign Against Homophobia (Skype call, 13 May 2016); Hungarian LGBT Alliance, above n 3; Justice for Sisters, above n 1; Malta LGBT Movement, above n 3; LGBT Centre Mongolia, above n 2; Pink Armenia, above n 5; interview anonymous NGO from Nigeria (Questionnaire, 2 June 2016).

8   See especially, Ronald Holzhacker "Transnational Strategies of Civil Society Organizations Striving for Equality and Nondiscrimination: Exchanging Information on New EU Directives, Coalition Strategies and Strategic Litigation" in Laszlo Bruszt and Ronald Holzhacker (eds) *Transnationalization of Economies, States, and Civil Societies: New Challenges for Governance in Europe* (Springer, New York, London, 2009) 219 at 218; Ryan R Thoreson *Transnational LGBT Activism: Working for Sexual Rights Worldwide* (University of Minnesota Press, Minneapolis, 2014) at 123.

this analysis shows that LGBTI gatekeeper NGOs work to develop information sharing and partnership on a horizontal trajectory. Gatekeeper NGOs invest in creating venues where activists can meet and share information and learn from one another; and they also strive to create connections between activists working in the same region to learn from one another.

The horizontal collaboration between LGBTI NGOs in Western Europe has been highlighted by some authors.[9] My findings confirm this horizontal collaboration between Western European LGBTI NGOs. For example, the interviewee from LGBT Denmark says that they have close collaboration with other NGOs based in Scandinavian states to coordinate their advocacy and be more effective at the UN.[10] But this is not all. LGBTI gatekeeper NGOs work to develop and strengthen the horizontal networking because LGBTI advocacy is stronger when peripheral NGOs work together on projects tailored for their specific needs. Ultimately, they have the aim of building a stronger, more democratic and more effective TAN, from below.

LGBTI NGOs are naturally drawn to collaborate with their colleagues working in neighbouring states. First, horizontal collaborations are particularly useful among NGOs working in the same sub-region because they share common struggles. The interviewee from the Polish organization Campaign Against Homophobia explains that they collaborate with organizations in Croatia, Lithuania, Latvia and Hungary. Their cooperation and working relationships are strong because they come from similar situations, similar struggles and consequently they have similar methods of work.[11] The interviewee from Pink Armenia shares the same position. They collaborate with organizations in Moldova, Ukraine, Georgia, Belarus and Azerbaijan within a frame of a coalition called Eastern Coalition for LGBT Equality.[12] The reason for this coalition is that the NGOs in the region have a shared history. Through such horizontal networking, NGOs can peer-mentor each other because, in the words of the Armenian interviewee, "there are NGOs that passed on what we are going through now".[13] In particular, the interviews from these two NGOs highlight that they met with their colleagues in neighbouring states during conferences and workshops, and they have then established a long-lasting collaboration with them.

Second, horizontal networking among peripheral NGOs is useful to create a common front and to speak with one voice before regional organizations. The interviewee from Saint Lucia comments that they collaborate closely with NGOs

---

9 See for example, Ronald Holzhacker, above n 8; Phillip M Ayoub "Cooperative Transnationalism in Contemporary Europe: Europeanization and Political Opportunities for LGBT Mobilization in the European Union" (2013) 5(2) *European Political Science Review* 279.
10 Interview LGBT Denmark (Skype call, 2 April 2016).
11 Campaign Against Homophobia, above n 7.
12 See also, Swedish: National Association for Sexual Equality "Eastern Coalition for LGBT Equality" (10 November 2015) RFSL www.rfsl.se/en/organization/international/eastern-coalition/ (Retrieved 27 July 2018).
13 Pink Armenia, above n 5.

in Jamaica, Barbados, Dominica and Antigua to coordinate a common strategy to work towards regional policies on SOGI issues in the Organization of the Eastern Caribbean States.[14] Furthermore, both interviewees from GALANG and Justice for Sisters say they are part of a South East Asian human rights network called ASEAN Sexual Orientation, Gender Identity and Expression (SOGIE) Caucus. In 2010, the sixth ASEAN People's Forum was held in Vietnam, and on that occasion a coalition of NGOs and sympathetic states managed to include SOGIE issues in the final document of the forum. The following year, in 2011, the ASEAN People's Forum was held in Jakarta, and several NGOs hosted a workshop on SOGIE.[15] The NGOs participating in these two events established the ASEAN SOGIE Caucus,[16] with the goal of including SOGIE in the programme of work of the ASEAN. In 2012, the ASEAN SOGIE Caucus lobbied to include LGBTI issues in the ASEAN Human Rights Declaration. At that time the advocacy was unsuccessful and the work of including LGBTI matters in ASEAN's human rights work is still ongoing.[17] Even though the advocacy action was not successful in the short-term, it helped to create horizontal networking among peripheral NGOs working in South East Asia to continue advocating for LGBTI rights before regional organizations.

Finally, it should be noted that horizontal networking does not only occur among neighbouring NGOs. The interviewee from the Australian Lesbian Medical Association (ALMA) – an NGO with ECOSOC consultative status since 2013, but not identified as a gatekeeper NGO for the purposes of this analysis – says that when they are approached by NGOs working in states that enforce homo- and transphobic laws, they can mentor them and provide moral support.[18]

In sum, some horizontal networking, such as the Eastern Coalition for LGBT Equality and the ASEAN SOGIE Caucus, develops spontaneously because of favourable political opportunities that facilitate them.[19] For example, LGBTI activists from neighbouring states come together at specific advocacy actions or meet at conferences. They also use the working relationships they developed face-to-face to build an enduring horizontal network. The ensuing section discusses that part of the horizontal networking is developed as a strategic choice by LGBTI gatekeeper NGOs.

14 Interview anonymous NGO from Saint Lucia (Skype call, 17 June 2016).

15 Ging Cristobal "Inclusion of the Human Rights of LGBTIQ People in the Final Statement at the 7th ASEAN People's Forum" (11 May 2011) OutRight Action International formerly known as International Gay and Lesbian Human Rights Commission https://iglhrc.wordpress.com/2011/05/11/inclusion-of-the-human-rights-of-lgbtiq-people-in-the-final-statement-at-the-7th-asean-people%e2%80%99s-forum/ (Retrieved 27 July 2018).

16 Justice for Sisters, above n 1.

17 Interview GALANG Philippines (Skype call, 25 May 2016); Justice for Sisters, above n 1. On the ASEAN Human Rights Declaration and SOGIE inclusion see also, Catherine Shanahan Renshaw "The ASEAN Human Rights Declaration 2012" (2013) 13 *Human Rights Law Review* 557.

18 Interview Australian Lesbian Medical Association (ALMA) (Skype call, 23 March 2016).

19 Ronald Holzhacker, above n 8, at 235.

How LGBTI gatekeeper NGOs build the network in practice

I asked my interviewees, both from LGBTI gatekeeper NGOs and peripheral NGOs, how they work together. The interviewees confirm the hypothesis that gatekeeper NGOs work to build the network horizontally, and I identify four recurring themes: training, funding, legal status and identity. The four aspects are addressed in turn.

Training

Some of the interviewees from gatekeeper NGOs highlighted that they invest in training and capacity building.[20] Preferred venues for capacity building are international conferences, meetings and training sessions. Each year ILGA-Europe organises a conference attended by hundreds of activists from all over Europe. During these conferences, ILGA-Europe organises training seminars in which activists from peripheral NGOs can learn how European human rights institutions function. This type of learning and networking continues outside the conferences with internet meetings, and during Pride Parades, where LGBTI activists go and support their colleagues. The interviewee from ILGA-Europe points out that occasions such as conferences and meetings provide great opportunities for networking, exchanging ideas and meeting face-to-face.[21] In addition, ILGA-Europe can facilitate the organization of sub-regional conferences, for example, in Eastern Europe and in the Balkan region. They can facilitate the communications between peripheral NGOs and, in general, they can facilitate a process of 'cross-fertilisation' in which peripheral NGOs learn from the experience of other peripheral NGOs.[22]

One of the interviewees from the Swedish National Association for Sexual Equality (RFSL) – ECOSOC consultative status since 2007, but not identified as a gatekeeper NGO – also maintains that they collaborate directly with NGOs in specific states, and that these projects focus on capacity building, with the aim of enabling peripheral NGOs to improve their own independent advocacy.[23] The interviewee from Blue Diamond Society confirms the importance of these initiatives by saying that they attended a training course sponsored by RFSL where not only could they learn about leadership and public speaking, but they could also network with other activists. The RFSL training course had a massive impact on their ability to advocate for themselves with regard to the skills learned and the working relationships established. In the words of the interviewee:[24]

---

20 ILGA-Europe (Skype call, 21 August 2015), above n 4; ILGA-Europe (Skype call, 21 August 2015), above n 4; interview ILGA-Europe (Phone call, 12 November 2015); interview Swedish Federation for LGBTQ Rights (RFSL) (Skype call, 3 May 2016).
21 ILGA-Europe (Skype call, 21 August 2015), above n 4.
22 Ibid.
23 Swedish Federation for LGBTQ Rights (RFSL) (Skype call, 3 May 2016), above n 20.
24 Blue Diamond Society, above n 1.

I met people from Europe, people working at the UN, OutRight, people from Austria. . . . It was a great opportunity for me to highlight my concerns, my issues, to learn from [others]. RFSL was one of my biggest tutors to learn how to advocate for my rights.

Funding

Another aspect of building the network horizontally relates to access to funding. Interviewees from gatekeeper NGOs and from NGOs with ECOSOC status highlight that they support the network horizontally by supporting peripheral NGOs to obtain grants. The interviewee from RFSL notes that they assist NGOs in drafting their grant applications to fund their projects.[25] Moreover, the interviewee from ILGA World reports that the organization supports NGOs and LGBTI activists by putting them in contact with one another. In particular, regional or global ILGA conferences are venues for activists and NGOs to meet and create working relationships. The interviewee continues by saying that ILGA provides travel grants and scholarships for activists to participate in ILGA's conferences and on these occasions activists are able to meet with funders, establish working relationships with them, discuss projects and possibly obtain further grants for their projects.[26]

Furthermore, the experience of LGBT Centre Mongolia with OutRight corroborates the view that gatekeeper NGOs support the network horizontally through increasing peripheral NGOs access to funding. The interviewee from LGBT Centre Mongolia explains that although OutRight is not a funding agency, it can raise funding and then use it for various projects. For example, LGBT Centre Mongolia was awarded the Felipe de Souza prize in 2011, from OutRight.[27] The Mongolian interviewee says that when they went in New York to receive the prize they had the chance to network with activists and other fundraising agencies. In the words of the interviewee: "During those three weeks at the US I met many founders, I was finally able to convince one of the founders, Open Society, to fund our organization".[28] Finally, the Mongolian activist states that OutRight put them in contact with various helpful allies in the region – such as LGBTI NGOs based in other East Asian states, and possible donors – with the aim of both sharing information and know-how and the possibility to gather resources.[29]

---

25 Swedish Federation for LGBTQ Rights (RFSL) (Skype call, 3 May 2016), above n 20.
26 Interview ILGA-World (Skype call, 13 April 2016).
27 Otgonbaatar Tsedendemberel and Munkhzaya Nergui "Felipa de Souza Awardees: The LGBT Centre in Ulaanbaatar, Mongolia" (7 March 2011) OutRight (formerly IGLHRC) https://iglhrc.wordpress.com/2011/03/07/felipa-de-souza-awardees-the-lgbt-centre-in-ulaanbaatar-mongolia/ (Retrieved 27 July 2018).
28 LGBT Centre Mongolia, above n 2.
29 Ibid.

Legal status

The ability to gather funding relies on legal status. Some governments place limitations on the freedom of association, assembly and speech of LGBTI advocates.[30] The consequence is that when groups are not recognised as legal entities, they find it difficult to obtain funding because they are not formally accountable. Again, the interviewee from LGBT Centre Mongolia states that they have been helped by OutRight. Initially, in the mid-2000s, the LGBT Centre Mongolia tried unsuccessfully to register the organization as a legal entity in Mongolia. The Mongolian authorities maintained that the name of the organization conflicted with "Mongolian custom and traditions".[31] The organization then reached out to OutRight which sent letters to various Mongolian authorities, such as the Minister of Justice and the State Secretary, asking them to comply with international human rights law obligations related to the rights of freedom of expression, assembly and organization. The interviewee says that such an action was successful and today LGBT Centre Mongolia is a registered legal entity.[32]

The lack of legal status is an obstacle to the development of transnational LGBTI advocacy. If governments do not allow LGBTI NGOs to legally exist at the national level, the pressure from below is weak.[33] The gatekeeper NGOs interviewed acknowledge such limit, as they report that the legal status is not a requirement to be part of the LGBTI network. Indeed, they welcome activists in the network, even when sexually and gender diverse groups are not able to register as a legal entity. For example, the interviewee from ILGA-Oceania highlights that it is not strictly necessary to have a legal status to be part of the ILGA system; it could be enough on some occasions to have some sort of accountability, such as a webpage or a Facebook group.[34]

Furthermore, ILGA's interviewee stresses that they are contacted by groups that do not have a legal status and have particular difficulties because of the restrictions imposed by their central governments. To overcome these limits, ILGA promotes peer-mentoring by putting them in contact with NGOs in the region or in neighbouring states. In doing so, peripheral NGOs can learn from previous experiences of their neighbours. Moreover, the interviewee adds that activists can enjoy ILGA's scholarships to travel and to stay at conferences even when they do not belong to a formal NGO.[35] These findings show that gatekeeper NGOs try to increase the participation of peripheral NGOs to network, even in an informal way.

---

30 Lynette J Chua and David Gilbert "Sexual Orientation and Gender Identity Minorities in Transition: LGBT Rights and Activism in Myanmar" (2015) 37 *Human Rights Quarterly* 1 at 6.
31 "Mongolia: Register LGBT Centre" (20 July 2009) OutRight (formerly IGLHRC) www.outrightinternational.org/content/mongolia-register-lgbt-centre (Retrieved 27 July 2018).
32 LGBT Centre Mongolia, above n 2.
33 See Timothy Hildebrandt "Development and Division: The Effect of Transnational Linkages and Local Politics on LGBT Activism in China" (2012) 21(77) *Journal of Contemporary China* 845 at 864.
34 Interview ILGA-Oceania (Skype call, 29 April 2016).
35 ILGA-World (Skype call, 13 April 2016), above n 26.

Identity

Peripheral NGOs need to frame their identities and their claims in ways that attract transnational cooperation.[36] That is, sexually and gender diverse groups need to use the Western LGBTI label to be accepted in the LGBTI TAN. However, my findings suggest that this is not always the case. One of the interviewees from RFSL reports that they can connect via internet and collaborate with groups of people that are not structured in legal entities or that are not as open as LGBTI organizations in their states of origin. In this way, they can allow sexually and gender diverse groups to access their resources without forcing them to self-identify with the Western 'LGBTI' label that would put them at high risk of criminal persecution and violence.[37]

Furthermore, one interviewee from ILGA reports that the organization is well aware of the fact that sexually and gender diverse communities in the Pacific need to be welcomed in the ILGA system with their specific identities and issues. They explain that their work focuses on holding consultations with tribal groups in New Zealand, Papua New Guinea, Tonga, Samoa and other Pacific islands to create a gender terminology on how Pacific populations identify transgender identities. They hold consultations with these communities in the Pacific and try to get to know about their stories, traditions and desires. The final goal is to assure that nobody is left behind and that every culture, ethnicity and tribe is recognised in the ILGA system.[38]

In sum, it emerges from the interviews that gatekeeper NGOs invest in creating spaces in which peripheral NGOs can meet, create working relationships and are put in contact with, and trained to better address, donors. These aspects help to create more democratic LGBTI TANs for two reasons. On the one hand, peripheral NGOs are stronger domestically and are better connected with one another, and therefore LGBTI gatekeeper NGOs retain relatively less intense ties and they progressively lose their ability to control the flow of knowledge and resources of the network. On the other hand, when peripheral NGOs learn how to advocate for their own rights before international organizations, when they know how to write successful grant applications and are put in connection with international donors, they have less need for gatekeeper NGOs to function as bridges between them and external allies. Consequently, gatekeeper NGOs' exclusive ties are slowly chipped away. Because LGBTI gatekeeper NGOs have less intense and less exclusive ties, they partially relinquish their social power, and therefore they foster the democratic legitimacy of their network. Figure 3.1 represents a revised version of Figure 2.1 in Chapter 2 and it shows that with more horizontal ties and with some forms of connections between peripheral NGOs and external allies, gatekeeper NGOs are relatively less central in the network.

---

36 Clifford Bob *The Marketing of Rebellion: Insurgents, Media, and International Activism* (Cambridge University Press, Cambridge, New York, 2005) at 4.
37 Swedish Federation for LGBTQ Rights (RFSL) (Skype call, 3 May 2016), above n 20.
38 Interview ILGA-World (Skype call, 3 April 2016).

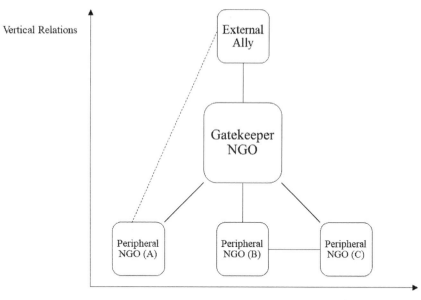

Figure 3.1 Gatekeeper NGOs' social power (revised): less intensity and less exclusiveness of ties

Even though gatekeeper NGOs maintain the same number of ties with other nodes of the network, its ties are relatively less intense because peripheral NGO (B) and (C) are now connected, which means that there is one more tie that does not involve the gatekeeper NGO. Second, the new relationship with peripheral NGO (A) and the external ally (signalled with a dash line) signifies that peripheral NGO (A) establishes some forms of working relationship with an international ally. In this way, the gatekeeper NGO has partially decreased its exclusive connection with the external ally because, for example, peripheral NGO (A) has been trained to write their own report or deliver a speech for the UPR process.

I argue that such strategy of building the LGBTI network from below has consequences on the agenda setting. Later in the book I discuss in more detail the process that leads to the agenda setting of the LGBTI TANs, while in the ensuing sub-paragraphs I provide some empirical examples of LGBTI gatekeeper NGOs promoting the horizontal development of the LGBTI TAN working at the UN to further support my horizontal networking arguments.

An early example of how the LGBTI network works in practice

Joachim notes that NGO access to international human rights conferences is important because they are opportunities to "introduce and circulate" new ideas.[39] Indeed, the first UN meeting where a governmental delegate – the Dutch junior minister Annelien Kappeyne van de Coppello – petitioned lesbian rights was at the 1985 UN World Conference on Women.[40] And again, ten years later in 1995, 11 lesbian gay and bisexual organizations were accredited to the World Conference on Women in Beijing.[41] During the fall of 1994, in preparation for the conference, OutRight worked closely with ILGA to put together a petition to ask the governments to:[42]

> [R]ecognize the right to determine one's sexual identity; the right to con-trol one's body, particularly in establishing intimate relationships; and the right to choose if, when, and with whom to bear or raise children, as funda-mental components of the human rights of all women regardless of sexual orientation.

The petition was an early attempt by an NGO to lobby for recognition of the rights of lesbian and bisexual women to form a family. The petition gathered approximately 6,000 signatures from all over the world, and it was one exam-ple of NGOs working in a network to pressure governments and international organizations. OutRight coordinated the advocacy action from peripheral LGBTI NGOs and activists to show that the support was coming from different regions.

The draft Platform of Action of the Beijing World Conference on Women called on governments to both eradicate discrimination in employment based on sexual orientation and to prevent persecutions based on sexual orientation, but all the references to sexual orientation were omitted from the final document because of the divisions among delegates.[43] Two reasons are identified to explain this omis-sion. On the one hand, Mertus claims that few mainstream NGOs were willing to "risk their own reputation" by strongly supporting the debate on sexual orienta-tion.[44] And, on the other hand, some authors explain that a coalition of Catholic and Islamic states with right-wing and ultra-conservative NGOs, united under the leadership of the Holy See, strongly opposed the debate on sexual orienta-tion[45] and criticised lesbian delegates at the Beijing conference for their alleged

---

39 Jutta Joachim *Agenda Setting, the UN, and NGOs: Gender Violence and Reproductive Rights* (Georgetown University Press, Washington, 2007) at 24.

40 See, Joke Swiebel "Lesbian, Gay, Bisexual and Transgender Human Rights: The Search for an International Strategy" (2009) 15(1) *Contemporary Politics* 19 at 25.

41 Douglas Sanders "Getting Lesbian and Gay Issues on the International Human Rights Agenda" (1996) 18 *Human Rights Quarterly* 67 at 90.

42 Françoise Girard "Negotiating Sexual Rights and Sexual Orientation at the UN" in Richard Parker, Rosalind Petchesky, and Robert Sember (eds) *Sex Politics: Reports from the Front Lines* (Sexuality Policy Watch, Rio de Janeiro, 2008) 311 at 331.

43 Douglas Sanders, above n 41, at 90.

44 Julie Mertus "Applying the Gatekeeper Model of Human Rights Activism: The US-Based Movement for LGBT Rights" in Clifford Bob (ed) *The International Struggle for New Human Rights* (University of Pennsylvania Press, Philadelphia, 2009) 52 at 65.

45 Françoise Girard, above n 42, at 335–337; Amnesty International Press Release *UN Com-mission on Human Rights: Universality under Threat over Sexual Orientation Resolution*

"attack on the values, cultures, traditions and religious beliefs of the vast majority of the world's peoples".[46] The advocacy around the Beijing World Conference on Women is a good early example of NGOs networking, which becomes more and more common after the failed attempt of the so called 'Brazilian resolution'.

Brazilian resolution

In April 2003, at the 59th session of the Commission on HR, Brazil proposed draft resolution E/CN.4/2003/L.92, calling upon all states "to protect the rights of all persons regardless of their sexual orientation".[47] Brazil presented the resolution as a natural continuation of its commitment against sexual orientation discrimination in international fora, as Brazil spoke in favour of sexual rights and sexual orientation at the Beijing Platform of Action; Declaration of Commitment on HIV/AIDS; and UN International Conference Against Racism, Racial Discrimination, Xenophobia and Related Intolerance. Girard reports that Brazilian diplomats did not work closely with allied state delegates or NGOs because they believed the resolution on non-discrimination on the grounds of sexual orientation would have been a simple corollary of the general non-discrimination principle. In Girard's opinion this lack of communication is one of the causes of the failure of the draft resolution. For example, Sweden and Canada were disappointed when Brazil took the leadership of the resolution without consultation.[48] However, once Brazil started the conversation on a possible resolution on sexual orientation, many NGOs mobilised.

Amnesty, Action Canada for Population and Development, and other NGOs organised informal discussions with states' delegates to build the support for the draft resolution.[49] NGOs lobbied for the inclusion of "gender identity" in the draft resolution but Ireland opposed it, and the expression "gender identity" was not included in the draft.[50] Eventually, the Brazilian resolution was supported by 20 states[51] but opposed by the Holy See[52] and by Pakistan on behalf of the Organization of Islamic Conference (OIC).[53] The Pakistan ambassador and one African diplomat said there were no homosexuals in their states and the

---

(AI Index: IOR 41/013/2003 2003) at 2; Ignacio Saiz "Bracketing Sexuality: Human Rights and Sexual Orientation: A Decade of Development and Denial at the UN" (2004) 7 *Health and Human Rights* 48 at 57–58.

46 Clifford Bob *The Global Right Wing and the Clash of World Politics* (Cambridge University Press, New York, 2012) at 37.

47 E/CN.4/2003/L.92 *Human Rights and Sexual Orientation* (Comm on HR, 2003) at [3].

48 Françoise Girard, above n 42, at 341–342.

49 At 434.

50 At 343.

51 E/2003/23 and E/CN.4/2003/135 *Report on the Fifty-Ninth Session* (Comm on HR, 2003) at [575]. See also Appendix 4.

52 ARC "The United Nations and the Advancement of LGBT Rights" http://arc-international.net/network-development/conference-presentations/presentation-un-mechanism (Retrieved 27 July 2018).

53 Amnesty International *Human Rights and Sexual Orientation and Gender Identity* (2004) at 2. For further readings see also, Vanja Hamzić "The Case of 'Queer Muslims': Sexual

representative from the Holy See argued that the text could condone paedophilia.[54] Pakistan proposed a no-action motion, which was barely defeated.[55] The opposing states then "threatened to bring hundreds of amendments to the text",[56] so the Commission on HR decided to postpone the decision to the following session in 2004.[57]

Before the 60th session of the Commission on HR, in February and March 2004, NGOs lobbied the members of the Commission on HR to pass the Brazilian resolution. Allied Rainbow Communities International (ARC) sponsored an international consultation to support the resolution, which was held in Rio de Janeiro and gathered key stakeholders from all over the world.

Moreover, numerous NGOs submitted written statements to the Commission on HR to raise the awareness on the Brazilian resolution. First, HRW called the Commission on HR to adopt a resolution that expresses concern on discrimination on the grounds of SOGI and requested the High Commissioner of Human Rights to investigate human rights violations based on SOGI.[58] Second, the American Psychological Association urged the Commission on HR to adopt the resolution on human rights and sexual orientation and to take further actions to contribute to the "human rights, health, and wellbeing of lesbian, gay, bisexual people and others who desire or engage in same-sex relationships".[59] Third, the Transnational Radical Party (TRP) expressed their concerns on how LGBT individuals are discriminated against in numerous states and encouraged the Commission on HR to include the notion of "gender identity" in the final draft of E/CN4/2003/L92. Interestingly, TRP commented that debate on marriage equality for lesbian women and gay men was rising among various states and stated that "the time is ripe to promote such a debate also within the United Nations system".[60] This is one of the sporadic examples of NGOs commenting on marriage equality in a written statement. Fourth, the Canadian HIV/AIDS Legal Network called the Commission on HR to support the Brazilian resolution because the prohibition of discrimination on the grounds of sexual orientation is crucial to address HIV/AIDS issues.[61]

Orientation and Gender Identity in International Human Rights Law and Muslim Legal and Social Ethos" (2011) 11 *Human Rights Law Review* 237 at 252.

54 Françoise Girard, above n 42, at 344.

55 E/2003/23 and E/CN.4/2003/135, above n 51, at [576].

56 Michael O'Flaherty and John Fisher "Sexual Orientation, Gender Identity and International Human Rights Law: Contextualising the Yogyakarta Principles" (2008) 8(2) *Human Rights Law Review* 207 at 229.

57 E/2003/23 and E/CN.4/2003/135, above n 51, at [582].

58 E/CN.4/2004/NGO/232 *Written Statement Submitted by Human Rights Watch (HRW)* (Comm on HR, 2004) at 3–4.

59 E/CN.4/2004/NGO/259 *Written Statement Submitted by the American Psychological Association* (Comm on HR, 2004) at 3.

60 E/CN.4/2004/NGO/191 *Written Statement Submitted by the Transnational Radical Party* (Comm on HR, 2004) at 3.

61 E/CN.4/2004/NGO/187 *Written Statement Submitted by the Canadian HIV/AIDS Legal Network* (Comm on HR, 2004). Also Amnesty International issued a report, which was not submitted to the Commission on HR as a written statement, but it shows the

The anti-LGBTI rights coalition also mobilised with the aim of blocking the Brazilian resolution. They tried to block any reference to the prohibition of discrimination on the grounds of sexual orientation by using the usual slippery slope argument. Before the 60th session of Commission on HR, the Pakistan ambassador sent a letter to all the other ambassadors in Geneva to warn them that sexual orientation is not defined in any UN documents and that sexual orientation may lead to "grossly errant behaviour like paedophilia".[62] Finally, the letter explained that sexual orientation issues should be regulated at the national level and that the resolution on sexual orientation threatens the "concept of traditional family".[63]

Moreover, the Permanent Mission of the Holy See at the UN in Geneva maintained that such a resolution would lead to the interpretation of the right to marry and to found a family without discrimination on the grounds of sexual orientation.[64] The Egyptian activist Bahgat notes that "[t]he resolution itself was not well conceived. . . . The opposition said it led the way to marriage, and they had a point".[65] In the book, I argue that the opportunities and constraints posed by international organizations, conservative/religious NGOs and states shape the way in which TANs present their legal analysis to advance LGBTI rights. In general, LGBTI gatekeeper NGOs frame LGBTI issues as an anti-discrimination claim because it matches well-established human rights principles and it is a framework that international organizations and states can accept. However, Bahgat's observation highlights the pitfall of adopting an approach based on the prohibition of discrimination on the grounds of SOGII. Despite LGBTI activists' best efforts, SOGII anti-discrimination claims can still be perceived as provocative by some conservative/religious states as they allege it would lead to a genderless definition of marriage, which is a strong argument for anti-LGBTI TANs and governments.[66]

Especially because of the political pressures mobilised by the Holy See and by the OIC, Brazil decided not to propose the draft resolution again.[67] Although there was strong nongovernmental support, no other states took the lead and draft resolution E/CN4/2003/L.92 lapsed from the agenda of the Commission on HR.[68] However, these events galvanised a group of LGBTI NGOs, who became eager to obtain a UN resolution on human rights and SOGI.

---

support of the organization to the Brazilian resolution. Amnesty International documents that LGBT individuals can be executed, tortured, discriminated against and harassed because of their SOGI, and called on the 60th session of the Commission on HR to condemn human rights violations on grounds of SOGI. See, Amnesty International, above n 44, at 10.

62 Françoise Girard, above n 42, at 346.

63 At 346.

64 At 346. See also, Ignacio Saiz, above n 44, at 57.

65 Quotation reported in Françoise Girard, above n 42, at 349.

66 See Tina Fetner *How the Religious Right Shaped Lesbian and Gay Activism* (University of Minnesota Press, Minneapolis, 2008) at 111.

67 Françoise Girard, above n 42, at 347.

68 ARC, above n 52.

Mobilisation effect of the Brazilian resolution

The advocacy action that surrounded the Brazilian resolution did not produce a short-term legal change, and only in 2011 did the HR Council finally issue the first resolution on human rights and SOGI. However, Fisher, from ARC, comments that the advocacy conducted between 2003 and 2004 has some aspects of success, as it promoted a mobilisation effect within the LGBTI network.[69] The ensuing sub-paragraphs explain the effect of such mobilisation and its implications for my analysis.

First, ARC was formed in 2003 and organised the strategic meeting in Rio de Janeiro to build the support for the Brazilian resolution, which was the first major initiative the organization undertook. ARC reports that this initiative went beyond a single advocacy action. The following extract of ARC's website highlights this later point:[70]

> This initiative went beyond just strategizing about a particular advocacy opportunity. It also marked the beginning of an enhanced level of international cooperation and movement-building. One of the outcomes of that consultation was the launch of ARC's sexual orientation and gender identity listserv which has been [sic] become a vital tool for strategic engagement and networking internationally, linking hundreds of activists from all geographic regions.

Second, the NGOs and activists who engaged in coordinating the support for the Brazilian resolution were able to learn how the UN worked and used such know-how to keep lobbying the UN in the following years. In other words, the LGBTI NGOs acquired a valuable understanding on how to bring their claims before the UN system.[71]

Third, the efforts to gather support to the Brazilian resolution prompted NGOs to send written statements to the Commission on HR. Before 2003, only two written statements mentioned sexual orientation issues and in a rather superficial way.[72] However, in 2003 and 2004, four NGOs submitted written statements to the Commission on HR strategically presented their legal analysis to support the prohibition of discrimination on the grounds of SOGI. That is to say that the events of the Brazilian resolution promoted the visibility of LGBTI issues in the Commission of HR.

Finally, in December 2004, once it was already clear that the Brazilian resolution would not have been moved forward at the Commission of HR, a coalition

---

69 Françoise Girard, above n 42, at 353.

70 ARC "About Us" http://arc-international.net/about (Retrieved 27 July 2018).

71 Françoise Girard, above n 42, at 353.

72 E/CN.4/1997/NGO/29 *Written Statement Submitted by the International Federation of Jurists* (Comm on HR, 1997); E/CN.4/1998/NGO/3 *Written Statement Submitted by the Latin American Committee for the Defence of Women's Rights* (Comm on HR, 1998) at 2.

of NGOs met to seek a common approach. ARC organised the 'International Dialogue' in Geneva, which was a strategy meeting with other human rights and LGBTI activists. At the meeting, the NGO coalition decided to look at SOGI issues across all relevant thematic resolutions; to build support for a future SOGI resolution among various regions of the world, to demonstrate SOGI issues are not only Western concerns; and finally, to increase LGBT visibility at the UN.[73] In sum, the events of the Brazilian resolution gave to the LGBTI TANs the occasion to set up a common strategy.

One aspect of the three-point strategy is particularly relevant for this analysis. In 2004, the LGBTI TANs decided to build support for future SOGI resolutions among various regions of the world. Indeed, this chapter seeks to advance the claim that LGBTI gatekeeper NGOs work to strengthen the advocacy coming from non-Western and peripheral NGOs, and they do so by strengthening and developing the network horizontally. In the ensuing sub-paragraphs, I provide further support for this claim by providing evidence from the LGBTI transnational advocacy.

After the Brazilian resolution: continuous attempts to bring SOGII issues before the United Nations

After the failed attempt of the Brazilian resolution, bringing sexually and gender diverse issues before the UN was even harder because states and some mainstream human rights NGOs became reluctant to advance the issue because of the strong opposition.[74] However, the LGBTI TAN kept lobbying the Commission on HR first, and then the HR Council, to issue a resolution on human rights and SOGI in 2005 and 2006.

First, in 2005, the Canadian HIV/AIDS Legal Network urged the Commission on HR to adopt a resolution to affirm the principle of non-discrimination on the grounds of SOGI, and to request the OHCHR to gather information on human rights violations on the grounds of SOGI and to make recommendations to states.[75] Moreover, again in 2005, the LGBTI TAN, under New Zealand leadership, submitted a joint statement to the Commission on HR.[76] New Zealand, on behalf of 32 states,[77] expressed regret that the Commission on HR was still not ready to address a resolution on sexual orientation discrimination. The New Zealand delegate stressed that individuals suffer violence and discrimination because of their sexual orientation and it called the Commission on HR and its member states to recognise the principle of the prohibition of discrimination on the grounds of sexual orientation.[78]

---

73 Françoise Girard, above n 42, at 350.
74 At 352.
75 E/CN.4/2005/NGO/143 *Written Statement Submitted by the Canadian HAIV/AIDS Legal Network* (Comm on HR, 2005) at 5.
76 Clifford Bob, above n 45, at 59.
77 See Appendix 4.
78 A/CN.4/2005/SR.52 *Commission on Human Rights 61st Session: Summary Record of the 52nd Meeting* (2005) at [40]; ARC "2005 Joint Statement" (March 2005) http://

Second, in 2006, the LGBTI TAN attempted again to obtain a resolution on human rights and SOGI issues, but the tentative resolution "was caught up in the delays" associated with the reform of the Commission on HR.[79] Consequently, Norway proposed a joint statement supported by 54 states, including 18 members of the HR Council.[80] Norway delivered the joint statement during the third session of the HR Council in December 2006[81] and expressed "deep concern at these ongoing human rights violations"[82] against individuals because of their SOGI and urged the HR Council to pay due attention to these human rights violations.

LGBTI and human rights NGOs targeted the HR Council as a new potential avenue to advance LGBTI rights. Indeed, in 2006, seven NGOs jointly submitted a statement on the occasion of the inaugural session of the HR Council,[83] to highlight the important role of the HR Council in the standard setting of human rights violations, and especially in areas that have gone previously unaddressed, such as SOGI issues.[84] They expressed concerns at the fact that LGBT activists have often been prevented from accessing the work of the UN,[85] and they called upon UN member states to ensure that all individuals are treated as free and equal in dignity and rights.[86]

In sum, in 2005 and 2006, the LGBTI TAN kept targeting the HR Commission and then the HR Council to obtain a resolution on LGBTI peoples' human rights. The Commission on HR and the HR Council were not ready to discuss and vote upon a resolution on human rights and SOGI issues, and two states took the leadership to make a statement in favour of SOGI rights. However, the two states – New Zealand and Norway – were still part of the Western European and Others Group. As stated earlier, the LGBTI TAN decided to build support for a future SOGI resolution among various other regions of the world to demonstrate SOGI issues are not only Western concerns. Indeed, the LGBTI

---

arc-international.net/global-advocacy/sogi-statements/2005-joint-statement/ (Retrieved 27 July 2018).

79 Mindy Jane Roseman and Alice M Miller "Normalizing Sex and Its Discontents: Establishing Sexual Rights in International Law" (2011) 34 *Harvard Journal of Law and Gender* 313 at 362.

80 See Appendix 4.

81 A/HRC/3/SR.6 *Human Rights Council, Third Session, Summary Record of the 6th Meeting* (General Assembly, 2006) at [11].

82 HE Wegger CHR Strømmen and Norway "2006 Joint Statement" (1 December 2006) ARC http://arc-international.net/global-advocacy/sogi-statements/2006-joint-statement/ (Retrieved 27 July 2018).

83 A/HRC/1/NGO/47 *Joint Written Statement Submitted by Action Canada for Population and Development (ACPD), Canadian HIV/AIDS Legal Network, Centre for Women's Global Leadership (Global Centre, CWGL), Global Rights, International Service for Human Rights (ISHR), International Women's Health Coalition (IWHC), and New Ways: Women for Women's Human Rights* (HR Council, 2006). In addition to the seven NGOs with consultative status, another 40 NGOs have shared the view disclosed in the statement.

84 At 2.

85 At 3.

86 At 4.

TAN was already harbouring an advocacy action that aimed to bring LGBTI and human rights activists from non-Western states to the negotiating table.

The Yogyakarta Principles: overcoming obstacles with a global response

In 2005 and 2006, the global LGBTI TAN was preparing an advocacy action aimed at promoting the rights of LGBT people. At the same time, it also aimed to de-Westernise and decentralise the LGBTI advocacy. Bob highlights that "[f]rustrated by a decade of UN failure" to advance SOGI issues,[87] a coalition of NGOs, under the leadership of the International Service for Human Rights and the International Commission of Jurists, selected a group of 29 international human rights experts to draft the Yogyakarta Principles (YPs).[88] The document was drafted during a period of 12 months between 2005 and 2006 and was launched in March 2007 in Geneva, after the main session of the HR Council, in the presence of ambassadors, state delegates and UN functionaries.[89] The YPs identify states' obligation to respect and protect the human rights of all without discrimination on grounds of SOGI.[90]

The YPs are not the first nongovernmental declaration on human rights and SOGI, as the Declaration of Montreal was issued one year before by the participants of the International Conference on LGBT Human Rights.[91] However, the YPs have a major impact on the international human rights, while the Declaration of Montreal was a rather utopian and aspirational document, with a limited impact outside the LGBTI activist network.[92] The YPs are often cited by states[93] and by the HR Council during the UPR process.[94] The success of the YPs during the UPR process is also due to the constant work of NGOs that call upon states to embrace them.[95]

---

87 Clifford Bob, above n 45, at 55.
88 Michael O'Flaherty and John Fisher, above n 56, at 232.
89 At 273.
90 At 208.
91 "Declaration of Montreal on Lesbian, Gay, Bisexual, and Transgender Human Rights" (29 July 2006) www.declarationofmontreal.org (Retrieved 27 July 2018). See also, Francine D'Amico "LGBT and (Dis)United Nations: Sexual and Gender Minorities, International Law, and UN Politics" in Markus Thiel and Manuela Lavinas Picq (eds) *Sexualities in World Politics: How LGBTQ Claims Shape International Relations* (Routledge, London, New York, 2015) 54 at 59.
92 Ryan Richard Thoreson "Queering Human Rights: The Yogyakarta Principles and the Norm That Dare Not speak Its Name" (2009) 8(4) *Journal of Human Rights* 323 at 327.
93 Michael O'Flaherty and John Fisher, above n 56, at 238.
94 David Brown "Making Room for Sexual Orientation and Gender Identity in the International Human Rights Law: An Introduction to the Yogyakarta Principles" (2010) 31 *Michigan Journal of International Law* 821 at 825–826.
95 A/HRC/11/37 *Report of the Human Rights Council on Its Eleventh Session* (HR Council, 2009) at [195]; A/HRC/12/50 *Report of the Human Rights Council on Its Twelfth Session* (HR Council, 2010) at [258], [348], [420], [589], [615], [656]; A/HRC/13/56 *Report*

Moreover, governments and international organizations accepted the YPs because the principles were strategically formulated in a way that resembles a human rights treaty,[96] as a tool to reinforce the authority of the principles as "a statement of legal standards".[97] O'Flaherty was the chairperson of the group of experts that drafted the YPs; he reports that, when discussing the final version of the YPs, marriage equality was a highly debated topic that triggered discussions among the drafters. On the one hand, there were human rights activists who wanted to keep a low profile by not encompassing marriage equality. On the other hand, there were human rights experts and academics who instead pushed for an interpretation of international law in an inclusive manner by explicitly mentioning a genderless right to marry. Eventually, the opinion of the first group prevailed. The drafters did not include a positive obligation for states to allow LGBTI people to marry because they deemed that the international community would have not been ready to accept it.[98] Moreover, the drafters considered that holding back on marriage equality would have shown more consistency with existing international human rights law.[99] Indeed, part of the success of the YPs stems from the fact that there is no mention of the right to marry for LGBTI people,[100] and encompassing such right would have compromised the credibility of the document.[101]

Thus, Principle 24 (right to found a family) reads: "Everyone has the right to found a family, regardless of sexual orientation or gender identity",[102] including through adoption and assisted procreation. States are encouraged to ensure that any privilege and obligation available to heterosexual married couples, civil partners and de facto couples are equally available for their LGBTI counterparts. In other words, this recommendation ensures that married LGBTI couples are

---

of the Human Rights Council on Its Thirteenth Session (HR Council, 2011) at [447], [549]; A/HRC/14/37 *Report of the Human Rights Council on Its Fourteenth Session* (HR Council, 2012) at [271], [330], [358], [441], [688]; A/HRC/15/60 *Report of the Human Rights Council on Its Fifteenth Session* (HR Council, 2011) at [373], [309]; A/HRC/16/2 *Report of the Human Rights Council on Its Sixteenth Session* (HR Council, 2011) at [421], [509]; A/HRC/17/2 *Report of the Human Rights Council on Its Seventeenth Session* (HR Council, 2012) at [263], [410], [478]; A/HRC/18/2 *Report of the Human Rights Council on Its Eighteenth Session* (HR Council, 2012) at [247], [270], [291], [362], [420], [524], [539], [633]; A/HRC/19/2 *Report of the Human Rights Council on Its Nineteenth Session* (HR Council, 2012) at [696]; A/HRC/22/2 *Report of the Human Rights Council on Its Twenty-Second Session* (HR Council, 2013) at [771]; A/HRC/32/2 *Report of the Human Rights Council on Its Thirty-Second Session* (HR Council, 2016) at [521].

96 At 328.

97 Michael O'Flaherty and John Fisher, above n 56, at 234.

98 "Let People Be Who They Are: LGBTI Rights Are Human Rights (Michael O'Flaherty)" (Monash University, Melbourne, 20 November 2014) www.youtube.com/watch?v=R2fq8 W3p3Xw&feature=youtube_gdata_player (Retrieved 27 July 2018).

99 Michael O'Flaherty and John Fisher, above n 56, at 236.

100 Ryan R Thoreson, above n 92, at 328.

101 David Brown, above n 94, at 856.

102 *The Yogyakarta Principles* (2007) at [Principle 24].

treated equally with married heterosexual couples, without calling for a positive obligation to provide LGBTI couples with the right to marry.[103] Also the new and updated version of the YPs – the Yogyakarta Principles plus 10 (YPs+10), issued at the tenth anniversary of the initial document – do not openly invoke the right to marry for LGBTI people.[104] This is to say marriage rights for LGBTI people are very controversial even for LGBTI activists and scholars, who were not able to agree upon a positive obligation towards marriage equality in the YPs and YPs+10.

In any case, the example of the YPs shows that the LGBTI TAN provides a global response to the obstacles found at the UN. First, the YPs were discussed and adopted in Indonesia, in contrast with the previous NGO document (the Declaration of Montreal) which was adopted in Canada. Second, among the 29 experts who signed the YPs, the majority came from non-Western states,[105] while the rest came from Western states.[106] Also, among the 33 experts signing YPs+10, the majority are from non-Western states.[107] In addition, the YPs+10 were preceded by a period of consultation led by the International Service for Human Rights and ARC, during which anybody interested could submit proposals and suggestions to the Drafting Committee.[108]

These aspects demonstrate that the LGBTI TAN aims to show that LGBTI rights are not only a Western issue, in an attempt to 'de-Westernise' the LGBTI advocacy. The LGBTI TAN works better when peripheral NGOs are strong and visible and when they can advocate for LGBTI rights from below. Therefore, gatekeeper NGOs promote such LGBTI NGO support from the periphery. These themes are further described in the ensuing sections.

The Argentinian statement: non-Western states are pressured to take ownership of LGBTI issues

In 2008, on the occasion of the 60th anniversary of the Universal Declaration of Human Rights, the LGBTI TAN lobbied governmental delegates to support a resolution at the General Assembly to promote the rights of all persons, regardless of SOGI. However, the resolution lacked support and was then delivered

---

103 Michael O'Flaherty and John Fisher, above n 56, at 236.
104 *The Yogyakarta Principles plus 10*, Adopted on 10 November 2017, Geneva.
105 Moldova, Argentina, South Africa, Brazil, Pakistan, Kenya, India, Botswana, Thailand, Kenya, Costa Rica, Nepal, Bulgaria, Indonesia, Serbia, China and Poland.
106 Australia (2), Turkey, New Zealand, United Kingdom (2), United States, Austria, Ireland (2), Finland and Canada.
107 Signatories from non-Western states: Latvia, Argentina (2), South Africa (2), Indonesia, Brazil, Zimbabwe, Hungary, Kenya (2), Costa Rica, Botswana (2), Thailand (2), India (4), Nepal, Lithuania and Uganda. Signatories from Western states: Australia (3), Sweden, United Kingdom (2), Germany, United States of America (4) and Switzerland (3).
108 "Experts Release Much Anticipated Expansion of the Yogyakarta Principles", YP+10 website. Retrieved from: http://yogyakartaprinciples.org/principles-en/press-release/ (Retrieved 5 July 2018).

as a statement.[109] Initially, the French delegation pledged to promote this resolution,[110] but some LGBTI NGOs and some states, in particular the Norwegian mission at the UN, proposed that a non-European mission should have presented a possible SOGI resolution at the General Assembly.[111] This shift in the ownership of the resolution was meant to show that LGBTI rights are cross-regional issues, rather than only Western issues.

In December 2008, Argentina proposed a resolution at the General Assembly. The interviewee from the Unitarian Universalist Association (UUA) reports that their NGO, as well as other LGBTI and human rights NGOs, lobbied UN national missions to create enough support for the resolution to pass.[112] However, because there were not enough members to support it, the resolution then became a declarative statement.[113] Consequently, at the 63rd General Assembly Plenary meeting, Argentina spoke on behalf of 66 states in support of the protection of human rights without SOGI discrimination.[114] The declarative statement urged the HR Council to address human rights violations on the grounds of SOGI and asked member states to take necessary steps to decriminalise sexually and gender diverse behaviour.[115]

The statement attracted "vehement opposition",[116] and Syria, with another 57 states, made a counterstatement.[117] The Syrian representative reiterated the universality of human rights and expressed concerns in the attempt of some UN member states to introduce new notions that "had no legal foundation in any international law instruments",[118] and that therefore they fell in the domestic jurisdiction of member states. Moreover, Syria stated that the introduction of the notion of sexual orientation can lead to legitimising paedophilia. The Russian Federation, Belarus and the Holy See orally expressed support for the Syrian statement.[119]

Because the General Assembly is composed of all the UN member states, the consensus to pass resolutions is not easily reached. In addition, religious/conservative TANs can build a bloc of conservative states to bar the consensus

---

109 ARC "2008 Joint Statement: Joint Statement on Human Rights, Sexual Orientation and Gender Identity" http://arc-international.net/global-advocacy/sogi-statements/2008-joint-statement/ (Retrieved 27 July 2018).

110 Interview Unitarian Universalist Association (UUA) (Skype call, 5 April 2016).

111 Ibid.

112 Ibid.

113 Mindy Jane Roseman and Alice M Miller, above n 79, at 362.

114 See Appendix 4.

115 GA/10801 "General Assembly Adopts 52 Resolutions, Six Decisions Recommended by Third Committee on Wide Range of Human Rights, Social Humanitarian Issues" (18 December 2008) General Assembly Press Release www.un.org/News/Press/docs/2008/ga10801.doc.htm (Retrieved 27 July 2018).

116 Clifford Bob, above n 45, at 60.

117 Daniel Moeckli and others *International Human Rights Law* (2nd ed, Oxford University Press, Oxford, United Kingdom, 2014) at 314.

118 GA/10801, above n 115.

119 Ibid.

around LGBTI and progressive issues.[120] Therefore, even if gatekeeper NGOs work to build the support for LGBTI rights among peripheral NGOs and among non-Western state delegates, LGBTI resolutions struggle to gather enough support at the General Assembly because "[a] dozen conservative states can stop anything".[121] As a consequence, both the LGBTI TAN and the religious/conservative TAN need to fall back into promoting non-binding statements. Statements at the General Assembly do not need to be voted upon, and therefore they are easier to achieve as opposed to resolutions.

However, statements delivered at the General Assembly have no official status within international law.[122] Because LGBTI gatekeeper NGOs and the overall LGBTI TAN pressure international organizations to create new standards of protection for LGBTI individuals, declaratory statements at the General Assembly are symbolic but not sufficient tools to meet such a goal. Therefore, the ensuing section explains that the LGBTI TAN brought its advocacy agenda to the HR Council. This is because the HR Council provides more advocacy opportunities, and even though the HR Council's resolutions are not binding,[123] they contribute to the development of a body of soft-law norms on human rights protections.

LGBTI activism targets the Human Rights Council

Since 1979, some LGBTI activists tried unsuccessfully to prompt the UN to adopt an International Convention on the Elimination of All Forms of Discrimination Based on Sexual Orientation.[124] Part of the LGBTI network is remaining interested in lobbying the UN to create some sort of convention on the prohibition of discrimination on the grounds of SOGII.[125] However, a possible International Convention on SOGI would need to be voted upon by the majority of the General Assembly members. The LGBTI TAN cannot yet ensure such majority. In this chapter, I demonstrate that LGBTI gatekeeper NGOs are working slowly and patiently to create a solid support for LGBTI issues among all the regions of the world. To do so, gatekeeper NGOs build the network horizontally by empowering peripheral NGOs to advocate for their rights. A possible International Convention on SOGI issues remains a long-term goal,[126] and it might be

---

120 See also, Jennifer Butler "The Christian Right Coalition and the UN Special Session on Children: Prospects and Strategies" (2000) 8(4) *The International Journal of Children's Rights* 351 at 359.
121 At 358.
122 Mindy Jane Roseman and Alice M Miller, above n 79, at 369.
123 Permanent Mission of Switzerland to the United Nations Office *The Human Rights Council: A Practical Guide* (Geneva, 2015) at 5.
124 Phillip M Ayoub and David Paternotte "Challenging Borders, Imagining Europe: Transnational LGBT Activism in a New Europe" in Nancy Naples and Jennifer Bickham Mendez (eds) *Border Politics: Social Movements, Collective Identities, and Globalization* (New York University Press, New York, 2014) 230 at 239.
125 ILGA-World (Skype call, 13 April 2016), above n 26.
126 ILGA-World, above n 26 (Skype call, 13 April 2016). The interviewee from UUA adds that having another convention would mean instituting a new secretariat and a new monitoring

achieved when more UN members support LGBTI people's rights consistently. For now, the HR Council, with its 47 member states, provides more advocacy opportunities, as the majority requires a lower number of votes.[127]

The ensuing sub-paragraphs describe the advocacy action of the LGBTI TAN that led to the first HR Council resolution on human rights and SOGI. It is shown that the gatekeeper NGOs' strategy to build the LGBTI TAN horizontally is starting to bear fruit. It is described how LGBTI gatekeeper NGOs coordinated peripheral NGOs to pressure their governments from below, to influence the international human rights debate.

The first Human Rights Council Resolution on Human Rights, Sexual Orientation and Gender Identity

In March 2011, South Africa proposed a draft resolution that aimed to:[128]

> [E]stablish an open-ended intergovernmental working group to elaborate new concepts, such as sexual orientation, and others which may emerge in this regard, defining such concepts and their scope and parameters in international human rights law prior to their integration into existing norms and standards of international human rights law.

ARC noted that such a draft resolution would have meant the creation of an open-ended intergovernmental working group to define 'new concepts', such as sexual orientation. In other words, SOGI issues would not have been considered in any other UN forum or mechanism, "effectively creating a censor".[129] Jordaan reports that South Africa did not discuss the draft resolution with other members of the HR Council; instead, the South African delegation only discussed it with the members of the African Group. In his opinion, by creating the working group, South Africa was "trying to bury the issue for decades".[130]

Therefore, from March to June 2011, ARC worked closely with LGBTI activists in South Africa, Geneva and elsewhere to lobby the South African representatives to opt for focusing the resolution on "addressing violence, discrimination and related human rights violations on grounds of [SOGI]".[131]

---

body, while the UN is struggling to monitor the conventions that already exist. Therefore, there seems to be resistance because of the economical and bureaucratic aspects that such a new convention would entail. Unitarian Universalist Association (UUA), above n 110.

127 See in general, Theodor Rathgeber *Performance and Challenges of the UN Human Rights Council: An NGOs' View* (Friedrich Erbert Stifgung, 2013) at 4.

128 A/HRC/16/L.27 *The Imperative Need to Respect the Established Procedures and Practices of the General Assembly in the Elaboration of New Norms and Standards and Their Subsequent Integration into Existing International Human Rights Law* (HR Council, 2011).

129 ARC "17th Session of the Human Rights Council" (2011) http://arc-international.net/global-advocacy/human-rights-council/hrc17/ (Retrieved 27 July 2018).

130 Eduard Jordaan "The Challenge of Adopting Sexual Orientation Resolutions at the UN Human Rights Council" (2016) 8(2) *Journal of Human Rights Practice* 298 at 302.

131 ARC, above n 129.

The new draft resolution (A/HRC/17/L.9)[132] was praised by the LGBTI network as an "excellent text",[133] and it was voted upon and adopted by the HR Council, in June 2011, becoming the first UN resolution on discrimination and violence based on SOGI.[134] Resolution A/HRC/17/19 was introduced by Brazil and South Africa[135] and co-sponsored by another 45 state delegates.[136] During the HR Council meeting, seven NGOs delivered statements.[137] The 2011 resolution was adopted with a slight majority: 23 votes in favour, 19 against and three abstentions.[138] After the adoption of the resolution, a coalition of 16 NGOs[139] issued a joint press release on the resolution to congratulate South Africa, Brazil and the co-sponsoring states for taking the leadership on the issues of SOGI.[140]

Freedman comments that draft resolution 17/19 was successful because of the absence of strong opposing voices. Indeed, draft resolution 17/19 passed during the 'Arab spring', when the OIC, whose members have always blocked SOGI resolutions in the past, was experiencing internal division and OIC members were absent during the discussion.[141] Undoubtedly, the LGBTI TAN has benefited from the political opportunities provided by the absence of opposing states but acknowledging only the lack of opposition is an oversimplification.

The favourable political opportunity presented itself, but the gatekeeper NGOs seized it. ARC's work with South African LGBTI NGOs and other peripheral NGOs was crucial. The initial proposal of the South African delegates would have created a working group to elaborate 'new' concepts such as SOGI. As a response to the unsatisfactory draft resolution, ARC coordinated and supported the work

---

132 A/HRC/17/L.9 *Human Rights, Sexual Orientation and Gender Identity* (HR Council, 2011).

133 ARC, above n 129.

134 A/HRC/RES/17/19 *Human Rights, Sexual Orientation and Gender Identity* (HR Council, 2011).

135 A/HRC/17/2 *Report of the Human Rights Council on Its Seventeenth Session* (General Assembly, 2012) at [722]. See also South African representative's opening statement at ARC "SOGI Resolution – South Africa's Opening Statement" http://arc-international. net/global-advocacy/human-rights-council/hrc17/amb_matjila_statement/ (Retrieved 27 July 2018).

136 A/HRC/17/2, above n 135, at [722].

137 ARC, Blue Diamond Society, United & Strong Inc., Caribbean Forum for the Liberation of Genders and Sexualities, Global Action for Trans* Equality, Australian Coalition for Equality, and COC.

138 A/HRC/RES/17/19, above n 134. See also Appendix 4.

139 ARC, Amnesty, Coalition of African Lesbians, COC, Council for Global Equality, Global Action for Trans* Equality, Heartland Alliance for Human Needs and Human Rights, HRW, International Day Against Homophobia and Transphobia, OutRight, International Campaign Stop Trans Pathologization, International Commission of Jurists, International Service for Human Rights, Sexual Rights Initiative, Thailand's Sexual, Diversity Network, Transgender Europe.

140 ARC "Historic Decision at the United Nations!" (17 June 2011) http://arc-international. net/press_release_hrcresolution/ (Retrieved 27 July 2018).

141 Rosa Freedman "The United Nations Human Rights Council's Backwards Step on LGBT Rights" (7 June 2013) IntLawGrrls http://ilg2.org/2013/06/07/the-united-nations-human-rights-councils-backwards-step-on-lgbt-rights/ (Retrieved 27 July 2018).

of peripheral NGOs to pressure their government from below to frame a resolution that encompasses SOGI issues within the existing norms and standards of international human rights law. In the ensuing years, LGBTI gatekeeper NGOs continued to promote the advocacy of peripheral LGBTI NGOs to obtain two other HR Council resolutions on human rights and SOGI.

The second Human Rights Council Resolution on Human Rights, Sexual Orientation and Gender Identity

In June 2014, in a joint statement delivered at the 26th session of the HR Council, ILGA, with 13 co-sponsoring NGOs and with the support of 500 organizations from all over the world,[142] asked the HR Council to adopt a resolution "to ensure regular reporting, constructive dialogue and sustained, systematic attention to the breadth of human rights violations" on the grounds of SOGII.[143] ILGA coordinated a petition, which gathered signatories from hundreds of NGOs from more than 100 states, "from Australia to Zimbabwe, from St Lucia to Samoa, from Uruguay to Uganda",[144] and called for regular reporting on SOGII related human rights violations.

In September 2014, Brazil, Chile, Colombia and Uruguay introduced draft resolution A/HRC/27/L.27/Rev.1, which was co-sponsored by 46 states.[145] Egypt, with the support of Djibouti, Malaysia, Nigeria, South Sudan, Uganda and the United Arab Emirates, introduced six hostile amendments aiming to change any reference to discrimination on the grounds of SOGI with a generic "discrimination based on race, colour, sex, language, religion, political or other opinion, national or social origin, property, birth or other status",[146] and one amendment aiming to introduce a paragraph affirming state sovereignty in the protection of human rights.[147] These amendments would have vanquished the significance of the resolution by excluding any reference to SOGI. All seven amendments were rejected,[148] and at its 27th session, the HR Council adopted, with absolute majority (25 in favour, 14 against and seven abstentions),[149] the second

---

142 Lame Charmaine Olebile *26th session of the Human Rights Council, June 2014: NGO Joint Statement – Item 8 General Debate* (ILGA, Online, 2014) at 2–13.

143 At 1.

144 At 1.

145 A/HRC/27/2 *Report of the Human Rights Council on Its Twenty-Seventh Session* (HR Council, 2014) at 139.

146 A/HRC/27/L.45 *Human Rights, Sexual Orientation and Gender Identity* (HR Council, 2014); A/HRC/27/L.46 *Human Rights, Sexual Orientation and Gender Identity* (HR Council, 2014); A/HRC/27/L.47 *Human Rights, Sexual Orientation and Gender Identity* (HR Council, 2014); A/HRC/27/L.48 *Human Rights, Sexual Orientation and Gender Identity* (HR Council, 2014); A/HRC/27/L.50 *Human Rights, Sexual Orientation and Gender Identity* (HR Council, 2014); A/HRC/27/L.51 *Human Rights, Sexual Orientation and Gender Identity* (HR Council, 2014).

147 A/HRC/27/L.49 *Human Rights, Sexual Orientation and Gender Identity* (HR Council, 2014).

148 A/HRC/27/2, above n 164, at 140–143.

149 See Appendix 4.

resolution on human rights and SOGI.[150] Furthermore, the resolution called the OHCHR to produce a new report on discrimination and violence on individuals on the basis of their SOGI, which was released in May 2015.[151]

Some LGBTI NGOs welcomed the HR Council resolution and the OHCHR report. ILGA, with 11 co-sponsoring NGOs and 379 organizations,[152] commended the second resolution and OHCHR report as "additional positive steps forward".[153] However, the coalition of NGOs reiterated that LGBTI individuals suffer systematic abuses, and therefore the response of the HR Council should be systematic with the adoption of a resolution that ensures regular reporting and constructive dialogue on SOGI issues.[154] Such position is not shared by all the actors of the LGBTI network; nonetheless, the LGBTI TAN, under the leadership of gatekeeper NGOs, continued to advocate for regular reporting on SOGI human rights violations in 2016.

The third Human Rights Council resolution and the appointment of a Special Rapporteur

In 2016, ILGA advanced a second petition to ask the HR Council to issue a resolution on human rights and SOGII, and to institute a Special Rapporteur on SOGII human rights violations.[155] ILGA's petition gathered the support of 628 NGOs from 151 states;[156] in particular, ILGA stressed that 70% of the NGOs that signed it were from non-Western states.[157] In doing so, ILGA highlighted that NGOs from all over the world were involved in advocating for a SOGI resolution and a Special Rapporteur with a SOGI mandate, in line with the ongoing LGBTI gatekeeper NGOs' strategy to build the peripheral support for LGBTI rights to show that these are not only Western concerns. And indeed, in June 2016, the HR Council adopted the third resolution on the protection against SOGI violence and discrimination,[158] instituting the first Special Rapporteur on SOGI discrimination and violence.[159]

---

150 A/HRC/RES/27/32 *Human Rights, Sexual Orientation and Gender Identity* (HR Council, 2014).
151 A/HRC/29/23 *Discrimination and Violence Against Individuals Based on Their Sexual Orientation and Gender Identity: Report of the Office of the United Nations High Commissioner for Human Rights* (HR Council, 2015).
152 Danish Sheikh *29th Session of the Human Rights Council – June 2015: NGO Joint Statement – Item 8 General Debate* (ILGA, Online, 2015) at 4–12.
153 At 1.
154 At 1. See also, A/HRC/29/NGO/118 *Joint Written Statement Submitted by Amnesty International, Human Rights Watch* (HR Council, 2015) at 4.
155 ILGA *628 NGOs from 151 Countries Call for a SOGI Independent Expert at the UN, 27 June 2016* (ILGA, Online, 2016).
156 At 2–20.
157 Daniele Paletta "United Nations Makes History on Sexual Orientation and Gender Identity" (30 June 2016) ILGA http://ilga.org/united-nations-makes-history-sexual-orientation-gender-identity/ (Retrieved 27 July 2018).
158 A/HRC/RES/32/2 *Protection Against Violence and Discrimination Based on Sexual Orientation and Gender Identity* (HR Council, 2016). See also Appendix 4.
159 Daniele Paletta, above n 157.

At least since 1992, the LGBTI TAN lobbied the UN to adopt a special procedure on SOGI issues.[160] For example, many NGOs, in their written statements, called upon the HR Council to institutionalise a Special Rapporteur on LGBTI issues, or in general to incorporate SOGI issues in other Special Rapporteur mandates.[161] Moreover, the LGBTI network lobbied the UN to have a special mandate on SOGI issues because Special Rapporteurs are neither UN staff nor paid, which makes them more independent and they "speak their minds".[162] ILGA's interviewee confirms that a Special Rapporteur on SOGII discrimination mandate was a priority within the LGBTI network.[163] Finally, further proof of the importance of special procedures for the LGBTI TAN can be seen in the fact that LGBTI NGOs collaborated with various Special Rapporteurs.[164]

However, not every NGO within the LGBTI network necessarily agrees on the need for a Special Rapporteur on LGBT human rights violations. Notably, the Coalition of African Lesbians (CAL) released a brief just before the vote at the HR Council, in May 2016, to say "NO to a Special Rapporteur on Sexual Orientation, Gender Identity".[165] In particular, they maintained that the interest of sexually and gender diverse people would be better served by a Special

---

160 Nicole LaViolette and Sandra Whitworth "No Safe Haven: Sexuality as a Universal Human Right and Lesbian and Gay Activism in International Politics" (1994) 23 *Millennium-Journal of International Studies* 563 at 572.

161 A/HRC/29/NGO/106 *Written Statement Submitted by the Article 19 – International Centre Against Censorship* (HR Council, 2015) at 5; A/HRC/19/NGO/150 *Written Statement Submitted by the Canadian HIV/AIDS Legal Network* (HR Council, 2012) at 4; A/HRC/19/NGO/61 *Written Statement Submitted by the Commonwealth Human Rights Initiative* (HR Council, 2012) at 4; A/HRC/24/NGO/39 *Joint Written Statement Submitted by the International Service for Human Rights, the Action Canada for Population and Development, Amnesty International, the Asian Forum for Human Rights and Development, the Cairo Institute for Human Rights Studies, the Canadian HIV/AIDS Legal Network, Centro de Estudios Legales y Sociales (CELS) Asociación Civil, the Commonwealth Human Rights Initiative, Conectas Direitos Humanos, the East and Horn of Africa Human Rights Defenders Project, Groupe des ONG pour la Convention relative aux Droits de l'Enfant, the Human Rights House Foundation, the International Commission of Jurists, the International Federation for Human Rights Leagues, the International Rehabilitation Council for Torture Victims, the World Organization Against Torture, CIVICUS – World Alliance for Citizen Participation* (HR Council, 2013) at 3; A/HRC/25/NGO/176 *Joint Written Statement Submitted by the Asian Legal Resource Centre, Amnesty International, Cairo Institute for Human Rights Studies, the East and Horn of Africa Human Rights Defenders Project, International Service for Human Rights, Reporters Sans Frontieres International – Reporters Without Borders International, Article 19 – International Centre Against Censorship* (HR Council, 2014) at 4; A/HRC/29/NGO/109 *Joint Written Statement Submitted by the Freemuse – The World Forum on Music and Censorship, International PEN, the Article 19 – International Centre Against Censorship* (HR Council, 2015) at 4; A/HRC/20/NGO/11 *Written Statement Submitted by the International Commission of Jurists* (HR Council, 2012) at 4.

162 Unitarian Universalist Association (UUA), above n 110.

163 ILGA-World (Skype call, 13 April 2016), above n 26.

164 LGBT Denmark, above n 10; Hungarian LGBT Alliance, above n 3.

165 Coalition of African Lesbians (CAL) "ACTIVISTS BRIEF: Coalition of African Lesbians Says NO to a Special Rapporteur on Sexual Orientation, Gender Identity" (May 2016) Sexual Policy Watch http://sxpolitics.org/activists-brief-coalition-of-

Rapporteur on Sexuality and Gender. Such an alternative mandate would have offered protection to LGBT people as well as to many others who are oppressed because of their sexuality and gender, for example, "sex workers, women seeking abortion services and those offering these services, people living with HIV, intersex people, young people and others".[166] In particular, CAL noted that a special mechanism for LGBT rights would pass the message that the rights of LGBT people are more important than the rights of sex workers and other oppressed communities.

The position of CAL remains on the margin of the LGBTI network. Even though LGBTI gatekeeper NGOs consult with the rest of the network to coordinate and to create an advocacy agenda that allows most of the NGOs involved being satisfied, it would be impossible to have an advocacy agenda that accommodates everybody, all the time. There is always going to be someone who is unhappy with how LGBTI rights have been framed. In general, this book shows that LGBTI gatekeeper NGOs partially relinquish their social power and decentralise their position in the network. Nonetheless, this section on CAL's views on the Special Rapporteur on SOGI discrimination and violence represents an exception to my arguments. Even though gatekeeper NGOs partially relinquish their central power, they remain the primary decision-makers.

Conclusion

The book argues that the way in which TANs name LGBTI people's human rights violations, and frame LGBTI issues, shapes the international human rights debate, and subsequently the international human rights standard setting. This chapter has focused on the way in which gatekeeper NGOs and peripheral NGOs work together (internetwork relations) to advance LGBTI rights. To do so, this chapter analyses interviews, archival material from the UN, and some NGO webpages and press releases.

First, the interviews demonstrate that LGBTI gatekeeper NGOs strive to build the LGBTI TAN horizontally, by creating physical spaces for activists working in the same sub-region to meet and to create long-lasting working bonds, and by connecting peripheral NGOs with donors. Moreover, it is shown that LGBTI gatekeeper NGOs invest in the capacity building of peripheral NGOs by providing grants for peripheral NGOs to travel to Geneva and New York to participate in the international organizations' meetings and express their claims in person. They also sponsor training sessions for peripheral NGOs to learn how international organizations work and how to improve their oral and writing skills so that peripheral NGOs are better able to draft their own reports and deliver their own speeches before international organizations. Even though gatekeeper NGOs remain the central actors within the LGBTI network – because they maintain

---

african-lesbians-says-no-to-a-special-rapporteur-on-sexual-orientation-gender-identity/
14809 (Retrieved on 27 July 2018).
166 Ibid.

stronger relationships with some international organizations' functionaries and some states' delegates – these actions are fundamental for a democratic development of the network.

Second, this chapter studied the mobilisation effect of the failed attempt of the Brazilian resolution. It discovered that during and soon after the Commission on HR session in which Brazil tabled the first resolution on human rights and SOGI, gatekeeper NGOs worked to mobilise peripheral NGOs to pressure their own governments from below. These advocacy actions galvanised a group of LGBTI NGOs and activists to keep pushing the Commission on HR first and then the HR Council to issue SOGI resolutions. In particular, the events of the Brazilian resolution promoted gatekeeper NGOs to call for two meetings, one in Rio de Janeiro and one in Geneva, where the LGBTI TAN decided to develop the network from below by de-centralising and de-Westernising the LGBTI advocacy.

These findings demonstrate that gatekeeper NGOs relinquish part of their social power by decentralising their position in the network and by de-Westernising the LGBTI advocacy. Gatekeeper NGOs understand that their interference with non-Western governments can be detrimental for the LGBTI advocacy. Moreover, acting alone they would not be convincing enough, especially before some conservative/religious governments that see LGBTI issues as a Western threat. Further examples of these dynamics are the YPs, signed in Indonesia, and the SOGI statement delivered by Argentina at the General Assembly.

In this chapter I show that by developing LGBTI networks horizontally, gatekeeper NGOs enhance their democratic legitimacy and the efficiency of their advocacy. For example, in 2011, gatekeeper NGOs seized favourable political opportunities and coordinated peripheral NGOs to pressure their governments to include SOGI rights in the existing human rights system of norms, rather than creating a separate working group on 'new' rights. Furthermore, the example of the advocacy around the following two HR Council SOGI resolutions demonstrates that gatekeeper NGOs continued coordinating the work of peripheral NGOs. In particular, gatekeeper NGOs promoted petitions to demonstrate that LGBTI rights are not only Western rights. The role of peripheral NGOs to pressure their governments and the UN has been crucial to advance the creation of soft-law instruments for LGBTI human rights protection. If peripheral NGOs are weak or non-existent, they are not able to play such an important role.

In sum, the horizontal development of LGBTI TANs has two consequences in the advocacy agenda. On the one hand, stronger and empowered peripheral NGOs that work in consultation with gatekeeper NGOs can influence the advocacy agenda decision-making with their specific 'peripheral' perspectives. However, the advocacy action for pressuring the HR Council to create a special procedure on LGBT rights shows that after the consultations gatekeeper NGOs maintain the final decision and there are instances in which peripheral NGOs might be unsatisfied with the advocacy agenda. On the other hand, because gatekeeper NGOs aim to build the network horizontally, they advocate for those rights that enhance the domestic political opportunities of NGOs working in the periphery of the network.

In describing the advocacy actions around the three HR Council resolutions, the statements at the General Assembly, and the YPs and YPs+10, the chapter inevitably also describes the counter attacks of the conservative/religious NGOs and states. LGBTI gatekeeper NGOs frame LGBTI issues in a way that maximises their political opportunities and minimises adversities. This is because, even though this chapter mostly focuses on the internetwork relations between gatekeeper NGOs and peripheral NGOs, the reality is that the LGBTI TANs do not work in a vacuum. In the ensuing chapter I discuss in-depth how the conservative/religious NGOs and states influence the LGBTI advocacy.

4 The broader political context

How states and other NGOs influence LGBTI NGOs' issue framing

Introduction

This chapter focuses on the way in which political opportunities and constraints provided by international organizations, states and other NGOs outside the network (the broader political context) shape how LGBTI TANs chose their advocacy agendas. In particular, the themes of alliance and political alignment are discussed. Powerful international allies, such as some governments and some UN agencies, can legitimise and amplify LGBTI claims. At the same time, coalitions of opposing NGOs and states try to prevent them from advancing their advocacy agenda. Therefore, this chapter shows that LGBTI gatekeeper NGOs frame LGBTI issues in a way that maximises their political opportunities and minimises adversities. These dynamics impact the development of the international human rights debate. To do so, the chapter develops as follows.

First, this chapter opens by discussing the question of access. This brief discussion is relevant because when NGOs cannot access the UN, they have limited chances to impact the international human rights debate, which is the core research question of this research. It is shown that since 2006, all the LGBTI NGOs that applied for ECOSOC consultative status were eventually granted it. Some of these NGOs are the LGBTI gatekeeper NGOs, like ILGA, ILGA-Europe, OutRight and ARC. This happens also because a bloc of pro-LGBTI states voted upon granting ECOSOC status to LGBTI NGOs, and in doing so they overruled and bypassed the Committee on NGOs' recommendations.

Second, the chapter highlights that UN member states can be divided into three groups with regard to their positions on LGBTI rights. There is a bloc of states that are pro-LGBTI issues, another bloc that is anti-LGBTI rights and a third bloc of non-aligned states that are not consistent in their position on LGBTI people's issues. It is explained that LGBTI gatekeeper NGOs coordinate the work of peripheral NGOs to lobby non-aligned states to support LGBTI resolutions and amendments. Gatekeeper NGOs are instrumental in coordinating the transnational LGBTI advocacy. But because gatekeeper NGOs' interference with foreign – especially non-Western – governments can be counterproductive, LGBTI gatekeeper NGOs build the network horizontally to ensure that peripheral NGOs are able to lobby their own (non-aligned) governments from below.

However, it is also shown that LGBTI gatekeeper NGOs need to maintain a low profile to find a "minimum common denominator"[1] to create consensus among these non-aligned states. In other words, LGBTI gatekeeper NGOs seize opportunities and minimise adversity by framing LGBTI issues as a matter of fundamental human rights protection.

Third, the chapter discusses the advocacy around HR Council resolutions on traditional values and the protection of the family. In this book, I claim that LGBTI gatekeeper NGOs operate democratically and they use mainly, although not exclusively, a prohibition of discrimination framework to maximise their broader political opportunities. To further investigate these claims, I research the importance of the advocacy for the right to marry in the LGBTI transnational advocacy. In this chapter, I further analyse the theme of the right to marry by demonstrating that marriage and family inequality are strong arguments used by conservative/religious NGOs and states to undermine advocacy for LGBTI rights. In general, the LGBTI TANs tend to avoid invoking these rights. However, this chapter provides some evidence that, when responding to conservative/religious NGOs and states' attacks, LGBTI gatekeeper NGOs cautiously highlight that LGBTI parent-families exist and they should not be excluded from human rights protections. In other words, they respond to conservative/religious NGOs' attacks by maintaining a low profile. As a result of this conflict between conservative/religious positions and LGBTI rights positions, the HR Council Advisory Committee and the OHCHR have been able to maintain the view that international human rights law understands the notion of 'family' in a wide sense, a provision that would potentially (but not explicitly) include LGBTI parent-families.

This chapter shows that the broader political context in which LGBTI TANs operate influences the way in which LGBTI gatekeeper NGOs maximise their political opportunities and minimise the challenges. The processes under which resolutions and recommendations are drafted and then voted upon require a continuous negotiation between pro-LGBTI positions and anti-LGBTI positions. On the one hand, LGBTI gatekeeper NGOs can coordinate the work of peripheral NGOs to pressure non-aligned states from below, and, with the support of many international allies, they can push for setting human rights standards that protect LGBTI people. However, to do so, they need to maintain a low profile and frame LGBTI issues as fundamental rights protection. On the other hand, conservative/religious NGOs and states use a slippery slope argument based on marriage inequality to prevent LGBTI rights from further developing. LGBTI gatekeeper NGOs respond to conservative/religious attacks but they still enforce cautionary tactics. These dynamics explain that the right to marry is not developed in the international human rights debate, despite the debate on the right to equality for LGBTI people is gaining more and more ground. Finally, this chapter also shows that, despite the victories achieved by the LGBTI TAN, like the three HR Council's resolutions on human rights and SOGI, LGBTI activists still have an uphill battle at the UN.

---

1 Interview Unitarian Universalist Association (UUA) (Skype call, 5 April 2016).

LGBTI organization and access: the Economic and Social Council's consultative status

The ECOSOC is composed of 53 member states of the UN, voted by the General Assembly; each member has one representative. The ECOSOC "may make recommendations for the purpose of promoting respect for, and observance of, human rights and fundamental freedoms for all".[2] Among its various tasks, the ECOSOC organises human rights conferences and it assists other UN agencies to promote human rights,[3] where NGOs are invited as observers.[4]

During the drafting of the UN Charter, many governmental delegates wanted to formalise the UN's relationships with NGOs,[5] but some delegates did not want NGO involvement in political matters such as peace, security and disarmament. A compromise was found by providing only the ECOSOC with the power to make official relationships with NGOs, as opposed to the UN as a whole.[6] In this way, NGOs can only collaborate with the ECOSOC on matters falling in its competences, that is to say economic, social and human rights issues. However, as Theo van Boven notes, the distinction between economic, social and human rights issues, on the one hand, and peace and security issues, on the other hand, is not as defined as the drafters of the UN Charter wanted it to be. Thus, NGOs had a major impact in the creation and maintenance of peace and in the disarmament.[7]

Article 71 of the UN Charter calls upon the ECOSOC to make arrangements for consultation with NGOs,[8] and in 1946, in response to the request from a number of NGOs,[9] the General Assembly recommended that the ECOSOC adopt a "suitable arrangement to enable [NGOs] to collaborate".[10] In that same year, the ECOSOC finally arranged consultations with NGOs to access expert advice from NGOs and to allow NGOs to express their views.[11]

---

2 Charter of the United Nations, United Nations (signed 26 June 1945, entered into force 24 October 1945), Article 62(2).

3 Rhona K M Smith *Textbook on International Human Rights* (6th ed, Oxford University Press, Oxford, 2014) at 60.

4 E/RES/1996/31 *Consultative Relationship between the United Nations and Non-Governmental Organizations* (1996) at Article 41.

5 Bruno Simma and Hermann Mosler (eds) *The Charter of the United Nations: A Commentary* (Oxford University Press, Oxford, New York, 1995) at 904.

6 Ruth B Rusell *A History of the United Nations Charter* (Brookings Institution, Washington, 1958) at 800.

7 Theo van Boven "The Role of Non-Governmental Organizations in International Human Rights Standard-Setting: A Prerequisite of Democracy" (1989) 20 *California Western International Law Journal* 207 at 208.

8 Charter of the United Nations, United Nations (signed 26 June 1945, entered into force 24 October 1945) Article 71.

9 World Federation of Trade Unions, the American Federation of Labour and the International Cooperative Alliance.

10 A/RES/4(I) *Representation of Non-governmental Bodies on the Economic and Social Council* (1946) at [a]. Cited in, Anna-Karin Lindblom *Non-Governmental Organizations in International Law* (Cambridge University Press, Cambridge, New York, 2005) at 375.

11 E/43/Rev.2 *Arrangement for Consultation with Non-Governmental Organizations* (1946). Cited in E/INF/23 *Arrangement of the Economic and Social Council of the United Nations for Consultation with Non-Governmental Organizations* (1948) at [5].

In 1968, the ECOSOC revised the agreement of consultation,[12] and again in 1996, acknowledging the breadth of NGOs' expertise.[13] Since 1996, NGOs have been categorised into three groups. First, organizations that are concerned with most of the ECOSOC fields of interest and that hold general consultative status. Second, organizations that have particular competence in a few fields of the ECOSOC activities and that have special consultative status. Finally, organizations neither in the first group nor in the second, but that the ECOSOC considers can make an occasional and valuable contribution to its work, categorised as Rosters. The three groups can attend ECOSOC meetings. Organizations with general and special consultative status have the right to submit written statements to the ECOSOC. Only NGOs with general consultative status can make oral presentations during meetings.[14]

Recognition of the consultative status by the ECOSOC indicates the NGO's recognition as a legitimate international actor.[15] For LGBTI organizations, the ECOSOC consultative status carries even more important social meaning because "ECOSOC has been a deeply symbolic venue for LGBT NGOs seeking recognition in the human rights arena".[16]

The value of the ECOSOC status is not only symbolic. There are some similarities between NGOs with ECOSOC consultative status and gatekeeper NGOs. It takes time, resources and expertise to achieve ECOSOC consultative status and therefore usually Western, bigger and better funded NGOs obtain it.[17] If, on the one hand, not all the NGOs with consultative status are gatekeeper NGOs, on the other hand, all the NGOs identified as gatekeepers in this book have ECOSOC consultative status. TAN theories claim that gatekeeper NGOs have a central role in the network because they have more visibility and greater ties with international organizations and states. Having ECOSOC consultative status is an important requirement for NGOs to be perceived as credible and reliable actors by states and international organizations. In other words, the consultative status helps NGOs to acquire a gatekeeping position within the network.

When LGBTI NGOs can participate in intergovernmental meetings, submit reports and communications, and in general can get in contact with governments and international organization officials, they influence the process of

---

12　E/RES/1296(XLIV) *Arrangements for Consultation with Non-Governmental Organizations (Item 18)* (1968). See also, Antonio Cassese "How Could Nongovernmental Organizations Use UN Bodies More Effectively?" (1979) 1(4) *Universal Human Rights* 73 at 73–75.

13　E/RES/1996/31, above n 4. See also, Karin Ryan and Laurie Wiseberg "ECOSOC Resolution 1996/31: The End Result of the ECOSOC Review Process of Rules Governing NGO Relations with the United Nations" in *Human Rights, the United Nations and Nongovernmental Organizations* (The Carter Centre, Atlanta, 1997) 9.

14　E/RES/1996/31, above n 4, at [22] – [32].

15　Kerstin Martens "Bypassing Obstacles to Access: How NGOs Are Taken Piggy-Back to the UN" (2004) 5(3) *Human Rights Review* 80 at 82.

16　Ryan R Thoreson *Transnational LGBT Activism: Working for Sexual Rights Worldwide* (University of Minnesota Press, Minneapolis, 2014) at 200.

17　For example, among LGBTI NGOs with ECOSOC consultative status, only one is a non-Western NGO, and it is Associação Brasileira de Gays, Lésbicas e Transgeneros.

issue emergence and issue framing in the international human rights debate. It goes without saying that when NGOs have limited or no access to the work of international organizations, they cannot provide their input to shape the issue framing process in an effective and influential manner.[18] The ensuing sub-paragraphs discuss the access of LGBTI NGOs to the work of the UN. This is because access is the necessary, although not sufficient, condition for NGOs to influence the issue emergence and issue framing processes discussed in this book.

LGBTI NGOs' consultative status

In D'Amico's opinion, during the 1990s the international arena opened a political space for LGBTI TANs because with the end of the Cold War the UN shifted away from the focus on security.[19] In 1993, ILGA was the first LGBTI organization to be granted ECOSOC consultative status.[20] ILGA started applying for the ECOSOC consultative status since its foundation in 1978.[21] But its application was considered by the Committee on NGOs for the first time in 1991,[22] and again in 1993, when ILGA was granted Roster status.[23] Soon after, a coalition of American right-wing NGOs lobbied the UN to revoke ILGA's consultative status accusing ILGA of misconduct. This is because the ILGA had the North American Man Boy Love Association (NAMBLA), which supports intergenerational relationships, among its members.[24] Such an attack was probably part of a wider conservative agenda for preventing the development of sexual rights at the UN,[25] and even though ILGA expelled NAMBLA from its membership, ILGA's consultative status was suspended in 1994.[26]

---

18 Jutta Joachim *Agenda Setting, the UN, and NGOs: Gender Violence and Reproductive Rights* (Georgetown University Press, Washington, 2007) at 24.

19 Francine D'Amico "LGBT and (Dis)United Nations: Sexual and Gender Minorities, International Law, and UN Politics" in Markus Thiel and Manuela Lavinas Picq (eds) *Sexualities in World Politics: How LGBTQ Claims Shape International Relations* (Routledge, London, New York, 2015) 54 at 58.

20 Douglas Sanders "Getting Lesbian and Gay Issues on the International Human Rights Agenda" (1996) 18 *Human Rights Quarterly* 67 at 67.

21 David Paternotte "The International (Lesbian and) Gay Association and the Question of Paedophilia: Tracking the Demise of Gay Liberation Ideals" (2014) 17(1–2) *Sexualities* 121 at 130.

22 Douglas Sanders, above n 20, at 98.

23 In favour: Bulgaria, Chile, Costa Rica, Cuba, France, Greece, Ireland, Russian Federation, Sweden. Against: Iraq, Lesotho, Oman, Sudan. Abstaining: Ethiopia, Libyan Arab Jamahiriya, Philippines. E/1993/63 *Report of the Committee on Non-Governmental Organization* (ECOSOC, 1993) at 13.

24 Clifford Bob *The Global Right Wing and the Clash of World Politics* (Cambridge University Press, New York, 2012) at 47.

25 David Paternotte, above n 21, at 130.

26 E/1994/L.48 *Arrangement for Consultation with Non-Governmental Organizations: Status of the International Lesbian and Gay Association with the Council* (ECOSOC, 1994). See in general, Joshua Gamson "Messages of Exclusion: Gender, Movements, and Symbolic Boundaries" (1997) 11 *Gender & Society* 178 at 183–187.

Two other LGBTI NGOs obtained the consultative status in the 1990s, the International Wages Due Lesbians in 1998[27] and the Coalition of Activist Lesbians in 1999,[28] but most of LGBTI organizations with current consultative status were accredited in the 2000s and 2010s.[29]

NGOs apply for consultative status from the Committee on NGOs – a standing committee of the ECOSOC composed of 19 members. The Committee on NGOs must take into account the basic requirements spelled out in resolution 1996/31.[30] However, the Committee on NGOs' decisions can be "highly political".[31] It is a common practice for the Committee on NGOs' members to reject the application of NGOs that seek to undermine their authority,[32] or keep submitting questions to the NGOs as a pretext to slowing down the decision-making process.[33] Indeed, in 2006, the Committee on NGOs considered the application for consultative status of four LGBTI organizations – ILGA, ILGA-Europe, Danish National Association for Gays and Lesbians, and Lesbian and Gay Federation in Germany – and rejected all of them without allowing the usual time for questions and discussions.

When discussing ILGA's application, the representative from Iran urged the Committee on NGOs to recommend not granting consultative status because of ILGA's alleged support for paedophilia. The German delegate commented that Iran's recommendation was discriminatory and unprecedented because ILGA was not given the opportunity to respond to additional questions where delegates were not satisfied.[34] At the request of the Iranian delegation, the Danish National Association for Gays and Lesbians, the Lesbian and Gay Federation in Germany, and ILGA-Europe's applications for consultative status were also rejected.

A number of country delegates highlighted the unusual treatment reserved for LGBTI NGOs and protested that the rejection of LGBTI organizations was becoming a pattern of discrimination within the Committee on NGOs' work.

27　E/1998/INF/3/Add.2 *Résolutions et Décisions Adoptées par le Conseil Économique et Social à la Reprise de sa Session d'Organization pour 1998 et à sa Session de Fond de 1998* (ECOSOC, 1998) at 146.

28　E/1999/INF/2/Add.2 *Resolutions and Decisions Adopted by the Economic and Social Council at the 10th Meeting of Its Resumed Organizational Session for 1999 and at Its Substantive Session of 1999* (ECOSOC, 1999) at 184.

29　See also, Giulia Dondoli "Searching for an Advocacy Venue: How LGBTI Organizations Are Getting Access to the United Nations" (2016) 8(2) *Yonsei Journal of International Studies* 134.

30　For example, NGOs must be concerned with matters falling in the competence of the ECOSOC; the aims of the NGOs must be in line with the principles of the UN Charter; and NGOs must demonstrate their programme is relevant to UN work.

31　Kerstin Martens, above n 15, at 83.

32　Ibid.

33　Jurij Daniel Aston "The United Nations Committee on Non-Governmental Organizations: Guarding the Entrance to a Politically Divided House" (2001) 12(5) *European Journal of International Law* 943 at 950.

34　E/2006/32 (Part I) *Report of the Committee on Non-Governmental Organizations on Its 2006 Regular Session (New York, 19–27 January 2006)* (ECOSOC, 2006) at 17–19.

The Danish delegate defended their national NGO by protesting against the discriminatory conduct of some Committee on NGOs' members.[35] Romania and India stated that organizations should have the occasion to answer other questions, allowing further time for discussion as was the usual Committee on NGOs' procedure.[36] France noted that the rapid rejection was in violation of resolution 1996/31 because the NGO did not have "the opportunity to respond to any objections being raised"[37] in the Committee on NGOs before a decision.[38]

Human rights NGOs also voiced their concerns. In 2006, eight NGOs sent written comments to the Commission on HR and to the HR Council to point out that in that year the Committee on NGOs rejected application for consultative status for any LGBT NGO that applied for it[39] without allowing the usual hearing time for discussion.[40]

As a response to the unusually rapid rejections by the Committee on NGOs, some members of the ECOSOC voted on overriding the Committee on NGOs' recommendations. Usually, the ECOSOC would follow the recommendations proposed by the Committee on NGOs,[41] but in December 2006 at the 47th meeting of the ECOSOC, the EU members recommended that the decisions of the Committee on NGOs on the consultative status of Danish National Association for Gays and Lesbians, Lesbian and Gay Federation in Germany and ILGA-Europe be re-opened. The three NGOs were granted consultative status with three draft resolutions issued by the ECOSOC, subverting the Committee on NGOs' recommendations.[42] ILGA's application was not successful in 2006,[43] but eventually the ECOSOC granted ILGA the consultative status in 2011.[44]

After 2006, the ECOSOC granted consultative status to all the ten LGBTI NGOs that made applications.[45] Five had previously been rejected by the Com-

---

35 At [54].

36 E/2006/32 (Part II) *Report of the Committee on Non-Governmental Organizations on Its Resumed 2006 Session (New York, 10–19 May 2006)* (ECOSOC, 2006) at 14–16.

37 E/RES/1996/31, above n 4, at [15].

38 E/2006/32 (Part II), above n 36, at [48].

39 A/HRC/1/NGO/47 *Joint Written Statement Submitted by Action Canada for Population and Development (ACPD), Canadian HIV/AIDS Legal Network, Centre for Women's Global Leadership (Global Centre, CWGL), Global Rights, International Service for Human Rights (ISHR), International Women's Health Coalition (IWHC), and New Ways: Women for Women's Human Rights* (HR Council, 2006) at 3.

40 E/CN.4/2006/NGO/162 *Written Statement Submitted by the Transnational Radical Party (TRP)* (Comm on HR, 2006) at 2; A/HRC/1/NGO/33 *Written Statement Submitted by the Transnational Radical Party (TRP)* (HR Council, 2006).

41 Jurij Daniel Aston, above n 33, at 949.

42 E/2006/SR.47 *Provisional Summary Record of the 47th Meeting: Held at Headquarters, New York, on Monday, 11 December 2006, at 3 pm* (ECOSOC, 2007) at 2–4.

43 E/2006/SR.34 *Substantive Session of 2006, General Segment: Provisional Summary Record of the 34th Meeting* (ECOSOC, 2006) at 5–6.

44 E/2011/SR.43 *Provisional Summary Record of the 43rd Meeting: Held at the Palais des Nations, Geneva, on Monday, 25 July 2011, at 3 pm* (ECOSOC, 2011) at 5.

45 Coalition Gaie et Lesbienne du Québec (2007), E/2007/32 (Part I) *Report of the Committee on Non-Governmental Organizations on Its 2007 Regular Session* (New York, 22–31

mittee on NGOs and then the Committee on NGOs' decision was overturned by the ECOSOC.[46] Some conservative/religious state delegates applied the usual strategy of indefinitely delaying the process of granting consultative status with prolonged questions.[47] In response, representatives from Germany,[48] Canada, Norway, Brazil[49] and the United States[50] at the ECOSOC overturned the Committee on NGOs' recommendations or decided upon LGBTI NGOs' applications that were still under examination by the Committee on NGOs. Consequently, some members of the ECOSOC, such as the Russian Federation, Pakistan and Egypt, protested that overturning the Committee on NGOs' recommendations was disrespectful to the work of the Committee on NGOs and it was highly selective.[51]

January 2007) (ECOSOC, 2007) at 14. Swedish Federation for Lesbian, Gay, Bisexual and Transgender Rights, E/2007/SR.38 *Provisional Summary Record of the 38th Meeting: Held at the Palais des Nations, Geneva, on Friday, 20 July 2007, at 3 pm* (ECOSOC, 2007) at 11. Federación Estatal de Lesbianas, Gays, Transexuales y Bisexuales (2008), E/2008/INF/2/Add.1 *Resolutions and Decisions Adopted by the Economic and Social Council at Its Substantive Session of 2008* (30 June to 25 July 2008) (ECOSOC, 2008) at 126. COC (2008), E/2008/32 (Part II) *Report of the Committee on Non-Governmental Organizations on Its Resumed 2008 Session* (New York, 29 May – 6 June and on 25 June 2008) (ECOSOC, 2008) at 19. Associação Brasileira de Gays, Lésbicas e Transgêneros (2009), E/2009/32 (Part I) *Report of the Committee on Non-Governmental Organizations on Its 2009 Regular Session* (New York, 19–28 January and 2 February 2009) (ECOSOC, 2009) at 15. OutRight (2010), E/2010/32 (Part II) *Report of the Committee on Non-Governmental Organizations on Its 2010 Resumed Session* (ECOSOC, 2010) at 29. ILGA (2011), E/2011/SR43, above n 39, at 5. Australian Lesbian Medical Association (ALMA) (2013) and Homosexuelle Initiative Wien (2013), E/2013/32 (Part II) *Report of the Committee on Non-Governmental Organizations on Its 2013 Resumed Session* (New York, 20–29 May and 7 June 2013) (ECOSOC, 2013) at 33, 36. ARC (2014), E/2014/32 (Part II) *Report of the Committee on Non-Governmental Organizations on Its 2014 Resumed Session* (New York, 19–28 May and 6 June 2014) (ECOSOC, 2014) at 31.

46 Coalition Gaie et Lesbienne du Québec; Swedish Federation for Lesbian, Gay, Bisexual and Transgender Rights; Federación Estatal de Lesbianas, Gays, Transexuales y Bisexuales; Associação Brasileira de Gays, Lésbicas e Transgêneros; and ILGA.

47 For example, IGLHRC (now OutRight) was already asked 44 questions when the representatives from Egypt and Qatar posed further questions. Similarly, the representative of Bulgaria stated that ALMA had responded in a satisfactory manner to the 54 questions that the members posed over seven consecutive sessions; however, some members of the Committee on NGOs continued to defer the decision. See, E/2013/32 (Part II), above n 45, at 29, 33.

48 E/2006/SR.47, above n 42, at 2–4.

49 E/2007/SR.38, above n 45, at 5.

50 E/2008/INF/2/Add.1, above n 45, at 126; E/2010/SR.39 *Provisional Summary Record of the 39th Meeting: Held at Headquarters, New York, on Monday, 19 July 2010, at 10 am* (ECOSOC, 2010) at 5.

51 E/2006/SR.47, above n 42, at 2–4; E/2007/SR.38, above n 45, at 5; E/2008/SR.37 *Provisional Summary Record of the 37th Meeting: Held at Headquarters, New York, on Monday, 21 July 2008, at 3 pm* (ECOSOC, 2008) at 4–6; E/2010/SR.39, above n 50, at 6.

Currently, there are 4,513 NGOs accredited with consultative status,[52] 14 of which are LGBTI NGOs with special consultative status[53] and one with Roster status.[54] In addition, there are 18 organizations with consultative status that list SOGII issues as part of their advocacy.[55]

In sum, during the past decade, LGBTI gatekeeper NGOs have been granted more and more access to the work of the UN, especially due to the support of a

---

52 There are 149 organizations in general consultative status, 3,389 in special consultative status and 975 on the Roster. E/2016/INF/5 *List of Non-Governmental Organizations in Consultative Status with the Economic and Social Council as of 1 September 2016* (ECOSOC, 2016).

53 Coalition of Activist Lesbians (Australia) (1999); Allied Rainbow Communities International (2014); Lesbian and Gay Federation in Germany (2006); Danish National Association for Gays and Lesbians (2006); International Lesbian and Gay Association – Europe (2006); Coalition Gaie et Lesbienne du Québec (2007); Swedish Federation for Lesbian, Gay, Bisexual and Transgender Rights (2007); COC (2008); Federación Estatal de Lesbianas, Gays, Transexuales y Bisexuales (2009); Associação Brasileira de Gays, Lésbicas e Transgeneros (2009); International Gay and Lesbian Human Rights Commission (2010); International Lesbian and Gay Association (2011); Australian Lesbian Medical Association (2013); Homosexuelle Initiative Wien (2013).

54 International Wages Due Lesbians (1998).

55 Education International E/C.2/2015/2/Add.3 *Quadrennial Reports for the Period 2010–2013* (ECOSOC, 2014) at 18. Mexican Foundation for Family Planning E/C.2/2010/2/Add.47 *Quadrennial Reports for the Period 2005–2008* (ECOSOC, 2010) at 8. Society for the Psychological Study of Social Issues E/C.2/2016/2/Add.23 *Quadrennial Reports for the Period 2011–2014* (ECOSOC, 2015) at 9. Parliamentarians for Global Actions E/C.2/2015/2/Add.8 *Quadrennial Reports for the Period 2010–2013* (ECOSOC, 2014) at 10. Unitarian Universalist Association E/C.2/2014/2/Add.17 *Quadrennial Reports for the Period 2010–2013* (ECOSOC, 2013) at 11. MiRA Resource Center for Black Immigrant and Refugee Women E/C.2/2014/2/Add.13 *Quadrennial Reports for the Period 2009–2012* (ECOSOC, 2013) at 17. *Unión de Asociaciones Familiares*, and Humanist Institute for Cooperation with Developing Countries E/C.2/2015/2/Add.4 *Quadrennial Reports for the Period 2010–2013* (ECOSOC, 2014) at 14 and 20. Robert F. Kennedy Center for Justice and Human Rights E/C.2/2014/2/Add15 *Quadrennial Reports for the Period 2009–2012* (ECOSOC, 2013) at 24. International Planned Parenthood Federation (East and South-East Asia and Oceania region) E/C.2/2012/2/Add.22 *Quadrennial Reports for the Period 2007–2010* (ECOSOC, 2011) at 17. Women Against Rape, and 8th Day Center for Justice E/C.2/2007/2/Add.30 *Quadrennial Reports for the Period 2002–2005* (ECOSOC, 2007). Canadian HIV/AIDS Legal Network E/C.2/2007/2/Add.11 *Quadrennial Reports 2002–2005* (ECOSOC, 2006) at 2. Action Canada for Population and Development E/C.2/2009/2/Add.7 *Quadrennial Reports for the Period 2004–2007* (ECOSOC, 2008) at 2. International Blue Crescent Relief and Development Foundation E/C.2/2011/2/Add.20 *Quadrennial Reports for the Period 2006–2009* (ECOSOC, 2011) at 5. Hebrew Immigrant Aid Society E/C.2/2013/2/Add.7 *Quadrennial Reports for the Period 2008–2011* (ECOSOC, 2012) at 27. International Commission of Jurists E/C.2/2010/2/Add.51 *Quadrennial Reports for the Period 2005–2008* (ECOSOC, 2010) at 7. Liberal International E/C.2/2012/2/Add.2 *Quadrennial Reports for the Period 2007–2010* (ECOSOC, 2011) at 11. Children's Human Rights Centre of Albania E/C.2/2016/2/Add.5 *Quadrennial Reports for the Period 2011–2014* (ECOSOC, 2015) at 10.

number of UN member states that pushed aside the usual procedures to ensure access by LGBTI NGOs, and despite the protests of some other UN member states. Indeed, the UN members are divided between states that are hostile to LGBTI rights and some states that are supportive of LGBTI rights. Such division shapes the issue framing of the LGBTI TAN. To understand these dynamics, the ensuing sub-paragraphs address the theme of political alignments.

Political alignment and United Nations member states

UN states are divided in their support of LGBTI rights in three groups.[56] On one end of the spectrum there are states that always support LGBTI rights; on the other end there are states that always oppose LGBTI rights. Somewhere in the middle there are states that are inconsistent in their votes on the matter. This section discusses how this division in blocs shapes the advocacy of the LGBTI TAN working at the UN.

First, there are a number of states that consistently show support for LGBTI people's rights. States like Belgium, Canada, Chile, France, Germany, Mexico and the United Kingdom supported the 2003 Brazilian resolution, 2005 New Zealand statement, the 2006 Norway statement, the 2008 Argentinian statement, and the three HR Council's resolutions on SOGI discrimination and violence. Second, there are a number of UN members that always block any soft-law provisions aimed at expanding the rights protection of LGBTI people, for example Iraq, Saudi Arabia and United Arab Emirates. Finally, there is a third group of UN member states, which I call 'non-aligned', which are inconsistent with their votes. Sometimes they support SOGII statements or SOGII resolutions, but some others they vote against, abstain or leave the room. Some examples of non-aligned states are Burkina Faso, China and Thailand.[57]

The inconsistent voting behaviour of the third group is because some states do not have a particularly strong opinion on LGBTI issues. At the same time, they want to maintain good relationships with states that favour LGBTI rights and those that do not.[58] Notably, the United States supported neither the New Zealand statement nor the Argentinian statement during the Bush administration. The United States' position changed in 2009 with the beginning of the Obama administration, whose office pledged support for LGBTI rights,[59] and in the following years the United States has been one of the leaders of LGBTI rights at the UN. In the future, the United States' position might change again under the Trump administration.[60] For example, in September 2017, the United States

---

56 See also, Francine D'Amico, above n 19, at 61.

57 See Appendix 4.

58 Unitarian Universalist Association (UUA), above n 1.

59 Francine D'Amico, above n 19, at 60. See also, Holning Lau "Sexual Orientation: Testing the Universality of International Human Rights Law" (2004) 71(4) *The University of Chicago Law Review* 1689 at 1706.

60 Eduard Jordaan "The Challenge of Adopting Sexual Orientation Resolutions at the UN Human Rights Council" (2016) 8(2) *Journal of Human Rights Practice* 298 at 304.

voted along with Saudi Arabia and the United Arab Emirates against a HR Council resolution to ensure that capital punishment is not applied discriminatorily "based on gender or sexual orientation".[61] The shift of such a powerful actor in the international relations will most likely result in a reshuffle of the three blocs.

LGBTI gatekeeper NGOs focus their attention in this third group of non-aligned states. The first group of states usually supports SOGII resolutions and does not need to be convinced in their votes. The second group of states is usually against LGBTI rights, and an advocacy action to convince them would be a waste of resources. Instead, the third group of non-aligned states provides some room for negotiation. The LGBTI TAN, under the leadership of LGBTI gatekeeper NGOs, works to patiently lobby the states of the third group to vote in favour of LGBTI rights.[62]

However, pressuring non-aligned states means that LGBTI TANs need to create issue framing that provides a 'bridge' to promote consensus,[63] which means focusing on fundamental protection.[64] In other words, searching for the support of non-aligned states means focusing on a "minimum common denominator",[65] that is, a minimum standard of protection upon which the non-aligned states can agree.

Even though gatekeeper NGOs and NGOs with consultative status have an important role in the LGBTI advocacy, they are not the only NGOs that can access the work of the UN. The example of the Resolution on Extrajudicial, Summary or Arbitrary Executions (2010) discussed next exemplifies how LGBTI TANs can influence the vote of non-aligned states promoting a fundamental rights framework. In particular, the next section further challenges the gatekeeper/peripheral NGOs' dichotomy by showing that LGBTI gatekeeper NGOs work to empower peripheral NGOs to lobby their own (non-aligned) governments from below.

Resolution on Extrajudicial, Summary or Arbitrary Executions: non-aligned states

Since 1992, the General Assembly has adopted resolutions on extrajudicial, summary or arbitrary executions every two years.[66] Since 2002, the resolution has included "sexual orientation" among the grounds on which killings are often based.[67] However, in November 2010, Mali and Morocco proposed an

61 A/HRC/36/L.6 *The Question of the Death Penalty* (HR Council, 2017) at 2.

62 Interview ILGA-World (Skype call, 13 April 2016).

63 Jutta Joachim, above n 18, at 30.

64 Ryan R Thoreson, above n 16, at 218.

65 Unitarian Universalist Association (UUA), above n 1.

66 Philip Alston and Ryan Goodman *International Human Rights: The Successor to International Human Rights in Context* (Oxford University Press, Oxford, 2013) at 227.

67 A/RES/57/214 *57/214 Extrajudicial, Summary or Arbitrary Executions* (General Assembly, 2003); A/RES/59/197 *59/197 Extrajudicial, Summary or Arbitrary Executions* (General Assembly, 2005); A/RES/61/173 *61/173 Extrajudicial, Summary or Arbitrary Executions* (General Assembly, 2007); A/RES/63/182 *63/182 Extrajudicial, Summary or Arbitrary*

amendment to draft resolution A/C.3/65/L.29/Rev.1[68] to omit the expression "discriminatory reasons, including sexual orientation" and replace it with "discriminatory reasons on any basis".[69] The representative from Benin, on behalf of the African Group of States, the OIC and the Group of Arab States, stated that such an amendment would ensure that all the forms of discrimination are addressed, without creating an "undefined and controversial notion" such as sexual orientation, which they claimed should not be included in the resolution.[70] The vote was recorded, and the amendment passed with 79 votes to 70 and 17 abstentions.[71]

The vote in November provoked a big reaction among LGBTI gatekeeper NGOs. OutRight and ARC set up a petition that gathered over 3,400 signatories[72] and called upon their NGO partners to lobby their governments to restore "sexual orientation" in the draft resolution. Numerous NGOs from various regions answered the action alert and wrote to ministers of foreign affairs and ambassadors of Bolivia, Philippines, Jamaica, Saint Lucia, Singapore, South Africa and Thailand.[73]

Eventually, at the following meeting in December 2010, the United States suggested adding "because of their sexual orientation",[74] and the amendment was voted with 122 in favour, one against and 62 abstentions.[75] As proof of the efficiency of the LGBTI TAN pressure, it should be noted that in the November vote, Philippines, Singapore and Thailand abstained; Bolivia did not vote; and South Africa, Jamaica and Saint Lucia voted in favour of eliminating sexual orientation from the draft resolution. In the December vote, all these aforementioned states voted to restore sexual orientation in the draft resolution. This shows the

---

Executions (General Assembly, 2009); A/RES/65/208 *65/208 Extrajudicial, Summary or Arbitrary Executions* (General Assembly, 2011); A/RES/67/168 *67/168 Extrajudicial, Summary or Arbitrary Executions* (General Assembly, 2013); A/RES/69/182 *69/182 Extrajudicial, Summary or Arbitrary Executions* (General Assembly, 2015).

68 A/C.3/65/L.29/Rev.1 *Extrajudicial, Summary or Arbitrary Executions* (General Assembly, 2010).

69 A/C.3/65/L.65 *Mali and Morocco: Amendment to Draft Resolution A/C.3/65/L.29/Rev.1* (General Assembly, 2010).

70 A/C.3/65/SR.46 *Summary Record of the 46th Meeting (16 November 2010)* (General Assembly, 2011) at [26].

71 See Appendix 4.

72 Jessica Stern "Civil Society Pressures Governments to Successfully Reverse Discriminatory Vote at UN" (21 December 2010) OutRight www.outrightinternational.org/content/civil-society-pressures-governments-successfully-reverse-discriminatory-vote-un (Retrieved 28 July 2018).

73 ARTEAGA and others "Read the Formal Communications from Human Rights Defenders in Countries that Lobbied Their Governments on this Vote" (2010) OutRight www.outrightinternational.org/sites/default/files/469-2.pdf (Retrieved 14 March 2017).

74 A/65/L.53 *United States of America: Amendment to Draft Resolution III Recommended by the Third Committee in Its Report Contained in Document A/65/456/Add.2 (Part II)* (General Assembly, 2010).

75 A/65/PV.71 *Official Record of 71st Plenary Meeting (21 December 2010)* (General Assembly, 2010) at 20. See also Appendix 4.

positive effect of the NGOs' lobby, when voicing LGBTI rights with a fundamental protection framework. Indeed, as Cary Alan Johnson from OutRight pointed out at the aftermath of the advocacy:[76]

> This [amendment], of course, could not have happened without the concerted and passionate efforts of several governments. But what this victory also demonstrates is the power of civil society at the UN and working across countries and regions to demand that their own governments vote to protect LGBT lives.

The significance of these events is twofold. First, because of their Western NGO status, LGBTI gatekeeper NGOs work better in coordinating the advocacy of peripheral NGOs rather than openly interfering with non-Western states decisions. Gatekeeper NGOs are instrumental to organise and coordinate advocacy actions. At the same time, LGBTI gatekeeper NGOs strongly rely on the peripheral partners to lobby their own governments to make governmental delegates vote in favour of a resolution or, as in this case, an amendment. Peripheral NGOs are better placed to lobby their national governments from below and governments can be more willing to listen to domestic pressure rather than foreign pressure. Therefore, it is in the interest of LGBTI gatekeeper NGOs to build the advocacy capacity of peripheral NGOs, ultimately to develop a stronger and more effective network.

Second, the gatekeeper and peripheral NGOs' advocacy can be more successful with states that are not strongly against LGBTI rights. Philippines, Singapore, Thailand, South Africa, Jamaica, Saint Lucia and Bolivia can be considered non-aligned states as they often abstained, or they have been inconsistent with their votes, during SOGII statements or resolutions.[77] Because of their position as 'non-aligned', the LGBTI TAN has been able to lobby them to change their vote. To be convincing in their advocacy, LGBTI gatekeeper NGOs needed to find a common ground. The resolution on extrajudicial, summary or arbitrary execution triggered oppositions from some African and Islamic states because it included explicitly the prohibition of discrimination on the grounds of sexual orientation. Nonetheless, the right to life, as spelled out in resolution A/RES/65/208,[78] has been widely accepted as a universal right.[79] Therefore, such a fundamental rights frame has facilitated the work of the LGBTI TAN to create enough support for the resolution.

The political alignment of UN member states on LGBTI issues not only contributes to shape the advocacy agenda of the LGBTI TAN, but allies to LGBTI

---

76 Jessica Stern, above n 72.
77 See Appendix 4.
78 A/RES/65/208, above n 67, at [6(b)].
79 Thomas Risse-Kappen, Stephen C Ropp, and Kathryn Sikkink *The Power of Human Rights: International Norms and Domestic Change* (Cambridge University Press, Cambridge, 1999) at 2.

activists can also contribute to such processes, for better and for worse. These themes are discussed in the ensuing sub-paragraphs.

International organizations' agencies act as allies of LGBTI transnational advocacy networks

Political allies, such as international organizations' functionaries and powerful governments, can amplify and legitimise the issue framing developed by human rights activists.[80] Such external legitimation is useful to consolidate the message proposed by LGBTI TANs, and consequently to promote the protection of LGBTI rights. A clear example comes from the Sustainable Development Goals (SDGs) released in 2015.

In September 2015, all 193 members of the UN agreed to the SDGs by consensus, which came into force in January 2016.[81] The Millennium Development Goals (MDGs), which preceded the SDGs and set the UN goals for development between 2000 and 2015, were criticised for lacking a view of "*equitable development*".[82] This perspective was included in the post-2015 goals; indeed, SDG10 calls for reducing inequality within and among states in empowering and promoting "social, economic and political inclusion of all, irrespective of age, sex, disability, race, ethnicity, origin, religion or economic or other status".[83] Even though, during the negotiation, some LGBTI and human rights NGOs worked to promote the inclusion of SOGII discrimination in SDG10 and elsewhere vulnerable groups where specified,[84] neither SDG10 nor other SDGs openly mention LGBTI people's rights or SOGII discrimination.[85]

As a further example of the need to find a minimum common denominator to gather as much support as possible from non-aligned states, the international advocacy advisor from RFSL reports that, in consultation with other NGOs, RFSL decided not to lobby for specific SOGII language in the SDGs because they did not believe such an advocacy action would have ever had a successful outcome. The interviewee comments that an initial draft of the SDGs proposed a closed list of grounds of discrimination; i.e. without the usual reference to the

---

80 Jutta Joachim "Framing Issues and Seizing Opportunities: The UN, NGOs, and Women's Rights" (2003) 47(2) *International Studies Quarterly* 247 at 251.
81 UN "United Nations Sustainable Development Agenda" United Nations Sustainable Development www.un.org/sustainabledevelopment/development-agenda/ (Retrieved 28 July 2018).
82 Michael W Doyle and Joseph E Stiglitz "Eliminating Extreme Inequality: A Sustainable Development Goal, 2015–2030" (2014) 28(1) *Ethics and International Affairs* 5 at 6.
83 A/69/L.85 *Draft Outcome Document of the United Nations Summit for the Adoption of the Post-2015 Development Agenda* (General Assembly, 2015) at 21.
84 Human Rights Campaign "Op-ed: What Does the UN's Agenda 2030 Mean for LGBT People?" (30 September 2015) Human Rights Campaign www.hrc.org/blog/op-ed-what-does-the-uns-agenda-2030-mean-for-lgbt-people/ (Retrieved 28 July 2018).
85 Some LGBTI activists expressed their disappointment for the missed opportunity to include SOGI in the text of the SDGs. See for example, Kit Dorey *The Sustainable Development Goals and LGBT Inclusion* (Stonewall, Online, 2016).

prohibition of discrimination on grounds of "other status". Therefore, RFSL focused on lobbying state delegates to include an open list of discrimination in the SDGs, as is usual in human rights treaties. In the opinion of the interviewee, RFSL's advocacy action on the SDGs was not considered a failure because they decided to focus on making sure that the final draft included a language that can be used as a point of access for covering SOGII issues by interpretation.[86] RFSL lobbied for a minimum common denominator on which most states could agree. Even though it was important to not lose the "other status" expression, the SDGs failed to address SOGII issues and many UN functionaries voiced their support for LGBTI people's rights in the following months.

In the aftermath of the negotiation of the SDGs, UN functionaries and bodies of experts tried to make up for the lack of express acknowledgement of SOGII discrimination in the SDGs. First, just a few days after the SDGs were adopted, former UN Secretary General Ban Ki-moon spoke at the High Level LGBT Core Group Event and reiterated that the SDGs have one guiding principle, which is "to leave no-one behind".[87] In this way, the Secretary General restated his commitment to fight intolerance and hate against individuals because of their SOGI,[88] even though the SDGs failed to do so. Second, 12 UN agencies issued an unprecedented joint statement calling all states to uphold their international human rights obligations and end violence and discrimination against LGBTI individuals.[89] In particular, the joint statement stressed that LGBTI people's human rights violations impact societies and impair their progress towards achieving the SDGs.[90]

Finally, when it was clear that LGBTI people were left behind in the SDGs, the United Nations Development Program (UNDP) started to consult with LGBTI and human rights NGOs, including ILGA. Indeed, the UNDP, under the leadership of former UNDP Administrator Helen Clark, invited ILGA and other NGOs to meet and discuss a project to create an UNDP LGBTI Inclusion Index.[91] The initiative was started because there was already awareness among UN agencies that the SDGs failed to acknowledge LGBTI people's human rights. This is

---

86 Interview Swedish Federation for Lesbian, Gay, Bisexual, Transgender and Queer Rights (RFSL) (Skype call, 18 May 2016).

87 Ban Ki-moon "Statement: Secretary-General's Remarks at the High Level LGBT Core Group Event 'Leaving No-One Behind: Equality & Inclusion in the Post-2015 Development Agenda'" (29 September 2015) United Nations – Secretary General www.un.org/sg/statements/index.asp?nid=9064 (Retrieved 28 July 2018).

88 Ibid.

89 International Labour Organization, United Nation Office on Drugs and Crime, United Nation Human Rights Office of the High Commissioner, United Nations Development Program, UN Women, UNESCO, World Food Program, United Nation High Commissioner for Refugees, World Health Organization, UNICEF (United Nations Children's Fund), and UNAIDS *Ending Violence and Discrimination Against Lesbian, Gay, Bisexual, Transgender and Intersex People* (UN, Online, 2015).

90 At 1.

91 ILGA-World (Skype call, 13 April 2016), above n 62.

another example of external allies that attempt to advance LGBTI rights despite states' opposition.

In sum, LGBTI TANs can count on strong allies among UN functionaries. Once the UN member states failed to include SOGII-specific language in the SDGs in 2015, the UNDP, the Secretary General and a number of other UN agencies reinstated the need for states to end discrimination and violence against people because of their SOGII. However, despite the importance of these actions promoted by UN agencies to make up for the lack of SOGII inclusion in the SDGs, it remains the fact that UN states were not able to agree to include SOGII issues in the 2030 development agenda. As the interviewee from UUA eloquently summarises, although UN agencies can say that because the SDGs use a language of "leaving no-one behind" and "everybody is included" is enough to include LGBTI people, "our experience is that if you don't mention us, we are not included".[92] The ensuing section concludes the analysis of LGBTI TAN framing of LGBTI issues at the UN by discussing the resolutions on traditional values and on the protection of the family. It is shown that LGBTI NGOs and conservative/religious NGOs and states influence one another in their advocacy agendas and tactics.[93]

Marriage and family arguments used against LGBTI people's rights

LGBTI gatekeeper NGOs working at the UN can rely on framing LGBTI rights as fundamental protection as a way to gather the support of non-aligned states. Moreover, when UN member states did not explicitly include SOGII in the SDGs, many UN agencies showed their support for LGBTI activists by restating that the prohibition of discrimination on the grounds of "other status" needs to be interpreted as also covering SOGII. In general, LGBTI TANs need to maintain a low profile to promote the protection of the rights of LGBTI people in order to find a minimum common denominator that all or nearly all UN member states can agree upon. At the same time, when UN agencies function as allies of LGBTI TANs, they also amplify and consolidate a framing of LGBTI issues as fundamental protections.

In light of these considerations, it is crucial to discuss how marriage arguments play out in the advocacy agenda of LGBTI TANs. In this book, I argue that – due to the complex internetwork relations between gatekeeper NGOs and peripheral NGOs – LGBTI gatekeeper NGOs do not frame LGBTI rights as a marriage equality issue because they do not want to impose such a 'Western' advocacy item on their less powerful peripheral partners, and the promotion of the right to marry is a low priority in the advocacy agenda of both the LGBTI TANs.

However, LGBTI NGOs do not work in a vacuum and their choices are also influenced by the necessity to react to what happens around them. Therefore, the

---

92 Unitarian Universalist Association (UUA), above n 1.
93 See especially, Clifford Bob, above n 24, at 5.

ensuing sub-paragraphs show that because the religious/conservative TANs and governments consider that marriage inequality has a strong cultural resonance,[94] they use marriage inequality arguments instrumentally to block any advancement in the protection of LGBTI people's human rights. As a consequence, the LGBTI TANs react by stating that LGBTI parent-families need protection as any other family formation. Finding themselves in the middle between two opposing interests, international organizations' agencies seek a compromise.

Human Rights Council resolutions on traditional values

Resolution 17/19 on human rights and SOGI[95] paved the way for a panel discussion on the topic, which took place in March 2012 within the HR Council;[96] many states and some NGOs and activists participated at the panel.[97] The then Secretary General, Ban Ki-moon, sent a video message,[98] and the then UN High Commissioner for Human Rights, Navi Pillay, presented her report on violence and discrimination against individuals on the basis of their SOGI.[99] Some NGOs delivered statements during and after the panel. For example, the representative from the Coalition of African Lesbians maintained that LGBTI activists do not ask for special rights, rather they ask governments to "recognise equality and non-discrimination for all citizens",[100] and International Commission of Jurists, HRW and Amnesty stressed that human rights are universal, regardless of SOGI.[101]

During the panel discussion, a number of states left the HR Council chamber to signal their opposition to a discussion on human rights and SOGI. NGOs responded to such provocation saying that states may walk out of the room, but "they may never walk away from the responsibility to protect their own citizens from discrimination and violence".[102] However, the message of some states, that they did not want to accept the prohibition of discrimination on the grounds of

---

94 Tina Fetner *How the Religious Right Shaped Lesbian and Gay Activism* (University of Minnesota Press, Minneapolis, 2008) at 111.

95 A/HRC/RES/17/19 *Human Rights, Sexual Orientation and Gender Identity* (HR Council, 2011).

96 United Nations Human Rights Council *Panel on Ending Violence and Discrimination Against Individuals Based on Their Sexual Orientation and Gender Identity* (UN, Online, 2012).

97 A/HRC/19/2 *Report of the Human Rights Council on Its Nineteenth Session* (HR Council, 2012) at [103] – [106].

98 Ban Ki-moon "Secretary-General's Video Message to Human Rights Council Meeting on Violence and Discrimination Based on Sexual Orientation or Gender Identity" (7 March 2012) United Nations Web Services Section www.un.org/sg/STATEMENTS/index.asp?nid=5900 (Retrieved 28 July 2018).

99 A/HRC/19/41 *Discriminatory Laws and Practices and Acts of Violence Against Individuals Based on Their Sexual Orientation and Gender Identity* (OHCHR, 2011).

100 ARC "UN Human Rights Council: Landmark Report and Panel on Sexual Orientation and Gender Identity" (7 March 2012) ARC http://arc-international.net/global-advocacy/human-rights-council/hrc19/press-release/ (Retrieved 28 July 2018).

101 Ibid.

102 Ibid.

SOGI, was loud and clear. Indeed, the religious/conservative TANs and governments were already preparing a counter attack and they were mobilising to lobby the HR Council to limit the rights of LGBTI people.

Just a few months after resolution 17/19 on human rights and SOGI was adopted, a coalition of eight conservative NGOs expressed concern at the introduction of SOGI issues in the human rights debate. The NGOs asked the HR Council to resist creating new human rights categories, such as "sexual orientation". The NGOs supported their claims that international human rights law should not include sexual orientation as a prohibited ground of discrimination, by using concerns regarding marriage equality as a pretext.[103] The coalition of NGOs stated that:[104]

> [E]fforts to promote "new rights" for particular groups in society . . . will put into question the respect and protection for such foundational social institutions as the natural family, marriage between husband and wife, and the rights of the child.

The religious/conservative coalition of NGOs and governments, under the leadership of Russia,[105] lobbied the HR Council to promote a series of resolutions on traditional values to state that different traditions, costumes and religions share common values and that families and communities have an instrumental role in transmitting such common values. In 2009, HR Council adopted the first resolution on traditional values,[106] and adopted further resolutions again in 2011[107] and 2012.[108] With similar wording, these resolutions recognise that a better understanding and appreciation of traditional values shared by all humanity can contribute to the promotion and protection of human rights and fundamental freedoms. The resolutions also called the HR Council Advisory Committee[109] and the OHCHR[110] to gather information on best practices in the application of traditional values for the promotion of human rights.

---

103 See also, Tina Fetner, above n 94, at 111.
104 A/HRC/19/NGO/43 *Joint Written Statement Submitted by Caritas Internationalis (International Confederation of Catholic Charities), New Humanity, the Association Points-Coeur, the Associazione Comunità Papa Giovanni XXIII, the Company of the Daughters of Charity of St Vincent de Paul, the Dominicans for Justice an d Peace – Order of Preachers, the International Organization for the Right to Education and Freedom of Education (OIDEL), the World Union of Catholic Women's Organizations* (HR Council, 2012) at 3.
105 A/HRC/21/2 *Report of the Human Rights Council on Its Twenty-First Session* (HR Council, 2015) at [110].
106 A/HRC/RES/12/21 *Promoting Human Rights and Fundamental Freedoms through Better Understanding of Traditional Values of Human Kind* (HR Council, 2009).
107 A/HRC/RES/16/3 *Promoting Human Rights and Fundamental Freedoms through a Better Understanding of Traditional Values of Humankind* (HR Council, 2011).
108 A/HRC/RES/21/3 *Promoting Human Rights and Fundamental Freedoms through a Better Understanding of Traditional Values of Humankind: Best Practices* (HR Council, 2012).
109 A/HRC/RES/16/3, above n 107, at [6].
110 A/HRC/RES/21/3, above n 108, at [6].

The resolutions were clearly meant to undermine the right of LGBTI people, although they claimed to be promoting pro-family traditional values. The resolutions were aimed to reverse "today's revision by the countries of the Western Europe and the North America [sic] of the fundamental values of humanity".[111]

As a response, in 2011, LGBTI NGOs sent a number of written statements to the HR Council to address the meaning of "traditional values". Numerous NGOs, such as HRW, International Commission of Jurist and ILGA,[112] explained that traditional values are often invoked to justify practices that breach international human rights law standards,[113] and maintained that the interpretation of traditional values can create concerns for activists working in the sector of SOGI.[114] The coalition of NGOs called upon the HR Council to acknowledge that international law recognises that the word "family" has a plurality of meaning, including LGBTI parent-families,[115] and invoked a pluralistic definition of family.[116]

Possibly influenced by the LGBTI NGOs' submissions, the HR Council Advisory Committee issued two provisional reports, in 2011[117] and in 2012,[118] which did not fulfil the expectations of the conservative/religious states and NGOs. The HR Council Advisory Committee highlighted that LGBT people can encounter

---

111 Nataliya S Semenova and others "Traditional Values and Human Rights of LGBT under the Contemporary International Law" (2015) 6(5) *Mediterranean Journal of Social Sciences* 305 at 309. See also, Cai Wilkinson "Putting 'Traditional Values' into Practice: The Rise and Contestation of Anti-Homopropaganda Laws in Russia" (2014) 13 *Journal of Human Rights* 363 at 368.

112 A/HRC/AC/7/NGO/1 *Joint Written Statement Submitted by the Association for Women's Rights, the International Planned Parenthood Federation, Action Canada for Population and Development, the Asian Forum for Human Rights and Development, the Cairo Institute for Human Rights Studies, the Canadian HIV/AIDS Legal Network, the Centre for Reproductive Rights, the Centre for Women's Global Leadership, Development Alternatives with Women for a New Era, Human Rights Watch, the International Commission of Jurists, the International Lesbian Gay Bisexual Transgender Intersex Association, the International Movement Against All Forms of Discrimination and Racism, the International Service for Human Rights, the International Women's Health Coalition, IPAS, Italian Association for Women in Development, the Federation for Women and Family Planning, the Swedish Federation for Lesbian Gay Bisexual Transgender Rights, Women for Women's Human Rights, – New Ways, the Women's International League for Peace and Freedom, Asian Pacific Forum on Women, Law and Development* (HR Council, 2011) at 2.

113 At 2. See also, *A/HRC/AC/8/NGO/4 Written Statement Submitted by the Canadian HIV/AIDS Legal Network* (HR Council, 2012) at 3.

114 A/HRC/AC/7/NGO/2 *Written Statement Submitted by the Association for Women's Rights in Development (AWID)* (HR Council, 2011) at 2.

115 At 6.

116 A/HRC/27/NGO/77 *Written Statement Submitted by the International Humanist and Ethical Union* (HR Council, 2014) at 4.

117 A/HRC/AC/8/4 *Preliminary Study on Promoting Human Rights and Fundamental Freedoms through a Better Understanding of Traditional Values of Humankind Prepared by Professor Vladimir Kartashkin, Rapporteur of the Drafting Group of the Advisory Committee* (HR Council, 2011).

118 A/HRC/AC/9/2 *Preliminary Study on Promoting Human Rights and Fundamental Freedoms through a Better Understanding of Traditional Values of Humankind* (HR Council Advisory Committee, 2012).

discrimination and harassment within their families and communities of origin,[119] and that in different cultural and traditional contexts various forms of families co-exist.[120] Therefore, without explicitly acknowledging LGBTI couples and parents, the HR Council Advisory Committee proposed an open definition of family that goes beyond the heterosexual nuclear family.

It is not possible to claim with certitude that the LGBTI TAN lobby had blocked further resolutions and reports on traditional values, but some hypotheses can be made. The website of the OHCHR reports that in November 2012, "in view of the challenges facing the drafting group in its efforts to reflect in the study the wealth of inputs provided by participants in the discussions",[121] the Advisory Committee requested that the HR Council postpone the finalisation of the study. As of July 2018, the Advisory Committee of the HR Council has not yet finalised its report on traditional values and human rights protection.[122]

Conservative/religious NGOs and states believed that in pressuring the HR Council to issue resolutions and reports on traditional values and human rights they would have obtained a clear statement that traditional values are instrumental to the enjoyment of human rights and that, in particular, the heterosexual family is one of the vehicles to transmit such traditional values. Indeed, some NGOs, such as Alliance Defending Freedom, Catholic Family (C-Fam) and Human Rights Institute, highlighted in written comments submitted to the HR Council Advisory Committee that traditional values, and in particular the heterosexual family as the fundamental unit of society, are instrumental to protect human rights.[123]

However, the conservative/religious initiative triggered the reaction of LGBTI NGOs and their allies. For example, the EU, Guatemala, Honduras, Amnesty and ARC submitted numerous written comments to the HR Council Advisory Committee to highlight that traditional values are often used to justify human rights violations against women and minorities, including sexual minorities.[124] Since the Advisory Committee was presented with many conflicting submissions, it decided to postpone the finalisation of the report and subsequently decided not to pursue the report at all.

Opposing TANs influence one another's advocacy agenda in a dynamic set of attack and counter attack.[125] There is no explicit reference to "traditional values" in any international human rights treaties and such a concept emerged in the HR

---

119 At [61].

120 At [59].

121 Human Rights Council Advisory Committee "Promoting Human Rights and Fundamental Freedoms through a Better Understanding of Traditional Values of Humankind" United Nations www.ohchr.org/EN/HRBodies/HRC/AdvisoryCommittee/Pages/Traditional-values.aspx (Retrieved 28 July 2018).

122 Ibid.

123 Ibid.

124 Ibid.

125 Clifford Bob, above n 24, at 5. See also Tina Fetner, above n 94, at xvii.

Council's agenda simultaneously with the SOGI issue debate[126] as a tool of the conservative TAN to bar the development of LGBTI rights. This book aims to show that LGBTI NGOs deem the advocacy for the right to marry is a low priority within their advocacy agenda at the UN. But because conservative/religious NGOs and states had expressly targeted LGBTI parent-families, the LGBTI TAN had to respond.

As a consequence of both pressures from the conservative/religious NGOs and LGBTI NGOs, it appears clear that UN bodies of experts, in particular the HR Council Advisory Committee, allied itself with the LGBTI NGOs. Even though I was not able to provide clear evidence that the HR Council was influenced by the LGBTI TAN, it emerges from the analysis of the events that the HR Council Advisory Committee's draft report on traditional values expressed similar concerns to those exposed by LGBTI NGOs in their written statements. In doing so, the HR Council Advisory Committee refuted the claims of the conservative/religious NGOs and states, as it did not declare that only married heterosexual couples and their genetically related children are protected by international human rights law. However, the HR Council Advisory Committee did not go as far as mentioning the rights of LGBTI couples and parent-families to be recognised as the LGBTI advocates might have wished it to do because it needed to find a compromise.

After 2012, there are no more recorded attempts of conservative/religious NGOs and governments to pursue further resolutions and reports on traditional values. Instead, conservative/religious NGOs and governments promoted new resolutions on the protection of the family, which are addressed next.

The two Human Rights Council resolutions on the protection of the family

After the HR Council passed resolution A/HRC/RES/27/32 on human rights and SOGI, the conservative/religious coalition of NGOs and states, under the leadership of the Organization of Islamic Cooperation (OIC), pressured the HR Council to issue two resolutions on the protection of the family.[127] The first resolution (A/HRC/RES/26/11) was adopted in 2014, and the HR Council convened a panel discussion on the protection of the family at its 27th session.[128] The panel discussion was then held in September 2014, with the participation of various NGOs; in particular, ARC also participated on behalf of International Service for Human Rights, OutRight and ILGA.[129] At the panel discussion,

---

126 Nataliya S Semenova and others, above n 111, at 307.
127 Robert C Blitt *Equality and Non-discrimination through the Eyes of an International Religious Organization: The Organization of Islamic Cooperation (OIC) Response to Women's Rights and Sexual Orientation and Gender Identity Rights* (ID 2814228 2016) at 44.
128 A/HRC/RES/26/11 *Protection of the family* (HR Council, 2014) at [1].
129 A/HRC/28/40 *Summary of the Human Rights Council Panel Discussion on the Protection of the Family: Report of the Office of the United Nations High Commissioner for Human Rights* (HR Council, 2014) at [4].

several delegations (not specified) pointed out that "HR Council resolution 26/11 did not refer to family diversity",[130] and they stressed the need to recognise the diversity of families, including same-sex couples.[131]

In July 2015, the HR Council issued a second resolution (A/HRC/29/22) on the protection of the family as the natural and fundamental group unit of the society, in focusing on issues related to single-headed households, protection of the children, disparity of household responsibilities between men and women, and the protection of disabled members of families. The conservative/religious organization C-Fam – an influential actor within the conservative/religious TAN working at the UN[132] – announced Resolution 29/22 as a "monumental development for the pro-family movement" at the UN.[133] Resolution 29/22 called the OHCHR to prepare a report on the subject,[134] and, to do so, the OHCHR sent a note verbale to call for states', NGOs' and stakeholders' submissions. Twenty-four states and 81 civil society organizations responded to the OHCHR.[135] In particular, Denmark pointed out that resolution 22/29 does not "properly recognise the fact that various forms of families exist".[136] Also, the United Kingdom, the United States and NGOs, such as Sexual Rights Initiatives, OutRight, Amnesty and ILGA, asked the OHCHR to consider LGBT parent-families.[137]

Consequently, the OHCHR issued report 31/37 on the protection of the family. In brief, the report stated that there is general consensus among UN documents that the concept of family must be understood in a "wide sense" as including various forms of families.[138] Although states maintain a margin of appreciation in defining the concept of family,[139] the report encouraged states to ensure that children born in LGBTI parent-families are not discriminated against

---

130 At [23].

131 At [5], [17], [23], [25].

132 Clifford Bob, above n 24, at 50.

133 Rebecca Oas "Big Win for Traditional Family at UN Human Rights Council" (2015) C-Fam <https://c-fam.org/friday_fax/big-win-for-traditional-family-at-un-human-rights-council/> (Retrieved 28 July 2018).

134 A/HRC/RES/29/22 *Protection of the Family: Contribution of the Family to the Realization of the Right to an Adequate Standard of Living for Its Members, Particularly through Its Role in Poverty Eradication and Achieving Sustainable Development* (HR Council, 2015) at [29].

135 UN Human Rights Council "Protection of the Family: Contribution of the Family to the Realization of the Right to an Adequate Standard of Living for Its Members, Particularly through Its Role in Poverty Eradication and Achieving Sustainable Development" www.ohchr.org/EN/HRBodies/HRC/Pages/ProtectionFamily.aspx (Retrieved 28 July 2018).

136 Signe Dam *Response by Denmark to Note Verbale of 2 September 2015 Regarding Human Rights Council resolution 29/22* (2015).

137 UN Human Rights Council, above n 121.

138 A/HRC/31/37 *Protection of the Family: Contribution of the Family to the Realization of the Right to an Adequate Standard of Living for Its Members, Particularly through Its Role in Poverty Eradication and Achieving Sustainable Development* (HR Council, 2016) at [24].

139 At [26].

because of the SOGII of their parents.[140] In so doing, the OHCHR demonstrated once again its alliance with the LGBTI TAN. Even though the resolutions and the report on the protection of the family were promoted with the aim of consolidating the ideal heterosexual married family as the fundamental group unit of society,[141] under the pressures of both states and NGOs, the OHCHR repeated that international human rights law protects various forms of families, not only heterosexual ones.

Conservative/religious voices were quick to express their disappointment. By February 2016, Global Helping to Advance Women and Children, the UN Family Rights Caucus, and 26 NGOs with consultative status submitted a written statement to complain that report 31/37 sought to advance the status of LGBT relationships in international law. The written statement claimed that the assumption that there is a general consensus within the UN on the existence of various forms of families is "false and disingenuous".[142] Similarly, the Society for the Protection of Unborn Children condemned the OHCHR's attempts "to create an opening for the recognition of family structures such as same-sex couples which have never been accepted in any binding UN treaty".[143]

In sum, the description of these events exemplifies that opposing TANs influence one another in a "dynamic set of relations".[144] LGBTI TANs, with the support of some governments, try to consolidate the prohibition of discrimination and the elimination of violence against individuals because of their SOGI. Such actions trigger the conservative/religious TANs' and governments' responses, which try to limit the rights of LGBTI people by consolidating the assumption that the heterosexual married family is the only normal and natural form of family. Consequently, the LGBTI TAN, which usually would not focus on marriage and family rights, asked the UN to acknowledge that LGBTI parent-families exist and need protection. Although it was not possible to find a clear cause-effect connection between the LGBTI NGOs' pressure and the response of UN organs, this section shows that both the HR Council Advisory Committee and the OHCHR acted as allies of the LGBTI TAN because they maintained that international human rights law recognises families as understood in a wide sense, potentially including LGBTI parent-families.

Conclusion

This book shows that the way in which LGBTI TANs strategically frame their claims as human rights violations influences the international human rights

---

140 At [42].
141 Robert C Blitt, above n 127, at 44.
142 A/HRC/31/NGO/155 *Joint Written Statement Submitted by Global Helping to Advance Women and Children* (HR Council, 2016) at 3.
143 A/HRC/NGO/193 *Written Statement Submitted by the Society for the Protection of Unborn Children (SPUC)* (HR Council, 2016) at 2.
144 Tina Fetner, above n 94, at xvii.

debate. Chapter 3 explains how dynamics related to internetwork relations between gatekeeper and peripheral NGOs influence LGBTI TANs' advocacy strategies. However, LGBTI TANs do not make their advocacy decisions in a vacuum and they need to consider the broad political opportunities and constraints offered by international organizations, governments and other NGOs. Hence, this chapter focuses on how the broader political context in which TANs operate shapes their advocacy. The chapter claims that LGBTI gatekeeper NGOs work to seize favourable political opportunities and minimise challenges. To do so, the chapter discusses several themes.

First, NGOs need to have access to the work of the UN to be able to influence the international human rights debate and to provide their inputs. The ECOSOC consultative status is the formal recognition of NGOs in the UN system and it allows them to submit oral and written statements to some UN organs. Since 2006, all LGBTI NGOs that applied for ECOSOC consultative status obtained it, also thanks to some sympathetic states that acted as allies of the LGBTI TAN and pressured the Committee on NGOs and the ECOSOC to grant access to LGBTI NGOs. The ECOSOC consultative status is important for NGOs to gain gatekeeping position within the network because they are perceived as credible and reliable actors by states and the UN. However, this chapter shows that gatekeeper NGOs are not the only NGOs that can access the work of the UN. Whether they have consultative status or not, LGBTI NGOs can lobby governmental delegates to vote in favour of resolutions, recommendations or amendments on SOGII issues. This aspect leads to the second consideration.

Second, LGBTI gatekeeper NGOs have a crucial role in coordinating and driving peripheral NGOs to pressure their own governments to advance the rights of LGBTI people. The example of the amendment to the Resolution on Extrajudicial, Summary or Arbitrary Executions demonstrates that it is particularly important for the overall network that peripheral NGOs are strong and able to advocate towards their own governments. This is because peripheral NGOs are in a better position to pressure their own governments. If peripheral NGOs are non-existent or weak, this advocacy from below cannot occur and the evolution of the international human rights debate on LGBTI rights would slow down. Moreover, this chapter explains that such advocacy actions work better in relation to non-aligned states. Consequently, gatekeeper NGOs need to focus on a "minimum common denominator", to gather the support of these non-aligned states.

Third, the chapter describes the attempts of some conservative religious states and NGOs to have the HR Council issue resolutions and recommendations on traditional values and the protection of the family. This coalition of states and NGOs, under the leadership of the Russian Federation and the OIC, tried to prevent the development of LGBTI rights by claiming that traditional values and the traditional heteronormative family are instrumental to the advancement of human rights. The LGBTI TANs and their international allies fought such resolutions and advocated for the recognition of the right of LGBTI parent-families to be protected. If, in general, I claim that LGBTI gatekeeper NGOs do not invoke the right to marry, opposing TANs influence one another's advocacy.

Therefore, LGBTI gatekeeper NGOs respond to conservative/religious NGOs and states' attacks by mentioning LGBTI parents' rights. Still, they do so by maintaining a prudent strategy and they do not strongly advocate for the right to marry. Because of this dynamic set of attacks and counter attacks, the OHCHR and the HR Council Advisory Committee declared that "family" should be interpreted in a wide sense.

Most notably, the analysis of the coalition of conservative NGOs and states' pressures to make the HR Council deliver resolutions on traditional values and on the protection of the family documents demonstrates that conservative NGOs and states have attempted to fight the LGBTI people's human rights' development. They have done so by juxtaposing the right to marry and the anti-discrimination principle, and by capitalising upon states' fears that the prohibition of discrimination on the grounds of SOGII will lead to a gender-neutral definition of the right to marry. The HR Council resolutions on human rights and SOGI have the same legal status of the HR Council resolutions on traditional values and on the protection of the family. It would be unfair to say that the SOGI resolutions are a victory for the LGBTI TAN, without acknowledging that the resolutions on traditional values and on the protection of the family are victories for the conservative/religious TAN. Therefore, the chapter highlights that LGBTI TANs are still facing a difficult battle for equality before the UN, despite a gradual consolidation of the prohibition of discrimination on the grounds of SOGII principle in the human rights debate.

Finally, the chapter discusses the fact that the LGBTI TANs can count on many powerful allies. UN functionaries, for example the Secretary General of the UN, and bodies of experts, such as the UN HR Council Advisory Committee, collaborate with LGBTI TANs to advance the rights of LGBTI people in the international human rights debate. However, it appears evident that these allies also need to maintain a low profile to find a compromise between pro-LGBTI positions and conservative/religious NGOs and governments.

Even though it is not always possible to identify a cause-consequence link between NGOs' advocacy and the outcomes of the drafting processes, this chapter helps to explain why the advocacy for the right to marry is so controversial for LGBTI transnational advocacy and why LGBTI gatekeeper NGOs, with the support of many powerful international allies, often need to frame LGBTI issues as fundamental human rights claims. These dynamics have consequences for the LGBTI TANs' agenda setting and subsequently in the international human rights debate. The next chapter further advances my arguments by spelling out the advocacy agenda of the LGBTI TANs working at the UN.

5 "With great power comes great responsibility"

The advocacy agenda of LGBTI transnational advocacy networks

Introduction

This chapter directly addresses the core question that underpins this book: What issues are advocated by LGBTI TANs, and how are these issues framed? In the previous chapters, I investigate how TANs set their advocacy agendas and frame LGBTI issues as human rights claims to understand the development of the international human rights debate. This chapter spells out, in detail, the advocacy agenda of the LGBTI TAN. With a combination of quantitative and qualitative analysis of NGO written and oral statements and interviews, it is shown that LGBTI gatekeeper NGOs strategically present their legal analysis to advance LGBTI people's rights by mainly using a prohibition of discrimination on the grounds of SOGII framework. Moreover, it is shown that the advocacy for the right to marry has a low priority in the advocacy agenda of the network.

To understand the significance of the prohibition of discrimination framework, the strategic choices behind the decision to adopt such a framework and the meaning of other rights invoked by LGBTI TANs, this chapter takes into consideration the dynamics discussed in Chapters 3 and 4 as interpretative lenses. To summarise, Chapter 3 discusses the internetwork relations between LGBTI gatekeeper and peripheral NGOs. It explains that LGBTI gatekeeper NGOs strive to build the LGBTI network horizontally, by building the capacity of the NGOs working in the periphery. This horizontal development strategy has two consequences for the advocacy agenda. On the one hand, stronger and more empowered peripheral NGOs can better influence gatekeeper NGOs' agenda decision-making. On the other hand, gatekeeper NGOs advocate for those rights that enhance the domestic political opportunities of the peripheral NGOs. But LGBTI NGOs do not work in a vacuum; rather they work in collaboration with, and in reaction to, other NGOs, states and international organizations. Therefore, Chapter 4 discusses how the broader political context of the UN influences the LGBTI TAN's advocacy agenda. Chapter 4 highlights that the LGBTI TAN and its allies frame LGBTI issues as fundamental protections to attract the support of non-aligned states and move forward with much needed resolutions and recommendations. Furthermore, even though the LGBTI TAN and allies keep a low profile, conservative/religious NGOs and governments use a slippery slope argument to bar any advancement of LGBTI rights protection. Building on the findings of Chapters 3 and 4, this chapter develops as follows.

First, the chapter investigates the work of LGBTI gatekeeper NGOs at the UN by analysing NGOs' written and oral statements. To ensure that the LGBTI TAN develops from below, the NGOs' written and oral statements advocate for those rights that enhance the domestic political opportunities of peripheral NGOs. To maximise their opportunities, gatekeeper NGOs frame LGBTI issues in terms that international organizations and states might "swallow".[1] Therefore, the chapter demonstrates that the NGOs' written and oral statements use predominantly an anti-discrimination framework because it is pragmatic, and it matches existing international human rights treaties. However, the chapter also explains that some gatekeeper NGOs should refrain from using a prohibition of discrimination framework, namely when commenting on non-Western states' (in particular from the anti-LGBTI bloc) human rights record. Indeed, during the UPR process, gatekeeper NGOs are very careful to use prohibition of violence and decriminalisation of same-sex sexual behaviours frameworks when they address the specific states' behaviours that are particularly against LGBTI rights, to avoid triggering unwanted backlashes.

Second, the chapter assesses the advocacy agenda of the broader LGBTI TANs by analysing the findings of the semi-structured interviews, with NGO staff members working mostly in peripheral NGOs.[2] When asked about their opinions on the most pressing issues for LGBTI communities, they expressed similar issues to the ones from the written and oral statements identified above, which is evidence in itself that gatekeeper NGOs listen to their peripheral partners. This finding consolidates the idea discussed in this book that LGBTI gatekeeper NGOs operate democratically. Nevertheless, one specification should be made. The interviewees mention discrimination on the grounds of SOGII as often as violence, visibility of sexually and gender diverse people and decriminalisation of same-sex sexual behaviours. In doing so, the interviewees demonstrate that they have a practical and multi-layered understanding of LGBTI issues.

Third, the chapter tackles the topics of the right to marry and its importance in the advocacy agenda of the LGBTI TAN. To do so, the chapter also discusses the advocacy for some forms of legal recognition of LGBTI couples' rights and family rights; for example, the right to adopt a child or the right to access assisted reproductive treatments. Western LGBTI advocacy is criticised for focusing on marriage equality and, in particular, for imposing the right to marry advocacy on non-Western NGOs. Because imposing marriage equality on the advocacy agenda of peripheral NGOs can be considered an interference and a misuse of power from gatekeeper NGOs, I discuss the right to marry as a way to test the democratic legitimacy of the LGBTI network.

---

1 Joke Swiebel "Lesbian, Gay, Bisexual and Transgender Human Rights: The Search for an International Strategy" (2009) 15(1) *Contemporary Politics* 19 at 28.

2 See Appendix 3.

Both Chapters 3 and 4 provided some evidence that LGBTI gatekeeper NGOs and their allies do not invoke the right to marry to minimise the backlash of conservative/religious blocs. With a combination of quantitative and thematic qualitative analysis of the NGOs' written and oral statements and the interviewees, finally, this chapter demonstrates that the right to marry has a low priority in the advocacy agenda of the LGBTI TAN. It is also shown that, despite its low priority, the interviewees do not have negative opinions on marriage institutions. This means that the right to marry is not opposed by LGBTI activists in principle. Some LGBTI transnational advocates consider that the right to marry, and in some cases the right to form a family, is something to be advocated for at the national level, if that is appropriate. Instead, transnational advocacy for the right to marry is not considered to be a good strategy and it does not win states' support.

In sum, the chapter spells out the advocacy agenda of the LGBTI TAN, in showing that the prohibition of discrimination on the grounds of SOGII is often the preferred framework to advocate for LGBTI rights at the UN. The chapter highlights the complexity of the LGBTI advocacy agenda, and it shows that gatekeeper NGOs do listen to the needs and desires of the peripheral NGOs, that they advocate for those rights that enhance the domestic political opportunities of peripheral NGOs and in particular that they do not impose marriage equality in the advocacy agenda of the broader network. These dynamics explain why the prohibition of discrimination on the grounds of SOGII is gaining traction in the international human rights debate, along with other important issues, such as the decriminalisation of same-sex sexual behaviours and the prohibition of violence based on SOGII, while other 'Western' conceptions of the 'gay agenda', namely the advocacy for the right to marry, have a low priority in the global LGBTI human rights advocacy at the UN.

NGOs' written statements

I selected NGOs' written statements sent to the HR Council by conducting several key word searches. I identified 92 written statements in the UN Official Documents System Search. Even though not all the NGOs that sent written statements to the HR Council are identified as gatekeeper NGOs, written statements are sent by LGBTI and human rights NGOs that have consultative status with the ECOSOC, and therefore they signal how bigger, more powerful and predominately Western NGOs frame LGBTI issues before the HR Council.

Out of the 92 written statements identified, three have scant reference to SOGII issues,[3] and therefore they cannot be the object of an in-depth analysis. The remaining 89 can be categorised into four groups. First, 16 written statements have LGBTI and SOGII issues as their primary focus; second, 28 written

---

3 A/HRC/25/NGO/133 *Written Statement Submitted by International Educational Development, Inc.* (HR Council, 2014); A/HRC/8/NGO/12 *Written Statement Submitted by Amnesty International* (HR Council, 2008); E/CN.4/2005/NGO/346 *Joint Written Statement Submitted by the Coordinating Board of Jewish Organizations (CBJO) and B'nai B'rith* (Comm on HR, 2005).

statements address LGBTI issues when reporting and commenting on human rights violations committed by specific states; third, 42 written statements discuss or mention LGBTI people's rights as an aspect of the main issue that was the focus of the communication. Finally, three written statements are addressed against LGBTI rights.[4] The ensuing section describes how NGOs frame LGBTI rights before the HR Council by analysing these 89 written statements.

How do NGOs frame LGBTI issues in their written statements?

I argue that LGBTI gatekeeper NGOs aim to develop networks horizontally, and to do so they advocate for rights that enhance the domestic political opportunity of peripheral NGOs, which in turn allow peripheral NGOs to thrive at home and ultimately allow the overall network to develop from below. Using social movement theories I identified these issues to be the development of sexual and gender diverse identities and visibility, pressure to allow LGBTI organizations to be formed and to participate in the political system, and decriminalisation of sexual and gender diverse behaviours.[5] Moreover, I specify that gatekeeper NGOs need to use consolidated human rights principles to match existing international human rights treaties and they do so by using mainly an anti-discrimination framework. The analysis of the following NGOs' written statements sent to the HR Council exemplifies these claims.

Among the 89 written statements, I identify 155 references to LGBTI people's rights and SOGII issues (see Figure 5.1). The majority of these remarks refer to the principle of anti-discrimination. NGOs refer to SOGII discrimination 58 times, which represents 37.4% of all the remarks. After the prohibition of discrimination on the grounds of SOGII, the second and third most advocated issues relate to LGBTI people's visibility and participation in their domestic political systems. Indeed, a total of 26 remarks (16.8%) deal with LGBTI people's right to association, peaceful assembly and expression. Moreover, 22 remarks (14.2%) regard the protection of LGBTI people from violence, intended as torture, ill-treatment, harassment and attacks against LGBTI individuals on the basis of their SOGII. Finally, the fourth most advocated issue is the decriminalisation of same-sex sexual behaviour, identified in 19 remarks (12.3%). In line with Adam, Duyvendak and Krouwel's work,[6] I classify these rights as enhancing the domestic political opportunities of sexually and gender diverse people because, as I explain later in the chapter, NGOs' written statements explain how these issues impair the development of LGBTI domestic mobilisation. The ensuing sub-paragraphs describe these findings and their significance.

---

4   See Appendix 2.

5   Barry D Adam, Jan Willem Duyvendak, and André Krouwel "Gay and Lesbian Movements beyond Borders? National Imprints of a Worldwide Movement" in Barry D Adam, Jan Willem Duyvendak, and André Krouwel (eds) *The Global Emergence of Gay and Lesbian Politics: National Imprints of a Worldwide Movement* (Temple University Press, Philadelphia, 1999) 344 at 350–360.

6   Ibid.

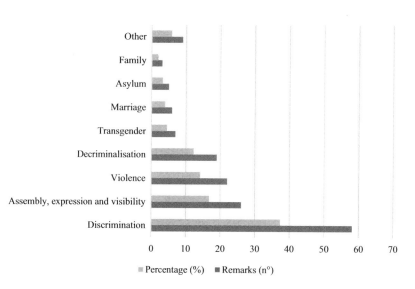

Figure 5.1 Summary of NGOs' written statements

The prohibition of discrimination principle in NGOs' written statements

The prohibition of discrimination on the grounds of SOGII is the prominent framework in the written statements because it is called upon both in written statements that have SOGII issues as their primary focus, and in those that as an aspect of the main issue that was the focus of the communication, or when reporting on specific states' human rights records. The three types of written statements are addressed in turn.

Written statements that focus on LGBTI rights

Out of the 89 written statements identified in this study, 16 have primary focus on LGBTI rights. These 16 discuss the prohibition of discrimination on the grounds of SOGII to some extent. Some of the written statements – submitted by the HRW,[7] Article 19,[8] Transnational Radical Party (TRP),[9] and Canadian HIV/AIDS Legal Network (CHLA)[10] – have the word 'discrimination'

---

7 E/CN.4/2004/NGO/232 *Written Statement Submitted by Human Rights Watch (HRW)* (Comm on HR, 2004).

8 A/HRC/29/NGO/106 *Written Statement Submitted by the Article 19 – International Centre Against Censorship* (HR Council, 2015).

9 A/HRC/1/NGO/33 *Written Statement Submitted by the Transnational Radical Party (TRP)* (HR Council, 2006); E/CN.4/2004/NGO/191 *Written Statement Submitted by the Transnational Radical Party* (Comm on HR, 2004); E/CN.4/2006/NGO/162 *Written Statement Submitted by the Transnational Radical Party (TRP)* (Comm on HR, 2006).

10 E/CN.4/2005/NGO/143 *Written Statement Submitted by the Canadian HAIV/AIDS Legal Network* (Comm on HR, 2005); E/CN.4/2004/NGO/187 *Written Statement Submitted by the Canadian HIV/AIDS Legal Network* (Comm on HR, 2004).

in the title, and they therefore discuss the prohibition of discrimination on the grounds of SOGII to a large extent. For example, the TRP maintains that the prohibition of discrimination on the grounds of sexual orientation is instrumental in addressing other human rights violations, such as the criminalisation of same-sex sexual conduct, violence against LGB people, and limited family rights for LGB people.[11] In other words, the central problem is discrimination on the grounds of sexual orientation. Other human rights violations stem from such fundamental inequality. In a similar manner, other NGOs highlight that prohibition of discrimination on the grounds of SOGII is instrumental in fighting the spread of HIV/AIDS infection[12] and improving the mental health of LGB people.[13]

Furthermore, even when the written statements do not have the word 'discrimination' in the title, they still discuss the prohibition of discrimination on the grounds of SOGII to some extent. For example, the written statement submitted by the Commonwealth Human Rights Initiative focuses on the decriminalisation of same-sex sexual conduct, but in the introduction of the text it explains that the criminalisation of same-sex sexual conduct "impinges on the right to equality and non-discrimination".[14] Similarly, the International Commission of Jurists (ICJ) focuses its written comments on the freedom of assembly and association for LGBT individuals, and explains that the restrictions on the right to assembly and association on LGBT activism "are in reality used as a pretext for discrimination on the basis of [SOGI]".[15]

Finally, the majority of the written statements that have LGBTI issues as the object of their message conclude their communication by encouraging the HR Council and UN states to combat discrimination on the grounds of SOGII.[16] This represents further evidence of the centrality of the anti-discrimination

---

11 A/HRC/1/NGO/33, above n 9, at 1; E/CN.4/2006/NGO/162, above n 9, at 1.

12 E/CN.4/2005/NGO/143, above n 10, at [8]; E/CN.4/2004/NGO/187, above n 10, at [8].

13 E/CN.4/2004/NGO/259 *Written Statement Submitted by the American Psychological Association* (Comm on HR, 2004).

14 A/HRC/19/NGO/61 *Written Statement Submitted by the Commonwealth Human Rights Initiative* (HR Council, 2012) at 1.

15 A/HRC/20/NGO/11 *Written Statement Submitted by the International Commission of Jurists* (HR Council, 2012) at 2. See also, A/HRC/20/NGO/13 *Written Statement Submitted by the International Commission of Jurists* (HR Council, 2012).

16 A/HRC/29/NGO/118 *Joint Written Statement Submitted by Amnesty International, Human Rights Watch* (HR Council, 2015) at 4; A/HRC/22/NGO/11 *Written Statement Submitted by the International Commission of Jurists* (HR Council, 2013) at 4; A/HRC/21/ NGO/62 *Written Statement Submitted by Liberal International* (World Liberal Union) (HR Council, 2012) at 4; A/HRC/19/NGO/150 *Written Statement Submitted by the Canadian HIV/AIDS Legal Network* (HR Council, 2012) at 4; A/HRC/1/NGO/47 *Joint Written Statement Submitted by Action Canada for Population and Development (ACPD), Canadian HIV/AIDS Legal Network, Centre for Women's Global Leadership (Global Centre, CWGL), Global Rights, International Service for Human Rights (ISHR), International Women's Health Coalition (IWHC), and New Ways: Women for Women's Human Rights* (HR Council, 2006) at 4; A/HRC/28/NGO/143 *Written Statement Submitted by the International Gay and Lesbian Human Rights Commission* (HR Council, 2015) at 3; A/HRC/29/ NGO/106, above n 8, at 5; E/CN.4/2004/NGO/187, above n 10, at 5; E/CN.4/2004/

framework in the 16 written statements that address LGBTI people's human rights violations. The fact that the prohibition of discrimination remains the prominent framework is also evident from the analysis of written statements that address SOGII as an aspect of the main issue of concern, or when reporting on specific states' human rights records. These written statements are addressed in the ensuing sub-paragraphs.

SOGII discrimination discussed in combination with other matters

The prohibition of discrimination on the grounds of SOGII is the prominent framework because it is also used in combination with other matters. First, NGOs highlight issues related to discrimination against LGBTI people when writing statements that are focused on discrimination in general. Indeed, some NGOs condemn SOGII discrimination when discussing discrimination in the context of enjoyment of the right to water and sanitation,[17] caste discrimination,[18] gender discrimination,[19] discrimination on grounds of ethnicity[20] and race,[21] and discrimination in Western Sahara.[22] These written statements implicitly demonstrate that NGOs are aware of the intersectional nature of discrimination.[23] Moreover, NGOs explicitly highlight the multi-layered nature of discrimination. Indeed, Amnesty claims that gender discrimination paired with SOGI discrimination can impair girls' right to education.[24] HelpAge mentions that a "range of intersecting forms of discrimination", including SOGI discrimination, can accumulate over time and limit the full enjoyment of human rights for older people.[25] The Asian Legal Resource Centre stresses that "[d]iscrimination against women in India

---

NGO/232 *Written Statement Submitted by Human Rights Watch (HRW)* (Comm on HR, 2004) at 3; E/CN.4/2005/NGO/143, above n 10, at [22(a)].

17 A/HRC/21/NGO/29 *Written Statement Submitted by the International Commission of Jurists* (HR Council, 2012).

18 A/HRC/22/NGO/81 *Written Statement Submitted by the International Movement Against All Forms of Discrimination and Racism (IMADR)* (HR Council, 2013); A/HRC/31/NGO/140 *Written Statement Submitted by the Human Rights Watch* (HR Council, 2016).

19 A/HRC/28/NGO/159 *Written Statement Submitted by Amnesty International* (HR Council, 2015).

20 A/HRC/11/NGO/25 *Written Statement Submitted by the Federation of Western Thrace Turks in Europe (ABTTF)* (HR Council, 2009) at 3.

21 A/HRC/16/NGO/73 *Joint Written Statement Submitted by the Organization for Defending Victims of Violence, the Khiam Rehabilitation Center for Victims of Torture, the Charitable Institute for Protecting Social Victims, the Network of Women's* (HR Council, 2011).

22 A/HRC/28/NGO/21 *Written Statement Submitted by the Federacion de Asociaciones de Defensa y Promocion de los Derechos Humanos* (HR Council, 2015).

23 See also, Mindy Jane Roseman and Alice M Miller "Normalizing Sex and Its Discontents: Establishing Sexual Rights in International Law" (2011) 34 *Harvard Journal of Law and Gender* 313 at 353.

24 A/HRC/29/NGO/114 *Written Statement Submitted by Amnesty International* (HR Council, 2015) at 2.

25 A/HRC/27/NGO/18 *Written Statement Submitted by the HelpAge International* (HR Council, 2014) at 2.

arises from multiple, intertwined, and pervasive sources" influenced by elements such as sexual orientation.[26]

Moreover, the prohibition of discrimination on the grounds of SOGII is the framework that is most used because NGOs explicitly call for the prohibition of discrimination on the grounds of SOGII as the key to access the full enjoyment of human rights for all.[27] Indeed, NGOs explicitly refer to the prohibition of discrimination on the grounds of SOGII for the full enjoyment of children's right to sexual and reproductive health,[28] human rights for migrants,[29] freedom of expression,[30] non-derogable rights during times of emergency[31] and the right to peace.[32] Similarly, NGOs also comment that the prohibition of discrimination on the grounds of SOGII is a gateway to the full enjoyment of human rights for all, in discussing states' reports in Egypt,[33] Colombia[34] and Bahrain.[35] In particular, SOGII discrimination can impair the full enjoyment of the right of women to

---

26 A/HRC/26/NGO/46 *Written Statement Submitted by the Asian Legal Resource Centre* (HR Council, 2014) at [2].

27 A/HRC/30/NGO/126 *Written Statement Submitted by Le Collectif des Femmes Africaines du Hainaut* (HR Council, 2015) at 3; E/CN4/1998/NGO/3 *Written Statement Submitted by the Latin American Committee for the Defence of Women's Rights* (Comm on HR, 1998) at 3.

28 A/HRC/22/NGO/88 *Written Statement Submitted by Plan International, Inc.* (HR Council, 2013).

29 A/HRC/26/NGO/81 *Written Statement Submitted by the Liberal International* (World Liberal Union) (HR Council, 2014).

30 A/HRC/31/NGO/179 *Written Statement Submitted by the Association for Progressive Communications (APC)* (HR Council, 2016) at 5.

31 E/CN.4/2005/NGO/122 *Written Statement Submitted by the International Commission of Jurists (ICJ)* (Comm on HR, 2005) at [4].

32 A/HRC/AC/7/NGO/3 *Joint Written Statement Submitted by the Commission of the Churches on International Affairs of the World Council of Churches (CCIA/WCC) and Others* (HR Council, 2011); A/HRC/20/NGO/59 *Joint Written Statement Submitted by the Commission of the Churches on International Affairs of the World Council of Churches (CCIA/WCC), and Others* (HR Council, 2012); A/HRC/AC/8/NGO/2 *Joint Written Statement Submitted by the Commission of the Churches on International Affairs of the World Council of Churches (CCIA/WCC) and Others* (HR Council, 2012); A/HRC/AC/9/NGO/3 *Joint Written Statement Submitted by the World Council of Churches (CCIA/WCC), and Others* (HR Council, 2012); A/HRC/22/NGO/156 *Joint Written Statement Submitted by the Commission of the Churches on International Affairs of the World Council of Churches (CCIA/WCC) and Others* (HR Council, 2013); A/HRC/AC/10/NGO/2 *Joint Written Statement Submitted by the Commission of the Churches on International Affairs of the World Council of Churches (CCIA/WCC) and Others* (HR Council, 2013); A/HRC/26/NGO/80 *Joint Written Statement Submitted by Asian Legal Resource Centre, and Others* (HR Council, 2014).

33 E/CN.4/2003/NGO/233 *Written Statement Submitted by International Federation of Human Rights Leagues (FIDH)* (Comm on HR, 2003); E/CN.4/2004/NGO/163 *Written Statement Submitted by the International Federation of Human Rights Leagues (FIDH)* (Comm on HR, 2004); E/CN.4/2005/NGO/156 *Written Statement Submitted by the International Federation of Human Rights Leagues (FIDH)* (Comm on HR, 2005).

34 E/CN.4/2005/NGO/255 *Written Statement Submitted by the Colombian Commission of Jurists (CCJ)* (Comm on HR, 2005).

35 E/CN.4/2005/NGO/154 *Written Statement Submitted by the International Federation of Human Rights Leagues (FIDH)* (Comm on HR, 2005).

reproductive health[36] and to access employment in Indonesia,[37] and right to a fair trial in the United States.[38]

Even though the right to anti-discrimination on the grounds of SOGII is the most often invoked, it is not the only one. The ensuing sub-paragraph discusses other rights invoked in the written statements.

Other issues: visibility, political participation and decriminalisation of sexually and gender diverse behaviours

The development and effectiveness of the LGBTI TAN can be impaired by many contingent difficulties of peripheral NGOs. Namely, Western tactics of visibility can be riskier for LGBTI activists working in some non-Western states; being identified as a sexually and gender diverse person can lead to violence, harassment, imprisonment or death; some states limit the rights of LGBTI people to association, assembly and speech. LGBTI gatekeeper NGOs' strategy consists of developing LGBTI networks horizontally, with the aim of developing a stronger and more effective advocacy from below. To build the capacity of NGOs working in the periphery of the network, LGBTI gatekeeper NGOs focus on the advocacy of rights that enhance the political opportunities of domestic NGOs. In the ensuing sub-paragraphs, I explain that gatekeeper NGOs advocate for freedom of association, assembly and expression; elimination of violence based on SOGII; and decriminalisation of sexually and gender diverse behaviours. Analysing the text of the written statements, I highlight how these NGOs' written comments aim to enhance the domestic political opportunities of LGBTI peripheral NGOs.

Out of the 155 remarks, 26 deal with the right of LGBTI people to freedom of association, peaceful assembly and expression. NGOs report that states can limit the right to freedom of assembly and association for LGBTI communities when they prevent LGBTI organizations from registering as associations, and ban Pride Parades,[39] when they enforce restrictions on journalists reporting on LGBT issues,[40] ban publications, shut down newspapers and block websites dealing with sexual orientation.[41] Most notably, the laws against the so-called Propaganda of Homosexuality unjustifiably limit the freedom of expression of LGBT people in Russia.[42]

Remarks addressing such issues are an important means of enhancing the domestic political opportunities of peripheral NGOs as they promote the visibility of sexually and gender diverse communities and the participation in the political system of their states. In particular, as the ICJ points out, states are

---

36 E/CN.4/2003/NGO/233, above n 33, at 3.
37 E/CN.4/2006/NGO/109 *Written Statement Submitted by the International NGO Forum on Indonesia Development (INFID)* (Comm on HR, 2006) at 2.
38 A/HRC/24/NGO/2 *Written Statement Submitted by Mouvement contre le Racisme et pour l'Amitié entre les Peuples* (HR Council, 2013) at 4.
39 A/HRC/20/NGO/11, above n 15, at 3.
40 A/HRC/26/NGO/20 *Written Statement Submitted by the International Educational Development, Inc.* (HR Council, 2014).
41 A/HRC/28/NGO/143, above n 16, at 2.
42 A/HRC/22/NGO/159 *Written Statement Submitted by the Human Rights House Foundation (HRHF)* (HR Council, 2013) at 4.

under the obligation to protect the freedom of association, peaceful assembly and expression of those minority groups that expose ideas not favoured by the majority or by the governments, such as sexually and gender diverse communities do, as essential means to democracy and pluralism.[43] Moreover, some NGOs clearly explain that when LGBTI individuals and organizations are not protected in their freedom of assembly, association and expression, they are subject to violence and harassment, which inevitably impair their ability to be visible in the society and to advocate for their rights. In fact, nine NGOs' written statements call upon states to protect human rights defenders working on SOGII issues.[44]

This leads to the third most addressed issue, the protection of LGBTI people from violence – meaning torture, ill-treatment, harassment and attacks against LGBTI individuals based on their SOGII – which is mentioned 22 times. The elimination of violence framework is often used by NGOs when discussing specific states' human rights reports. Indeed, among the 22 remarks on violence concerns, 14 are made in regard to the treatment of LGBTI people in Colombia,[45] United States of America,[46] Nepal,[47] Honduras,[48] Ireland,[49] Iran,[50]

---

43 A/HRC/20/NGO/11, above n 15, at 2.

44 A/HRC/21/NGO/62, above n 16; A/HRC/29/NGO/118, above n 16; A/HRC/16/NGO/104 *Joint Written Statement Submitted by the Front Line International Foundation for the Protection of Human Rights Defenders, the Center for Reproductive Rights, Inc, the BAO-BAB for Women's Human Rights* (HR Council, 2011); A/HRC/20/NGO/50 *Written Statement Submitted by CIVICUS – The World Alliance for Citizen Participation* (HR Council, 2012); A/HRC/24/NGO/39 *Joint Written Statement Submitted by the International Service for Human Rights, the Action Canada for Population and Development, Amnesty International, the Asian Forum for Human Rights and Development, the Cairo Institute for Human Rights Studies, the Canadian HIV/AIDS Legal Network, Centro de Estudios Legales y Sociales (CELS) Asociación Civil, the Commonwealth Human Rights Initiative, Conectas Direitos Humanos, the East and Horn of Africa Human Rights Defenders Project, Groupe des ONG pour la Convention relative aux droits de l'enfant, the Human Rights House Foundation, the International Commission of Jurists, the International Federation for Human Rights Leagues, the International Rehabilitation Council for Torture Victims, the World Organization Against Torture, CIVICUS – World Alliance for Citizen Participation* (HR Council, 2013); A/HRC/28/NGO/166 *Written Statement Submitted by the International Service for Human Rights* (HR Council, 2015); A/HRC/13/NGO/106 *Written Statement Submitted by Amnesty International* (HR Council, 2010); A/HRC/16/NGO/57 *Written Statement Submitted by the Asian Legal Resource Centre (ALRC)* (HR Council, 2011); A/HRC/4/NGO/81 *Written Statement Submitted by the International NGO Forum on Indonesian Development (INFID)* (HR Council, 2007).

45 A/HRC/13/NGO/106, above n 44, at 2; A/HRC/4/NGO/130 *Written Statement Submitted by the Colombian Commission of Jurists* (HR Council, 2007) at 2.

46 A/HRC/16/NGO/126 *Joint Written Statement Submitted by Action Canada for Population and Development, Madre, Inc, the Urban Justice Center* (HR Council, 2011) at 2.

47 A/HRC/16/NGO/57, above n 44, at 3; E/CN.4/2004/NGO/33 *Written Statement Submitted by the Asian Legal Centre (ALRC)* (Comm on HR, 2004) at [5].

48 A/HRC/25/NGO/36 *Written Statement Submitted by Amnesty International* (HR Council, 2014) at 3.

49 A/HRC/25/NGO/52 *Written Statement Submitted by the International Federation for Human Rights Leagues* (HR Council, 2014) at [14].

50 A/HRC/28/NGO/143, above n 16, at 2.

Gambia,[51] Poland,[52] Iraq,[53] Bahrain[54] and Egypt.[55] It is important that gatekeeper NGOs use a prohibition of violence framework when commenting on the human rights record of non-Western states. Four examples of written statements sent by OutRight and Amnesty clarify this latter point.

Two of the NGOs that I identified as gatekeeper NGOs, Amnesty and Out-Right, focus their written comments on non-Western states with a prohibition of violence framework. Indeed, a written statement sent by OutRight was mainly focused on the "plight" of LGBT people in Iraq; not once did it use the words "discrimination", "equality" or similar. Rather, the organization used a prohibition of violence framework, reporting of attacks, harassments and detentions of LGBT people in Iraq.[56] Similarly, Amnesty avoids writing about the prohibition of discrimination on the grounds of SOGII when discussing LGBTI human rights violations in Gambia[57] and Colombia,[58] preferring instead to talk about violence, torture and detentions. I consider this to be an example of good practice of LGBTI gatekeeper NGOs; they refrain from calling out foreign governments on their SOGII discrimination because these can sometimes be interpreted by some states as a threat to their traditional (heteronormative) understanding of family and marriage.[59] Instead, these two gatekeeper NGOs prefer to use a protection from violence framework, which is usually not perceived as a foreign value, rather as a universally accepted norm.[60]

However, in other occasions, both OutRight and Amnesty did not follow the same good practice. Indeed, OutRight calls upon the Islamic Republic of Iran to respect its international legal obligation "to treat all individuals equally, without distinction based on sexual orientation and/or gender identity",[61] to fight criminalisation of same-sex sexual conduct, torture and limited freedom of expression for LGBT people. Amnesty highlights that LGBTI people suffer discrimination and violence in Honduras[62] and calls upon the Nigerian government to repeal

---

51 A/HRC/28/NGO/170 *Written Statement Submitted by Amnesty International* (HR Council, 2015) at 3.
52 A/HRC/4/NGO/124 *Written Statement Submitted by the World Organization Against Torture* (HR Council, 2007) at 3.
53 A/HRC/S-22/NGO/5 *Written Statement Submitted by the International Gay and Lesbian Human Rights Commission (IGLHRC)* (HR Council, 2014).
54 E/CN.4/2005/NGO/154, above n 35.
55 E/CN.4/2003/NGO/233, above n 33; E/CN.4/2004/NGO/163, above n 33.
56 A/HRC/S-22/NGO/5, above n 53.
57 A/HRC/28/NGO/170, above n 51.
58 A/HRC/13/NGO/106, above n 44.
59 Dominic McGoldrick "The Development and Status of Sexual Orientation Discrimination under International Human Rights Law" (2016) 16(4) *Human Rights Law Review* 613 at 660; Ryan R Thoreson *Transnational LGBT Activism: Working for Sexual Rights Worldwide* (University of Minnesota Press, Minneapolis, 2014) at 123.
60 Lisa McIntosh Sundstrom "Foreign Assistance, International Norms, and NGO Development: Lessons from the Russian Campaign" (2005) 59(2) *International Organization* 419 at 421.
61 A/HRC/28/NGO/143, above n 16, at 3.
62 A/HRC/25/NGO/36, above n 48, at 3.

the infamous "Same Gender Marriage (Prohibition) Bill" and legislation that discriminates on the basis of SOGI.[63] As Chapter 2 explains, the boomerang pattern of action does not always work in transnational LGBTI advocacy because some governments gain national political support by resisting Western pressure to respect the human rights of LGBTI people.[64] Indeed, Amnesty's call to repeal the Nigerian "Same Gender Marriage (Prohibition) Bill" is particularly notable as a number of authors highlight how the interference of Western LGBTI NGOs caused a backlash from the Nigerian government and ultimately the reintroduction of the Bill.[65]

LGBTI gatekeeper NGOs frame LGBTI issues in a way that maximises their political opportunities and minimises adversities. In general, the prohibition of discrimination framework maximises LGBTI gatekeeper NGOs' political opportunities. However, despite LGBTI gatekeeper NGOs' best efforts, the prohibition of discrimination on the grounds of SOGII can still be perceived as provocative by some conservative/religious states. In the NGOs' written statements analysed in this section, I found that gatekeeper NGOs sometimes use a prohibition of violence framework, and some other times they use a prohibition of discrimination framework. The use of the prohibition of discrimination framework is in line with the majority of the LGBTI transnational advocacy. But because some conservative/religious states perceive the prohibition of SOGII discrimination to be problematic, gatekeeper NGOs could focus more on the prohibition of violence when they comment upon the human rights violations in some states, for example Iran and Nigeria.

Furthermore, when same-sex sexual activities are criminalised, LGBTI activists have limited political opportunities to develop and mobilise. This is because, as the Commonwealth Human Rights Initiative points out, the mere existence of laws criminalising same-sex sexual practices, whether enforced or not, "serve to stigmatise and further marginalise LGBTI persons and make it difficult for LGBTI persons to claim and assert their rights".[66] Because of its importance, the call for decriminalising same-sex sexual behaviour is often present both in written statements that address LGBTI rights in general[67] as well as country reports.[68]

---

63 A/HRC/11/NGO/49 *Written Statement Submitted by Amnesty International* (HR Council, 2009) at 5.

64 Ryan R Thoreson, above n 59, at 138.

65 See, Michael J Bosia "Strange Fruit: Homophobia, the State, and the Politics of LGBT Rights and Capabilities" (2014) 13 *Journal of Human Rights* 256 at 260; Paula Gerber and Joel Gory "The UN Human Rights Committee and LGBT Rights: What is it Doing? What Could it be Doing?" (2014) 14 *Human Rights Law Review* 403 at 419; Hakan Seckinelgin "Global Activism and Sexualities in the Time of HIV/AIDS" (2009) 15 *Contemporary Politics* 103 at 112.

66 A/HRC/19/NGO/61, above n 14, at 2.

67 A/HRC/19/NGO/150, above n 16; A/HRC/21/NGO/62, above n 16; A/HRC/1/NGO/47, above n 16; A/HRC/1/NGO/33, above n 9; A/HRC/29/NGO/118, above n 16; E/CN.4/2004/NGO/232, above n 16.

68 A/HRC/11/NGO/49, above n 63; A/HRC/24/NGO/27 *Written Statement Submitted by the Human Rights Law Centre* (HR Council, 2013); A/HRC/28/NGO/143,

Finally, some other issues are mentioned, such as marriage and family rights for LGBTI people, which I discuss more in-depth later in the chapter; asylum for persons fleeing persecution because of their SOGII;[69] and transgender people issues.[70] It should be noted that bisexual and intersex people are somewhat invisible within the advocacy agenda of the LGBTI and human rights NGOs who send written statements to the HR Council. There are no written statements specifically addressing bisexual and intersex people's issues, apart from the usual mention in the generic formula of 'LGBTI'. One exception is one written statement by the ICJ, which commends Australia and Nepal for including a third gender in their identification documents "beyond male and female in order to accommodate the gender identity of transsexual and intersex persons".[71] The fact that bisexual and intersex people's issues are sometimes invisible in the LGBTI advocacy confirms an observation also made by others.[72] However, the analysis of the NGOs' written statements shows a trend of an increasing inclusion of intersex status among the grounds of prohibited discrimination along with sexual orientation and gender identity. Indeed, before 2012, NGOs did not advocate for prohibition of discrimination on intersex status, and after 2012 six written statements included intersex status among the listed grounds of prohibited discrimination.[73]

In sum, this section provides some major findings for this book. I argue that the political opportunities provided by the international system shape the way in which LGBTI gatekeeper NGOs frame their claims. In other words, LGBTI gatekeeper NGOs frame LGBTI issues in a way that maximises their political opportunities. Following Swiebel's analysis,[74] I claim that the prohibition of

---

above n 16; A/HRC/28/NGO/170, above n 51; A/HRC/S-22/NGO/5, above n 53; E/CN.4/2003/NGO/233, above n 33; E/CN.4/2004/NGO/163, above n 33; E/CN.4/2005/NGO/261 *Written Statement Submitted by Transnational Radical Party* (Comm on HR, 2005).

69 A/HRC/26/NGO/81, above n 29, at 2; A/HRC/21/NGO/62, above n 16, at 4; A/HRC/1/NGO/33, above n 9, at 2. See also, A/HRC/31/NGO/181 *Written Statement Submitted by Servas International* (HR Council, 2016) at 4.

70 A/HRC/19/NGO/150, above n 16, at 4; A/HRC/29/NGO/106, above n 8, at 5; A/HRC/29/NGO/118, above n 16, at 4; E/CN.4/2004/NGO/187, above n 10, at 5; E/CN.4/2005/NGO/143, above n 10, at [20]; A/HRC/24/NGO/112 *Written Statement Submitted by Verein Sudwind Entwicklungspolitik* (HR Council, 2013) at 2.

71 A/HRC/21/NGO/29, above n 17, at 3.

72 See for example, Michael Boucai "Sexual Liberty and Same-Sex Marriage: An Argument for Bisexuality" (2012) 49 *San Diego Law Review* 415 at 453–454. See also, Emiel Maliepaard "Bisexual Citizenship in the Netherlands: On Homo-Emancipation and Bisexual Representations in National Emancipation Policies" (2015) 18(4) *Sexualities* 377 at 377–379. One of the interviewees commented that bisexual people issues are often overlooked by the wider LGBTI movement. Interview Bisexual Alliance Victoria (Skype call, 27 May 2016).

73 A/HRC/19/NGO/61, above n 14; A/HRC/25/NGO/130 *Joint Written Statement Submitted by CIVICUS – World Alliance for Citizen Participation* (HR Council, 2014); A/HRC/25/NGO/36, above n 48; A/HRC/27/NGO/77 *Written Statement Submitted by the International Humanist and Ethical Union* (HR Council, 2014); A/HRC/29/NGO/118, above n 16; A/HRC/30/NGO/126, above n 27. See also Appendix 2.

74 Joke Swiebel, above n 1, at 28.

discrimination framework facilitates the LGBTI advocacy. With a quantitative and qualitative analysis of the NGOs' written statements, I ultimately demonstrate that gatekeeper NGOs and NGOs with ECOSOC consultative status use mainly, although non-exclusively, a prohibition of discrimination framework to advocate for LGBTI rights before the HR Council. In addition, I argue that to ensure the success of the LGBTI transnational advocacy, LGBTI gatekeeper NGOs work to build the network horizontally by building the capacity of the domestic NGOs working at the periphery of the network. Through a combination of quantitative and thematic qualitative analysis of the NGO written statement I demonstrate that, as second, third and fourth most invoked rights, LGBTI gatekeeper NGOs advocate for prohibition of violence, the decriminalisation of same-sex sexual behaviour and the freedom of assembly, association and expression. They do so with the aim of enhancing the domestic political opportunities of LGBTI groups and human rights defenders.

The ensuing sub-paragraphs show that the gatekeeper NGOs frame LGBTI issues in a similar way to the oral statements they deliver during the UPR process. However, the structure of the UPR system produces some differences in the NGOs' advocacy. This is because during the UPR, NGOs comment upon specific states' human rights violations, rather than discussing general human rights principles, as they do in the written statements submitted to the HR Council. Second, the differences are also because during the UPR, NGOs and states' representatives have the chance to listen to each other's statements and influence each other's issue framing.

Universal Periodic Review: NGOs' oral statements

The UPR is a relatively new mechanism,[75] which aims to complement the work of the human rights treaties bodies.[76] States are required to prepare a national report on their human rights record, under previous consultation with national NGOs and human rights institutions.[77] In addition, NGOs can submit their own written reports to the OHCHR.[78] Rathgeber observes that states participating in the UPR are likely to raise concerns on SOGI issues when these have been previously raised by NGOs.[79] Therefore, it is particularly relevant to analyse NGOs' oral statements during the UPR process.

The HR Council holds a record of all the oral statements delivered by states and NGOs during the UPR process. I identified 301 paragraphs in which NGOs made

---

75 A/RES/60/251 *Human Rights Council* (General Assembly, 2006) at [5(e)].

76 Office of the United Nations High Commissioner for Human Rights *Working with the United Nations Human Rights Programme: A Handbook for Civil Society* (UN, Online, 2008) at 80.

77 A/HRC/RES/5/1 *Institution-Building of the United Nations Human Rights Council* (2006) at [15(a)].

78 At [15(c)].

79 Theodor Rathgeber *Performance and Challenges of the UN Human Rights Council: An NGOs' View* (Friedrich Erbert Stifgung, 2013) at 10–11.

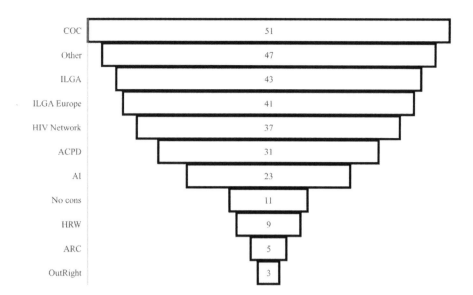

COC 51
Other 47
ILGA 43
ILGA Europe 41
HIV Network 37
ACPD 31
AI 23
No cons 11
HRW 9
ARC 5
OutRight 3

Figure 5.2 List of NGOs that delivered the oral statements

Note: "No cons" refers to NGOs without ECOSOC consultative status.

references to LGBTI issues. COC did not send third party intervention at the HR Council but is very vocal in speaking about LGBTI rights during the UPR, and COC delivered 51 oral statements on LGBTI issues. Moreover, ILGA and ILGA-Europe delivered 84 oral speeches on LGBTI rights during the UPR. In addition, there are another two NGOs that delivered many oral speeches on LGBTI issues and these are the CHLN and Action Canada for Population and Development (ACPD) with respectively 37 and 31 comments. The comments delivered by COC, ILGA, ILGA-Europe, CHLN and ACPD represent two-thirds of the total. Because COC, ILGA and ILGA-Europe are identified as gatekeeper NGOs for this research, analysing the NGOs' oral statements helps to clarify how LGBTI gatekeeper NGOs frame LGBTI issues at the UN (see Figure 5.2).

In comparison, Amnesty and HRW – which submitted the majority of the written statements just analysed above – delivered only 23 and nine oral speeches on LGBTI rights, respectively. When they do comment upon LGBTI rights, they do so along with other issues and in a rather superficial way. In other words, many of the comments delivered by Amnesty and HRW are limited to commend states that accept recommendations on LGBTI issues and criticise those states that did not accept recommendation on LGBTI rights.[80]

80 A/HRC/14/37 *Report of the Human Rights Council on Its Fourteenth Session* (HR Council, 2012) at [575]; A/HRC/16/2 *Report of the Human Rights Council on Its Sixteenth Session* (HR Council, 2011) at [535]; A/HRC/17/2 *Report of the Human Rights Council on Its Seventeenth Session* (General Assembly, 2012) at [359], [536]; A/HRC/19/2 *Report of the*

This rather superficial and scarce involvement of Amnesty and HRW on the advocacy for LGBTI rights during the UPR process is probably because these two NGOs have general human rights mandate and only limited time to speak. Therefore, Amnesty and HRW need to advocate for a range of different human rights violations, in defence of many vulnerable populations. Instead, COC, ILGA, ILGA-Europe, CHLN and ACPD can focus on LGBTI issues more thoroughly because of their sexuality and gender mandate. Considering that Amnesty and HRW have a crucial role in drawing states' attentions on human rights violations, the limited comments of Amnesty and HRW on SOGII issues might result in the marginalisation of these issues within the UPR system. Indeed, according to UPR Info – a Geneva-based NGO that monitors the UPR process – SOGI recommendations are the 22nd most frequent recommendations, out of 30. This means that SOGI recommendations are marginal within the UPR, as they represent only 2.39% of the total recommendations.[81]

In any case, when Amnesty and HRW do comment on LGBTI issues they focus primarily on anti-discrimination and decriminalisation claims.[82] This is in line with the general findings, which are discussed next.

The advocacy agenda at the Universal Periodic Review: prohibition of discrimination and domestic political opportunities

I coded the 301 paragraphs in Nvivo11 and I identified 689 references on LGBTI issues, made by NGOs. Similar to the analysis of the NGOs' written statements, the most mentioned issue is the prohibition of discrimination on the grounds of SOGII, invoked 176 times, and representing 25.6% of the total. Moreover, the

---

Human Rights Council on Its Nineteenth Session (HR Council, 2012) at [484], [752]; A/HRC/22/2 *Report of the Human Rights Council on Its Twenty-Second Session* (HR Council, 2013) at [438], [466], [468]; A/HRC/24/2 *Report of the Human Rights Council on Its Twenty-Fourth Session* (HR Council, 2014) at [850], [854]; A/HRC/25/2 *Report of the Human Rights Council on Its Twenty-Fifth Session* (HR Council, 2014) at [456]; A/HRC/29/2 *Report of the Human Rights Council on Its Twenty-Ninth Session* (HR Council, 2015) at [813]; A/HRC/30/2 *Report of the Human Rights Council on Its Thirtieth Session* (HR Council, 2016) at [439]; A/HRC/32/2 *Report of the Human Rights Council on Its Thirty-Second Session* (HR Council, 2016) at [1056].

81 UPR Info, "Statistics and Recommendations". Retrieved from: www.upr-info.org/database/statistics/ (Last accessed: 6 July 2018).

82 A/HRC/8/52 *Report of the Human Rights Council on Its Eight Session* (HR Council, 2008) at [536]; A/HRC/10/29 *Report of the Human Rights Council on Its Tenth Session* (HR Council, 2009) at [319]; A/HRC/15/60 *Report of the Human Rights Council on Its Fifteenth Session* (HR Council, 2011) at [588]; A/HRC/17/2, above n 80, at [359], [536]; A/HRC/22/2, above n 80, at [438], [466], [486]; A/HRC/24/2, above n 80, at [850], [854]; A/HRC/27/2 *Report of the Human Rights Council on Its Twenty-Seventh Session* (HR Council, 2014) at [581]; A/HRC/28/2 *Report of the Human Rights Council on Its Twenty-Eighth Session* (HR Council, 2015) at [485]; A/HRC/29/2, above n 80, at [813]; A/HRC/30/2, above n 80, at [493], [691]; A/HRC/31/2 *Report of the Human Rights Council on Its Thirty-First Session* (HR Council, 2016) at [894]; A/HRC/32/2, above n 80, at [1056], [1103].

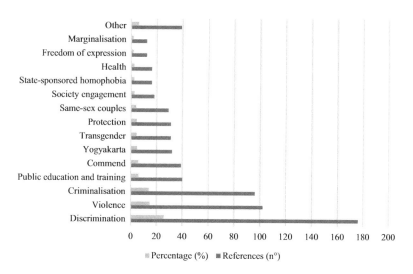

Figure 5.3 Summary of NGOs' oral statements

second and third most advocated issues are again the rights that Adam, Duyvendak and Krouwel claim would increase the domestic political opportunities of
LGBTI NGOs. Indeed, the second most advocated issue regards the protection
of LGBTI people from violence, intended as torture, ill-treatment and attacks
based on homo- and transphobic hate, mentioned 102 times (14.8%). The third
most advocated issue regards the decriminalisation of same-sex sexual behaviour,
mentioned 96 times (13.9%). Finally, the fourth most advocated issue is the recommendation to create public education campaigns and training for law enforce-
ment and public officials, which was not present in the analysis of the NGOs'
written statements submitted to the HR Council, but that still enhances the visibility of LGBTI people in society. This recommendation is made 40 times and
represents 5.8% of the total (see Figure 5.3).

The four most advocated issues are in line with social movement theories and
with the NGOs' written statements. Indeed, the analysis of the UPR documents
confirms that the majority of NGOs' oral statements frame LGBTI issues as
an anti-discrimination claim. Moreover, the second and third most advocated
issues – that are decriminalisation of same-sex sexual behaviour, fighting violence and harassment, and promoting training and public education campaigns
on SOGII – are all tools that allow participation of LGBTI people in society;
according to social movement theories, they should facilitate the development of
LGBTI social movements at the domestic level. In other words, these findings
further confirm that NGOs work to empower the LGBTI TAN from below.

However, there are some differences between the NGOs' written statements
and the NGOs' oral statements. These differences are due to the fact that, first,
the NGOs' written statements are a 'one-way' interaction: NGOs write their
opinions and send them to the HR Council, while the NGOs' oral statements
are part of a larger frame of interactions in which NGOs communicate with the

state under review as well as with the other states participating in the process. The second difference is that the NGOs' written statements are addressed to the HR Council and to UN member states in general, and therefore they address human rights in principle. Instead, during the UPR process, NGOs comment upon states' specific human rights violations, and therefore they discuss human rights in practice. These two differences are addressed in turn in the ensuing sections.

The ricochet effect between NGOs' and states' human rights framings

During the UPR, first states comment upon the human rights record of the state under review, and second, other stakeholders, among which are NGOs, are invited to express their comments and recommendations to the state under review. Therefore, the UPR process functions in a way that allows views to be exchanged both among states, and between NGOs and states under view. However, the UPR process allows for a third set of interactions to happen. Because NGOs deliver their statements after a first round of states' representatives' comments, NGOs' human rights framing is influenced by what these states have said before them. This section discusses these sets of interactions and their consequences for issue framing and emergence.

During the UPR process, NGOs not only comment upon the negative aspect of state behaviours, they also commend states for their achievements on LGBTI rights protection. I identified 39 times in which NGOs commended states' behaviours. For example, states are commended for supporting international statements or resolutions on LGBTI rights,[83] for legislating upon same-sex couples,[84] for fighting SOGII discrimination,[85] decriminalising same-sex sexual behaviour,[86] including third gender in the census,[87] promoting same-sex marriage recognition,[88] recognising SOGII as a ground for granting asylum,[89]

---

83 A/HRC/10/29, above n 82, at [374], [528]; A/HRC/11/37 *Report of the Human Rights Council on Its Eleventh Session* (HR Council, 2009) at [651]; A/HRC/12/50 *Report of the Human Rights Council on Its Twelfth Session* (HR Council, 2010) at [238], [275], [659]; A/HRC/13/56 *Report of the Human Rights Council on Its Thirteenth Session* (HR Council, 2011) at [341], [417], [697]; A/HRC/14/37, above n 80, at [293].
84 A/HRC/12/50, above n 83, at [348].
85 A/HRC/8/52, above n 82, at [229]; A/HRC/12/50, above n 83, at [532], [535]; A/HRC/13/56, above n 83, at [549]; A/HRC/15/60, above n 82, at [374], [691]; A/HRC/16/2, above n 80, at [509], [528]; A/HRC/17/2, above n 80, at [263]; A/HRC/18/2 *Report of the Human Rights Council on Its Eighteenth Session* (HR Council, 2012) at [270], [291]; A/HRC/19/2, above n 80, at [486]; A/HRC/21/2 *Report of the Human Rights Council on Its Twenty-First Session* (HR Council, 2015) at [730]; A/HRC/29/2, above n 80, [698].
86 A/HRC/8/52, above n 82, at [987]; A/HRC/32/2, above n 80, at [844].
87 A/HRC/17/2, above n 80, at [324].
88 A/HRC/19/2, above n 80, at [560], [696].
89 A/HRC/21/2, above n 85, at [515].

explicitly including SOGII grounds in hate crimes legislation[90] and for improving the rights protection of LGBTI people in general.[91]

Nonetheless, NGOs often note with regret that states refuse to accept recommendations on SOGII, which have been previously raised by states' representatives. For example, Serbia,[92] San Marino,[93] Turkey,[94] Malawi,[95] Honduras,[96] Ukraine,[97] Switzerland,[98] Belarus,[99] Liberia,[100] Botswana[101] Denmark,[102] Solomon Islands[103] and Singapore[104] are reprimanded for not accepting recommendations regarding the prohibition of discrimination on grounds of SOGII. Moreover, Belize,[105] Ghana,[106] Gambia,[107] Malawi,[108] Saint Lucia,[109] Indonesia,[110] Botswana,[111] Lebanon,[112] Singapore[113] and Liberia[114] are reprimanded for rejecting recommendations regarding the decriminalisation of same-sex sexual behaviours.

The fact that NGOs 'note with regret' that states under UPR do not accept other states' recommendations highlights two aspects: recommendation on SOGII issues are often rejected by states, and NGOs echo states' concerns. First, Schlanbusch claims that SOGI issues are marginal within the UPR system, as they are not often raised; when they are raised, the "recommendations are rejected to a much higher extent than recommendations in general".[115] This analysis does not provide a comparison between the rejection of SOGII issues and other

---

90 A/HRC/23/2 *Report of the Human Rights Council on Its Twenty-Third Session* (HR Council, 2013) at [627].
91 A/HRC/21/2, above n 85, at [759]; A/HRC/22/2, above n 80, at [737]; A/HRC/23/2, above n 90, [460]; A/HRC/25/2, above n 80, at [840]; A/HRC/26/2 *Report of the Human Rights Council on Its Twenty-Sixth Session* (HR Council, 2014) at [860]; A/HRC/27/2, above n 82, [349]; A/HRC/30/2, above n 80, [641].
92 A/HRC/10/29, above n 82, at [528].
93 A/HRC/14/37, above n 80, [441].
94 A/HRC/15/60, above n 82, at [553].
95 A/HRC/16/2, above n 80, at [396].
96 At [531].
97 A/HRC/22/2, above n 80, at [466], [468].
98 At [615].
99 A/HRC/31/2, above n 82, at [335].
100 A/HRC/30/2, above n 80, at [743].
101 A/HRC/23/2, above n 90, at [460].
102 A/HRC/32/2, above n 80, at [799].
103 At [974].
104 At [1103].
105 A/HRC/12/50, above n 83, at [274].
106 At [632].
107 A/HRC/14/37, above n 80, at [610].
108 A/HRC/16/2, above n 80, at [396].
109 A/HRC/17/2, above n 80, at [359].
110 A/HRC/21/2, above n 85, at [455].
111 A/HRC/23/2, above n 90, at [457].
112 A/HRC/31/2, above n 82, at [521].
113 A/HRC/32/2, above n 80, at [1103].
114 A/HRC/30/2, above n 80, at [743].
115 Mari Dahl Schlanbusch "Sexual Orientation and Gender Identity Rights in the Universal Periodic Review" (Master, University of Tromsø, 2013) at 53.

human rights issues, but the NGOs' oral statements surely show that states, even European states like Switzerland and Denmark, are still resistant to accepting recommendations on SOGII human rights violations.

Second, as highlighted above, states participating in the UPR are likely to raise concerns on SOGII issues when these have been previously raised by NGOs.[116] Moreover, social movement theories in general claim that when states adopt and repeat NGOs' frameworks, they can "amplify and legitimize"[117] NGOs' advocacy. Instead, this section on the NGOs' oral statements delivered at the UPR signifies that NGOs repeat and echo states' recommendations. In other words, during the UPR, first states express their views and propose recommendations to the state under review, then NGOs further comment upon the state under review. In this way, NGOs have the chance to listen to what states recommend before them and then adjust their own oral statements to repeat and reinforce the message. Therefore, not only do states amplify and legitimise NGOs' framework, NGOs also legitimise and amplify states' framework in a continuous ricochet effect of ongoing reciprocal reinforcement.[118]

In sum, as explained in other parts of this book, TANs do not work in a vacuum. Instead, the way in which gatekeeper NGOs frame LGBTI rights is influenced by the broader political context in which they operate. This section shows that because the UPR is a process characterised by the interaction between states and NGOs, gatekeeper NGOs' issue framings are influenced by states' framing, just as states' framing are influenced by NGOs' ones. That is to say that during the UPR, NGOs and states influence each other in a ricochet process by which "information and arguments ricochet rapidly across"[119] NGOs and states to protect LGBTI people's rights. There are other differences and similarities between the finding of the analysis of the NGO oral and written statements, which are due to the fact that during the UPR process, NGOs can comment upon specific states' human rights records. The ensuing session highlights these difference and similarities.

Differences and similarities between the oral and the written comments: human rights in practice

There are some differences between the analysis of the written statements submitted at the HR Council and the oral statements delivered during the UPR. Some of the differences, as the one just addressed above, are due to the fact that the UPR is a sort of 'conversation' between the state under review and the actors reviewing them. Therefore, states and NGOs can influence each other in their recommendations and framing. Another difference

---

116 Theodor Rathgeber, above n 79, at 10–11.
117 Jutta Joachim "Framing Issues and Seizing Opportunities: The UN, NGOs, and Women's Rights" (2003) 47(2) *International Studies Quarterly* 247 at 251.
118 Ronald Holzhacker "State-Sponsored Homophobia and the Denial of the Right of Assembly in Central and Eastern Europe: The 'Boomerang' and the 'Ricochet' between European Organizations and Civil Society to Uphold Human Rights" (2013) 35(1–2) *Law & Policy* 1.
119 At 2.

between the NGOs' written statements and the NGOs' oral statements stems from the fact that during the UPR process, NGOs address their comments towards specific states, and, therefore, they can speak of LGBTI human rights violation in a practical and targeted way. This second aspect is addressed in this section.

As highlighted above, the four most mentioned issues are similar between the findings of the oral and written statements. Still with some differences. The oral comments delivered by NGOs during the UPR confirm again that NGOs focused mostly on calling upon states to fight discrimination on the grounds of SOGII, and the SOGII framework is used in conjunction with other rights because the prohibition of discrimination is instrumental to the LGBTI people's full enjoyment of their rights. However, in the oral statements, NGOs refer proportionally less often to discrimination issues as opposed to the written statements. In other words, NGOs refer to SOGII discrimination 37.4% of the time in the written statements, and 25.4% during the oral statements. When NGOs call upon the protection of LGBTI people's rights in general in the written statements, they frame LGBTI people's rights as a prohibition of discrimination claim. When NGOs discuss LGBTI people's rights in detail, by referring to a specific state behaviour during the UPR, they still frame LGBTI issues as a discrimination claim, but not as much. Moreover, in the NGOs' written statements, the second most advocated issue was the right of assembly, expression and visibility of LGBTI people, while in the NGOs' oral statements these issues are mentioned only 12 times, representing the 1.7% of the total. Instead, the second and third most advocated issues in the NGOs' oral statements are protection from violence and decriminalisation of same-sex sexual behaviours. These are also in the top four of the analysis of the NGOs' written statements, but as third and fourth respectively. In other words, more than in the written statements, NGOs' oral statements address urgent threats to LGBTI people's safety.

The fact that NGOs' oral statements focus proportionally less on the prohibition of discrimination on the grounds of SOGII has the consequence that other issues, like protection from violence and decriminalisation of same-sex sexual behaviours, become more relevant. Moreover, because there is the focus on states' human rights records, in the oral statements, NGOs are much more able to articulate how these protections and rights should be developed in practice. This is well exemplified by the analysis of the prohibition of violence and decriminalisation frameworks.

First, NGOs' written statements often advocate for the protection of LGBTI people from violence, ill-treatments and attacks, but they do not quite conceptualise these attacks and violence as hate crimes. Instead, when discussing LGBTI issues orally, and especially when commenting upon state human rights records, NGOs are able to go more into the specific details of actually how to fight violence. The protection of LGBTI people from violence is also achieved through hate crimes legislation and investigation. Therefore, NGOs' oral statements called upon states to include SOGII grounds in their national hate crimes legislation[120] and investigate hate crimes committed against LGBTI people.[121]

Second, many NGOs' oral statements say that laws that criminalise same-sex sexual behaviours prevent LGBTI people from fully enjoying their rights. NGOs say that the decriminalisation of same-sex sexual behaviours is crucial to fight violence and harassment,[122] protect people's privacy,[123] effectively prevent and treat HIV/AIDS,[124] promote people's enjoyment of their social and economic rights,[125] fight homophobia[126] and guarantee the security of human rights defenders.[127] There is a strong connection between the discrimination and the decriminalisation advocacy frameworks. This is because when states enforce laws that discriminate against LGBTI people, to the point of criminalising same-sex sexual behaviours and occasionally transgender behaviours, LGBTI people are marginalised, stigmatised and prevented from fully enjoying their rights.[128]

Sometimes states are threatened by calls for the prohibition of discrimination on the grounds of SOGII because they fear the consequences that SOGII anti-discrimination would have in their family laws, and even because many states still consider 'SOGII' a foreign value. It is well documented in Chapters 3 and 4 of this book that the coalition of conservative/religious states and NGOs mobilises effectively against the right to anti-discrimination because they claim that the prohibition of discrimination on the grounds of SOGII will eventually lead to the right to marry for LGBTI people. In other words, the prohibition of discrimination on the grounds of SOGII is still very controversial for many states, and when NGOs deliver oral statements during the UPR to comment upon specific states' human rights behaviour, they avoid backlash by invoking the prohibition of violence and the decriminalisation of same-sex sexual behaviours.

In the NGOs' oral statements, the prohibition of discrimination on the grounds of SOGII is still the most often used framework, but there are many

---

120 A/HRC/8/52, above n 82, [538]; A/HRC/10/29, above n 82, [528], [653]; A/HRC/14/37, above n 80, [293], [576], [688]; A/HRC/16/2, above n 80, at [509]; A/HRC/18/2, above n 85, at [420]; A/HRC/19/2, above n 80, at [365]; A/HRC/21/2, above n 85, at [370]; A/HRC/22/2, above n 80, at [770]; A/HRC/26/2, above n 91, at [641]; A/HRC/27/2, above n 82, at [347], [388], [516]; A/HRC/29/2, above n 80, at [698]; A/HRC/30/2, above n 80, at [482], [641]; A/HRC/32/2, above n 80, at [680], [846].

121 A/HRC/13/56, above n 83, at [344]; A/HRC/15/60, above n 82, at [553]; A/HRC/22/2, above n 80, at [770]; A/HRC/23/2, above n 90, at [376]; A/HRC/24/2, above n 80, at [804]; A/HRC/25/2, above n 80, at [747]; A/HRC/26/2, above n 91, at [826].

122 A/HRC/10/29, above n 82, at [374]; A/HRC/11/37, above n 83, at [395].

123 A/HRC/10/29, above n 82, at [706]; A/HRC/15/60, above n 82, at [624].

124 A/HRC/13/56, above n 83, at [672]; A/HRC/14/37, above n 80, at [485].

125 A/HRC/17/2, above n 80, at [537].

126 A/HRC/22/2, above n 80, at [438].

127 A/HRC/24/2, above n 80, at [852].

128 See especially, A/HRC/10/29, above n 82, at [706]; A/HRC/11/37, above n 83, at [716]; A/HRC/15/60, above n 82, at [624]; A/HRC/22/2, above n 80, at [438].

occasions in which gatekeeper NGOs comment upon the human rights record of non-Western states and they focus on violence and decriminalisation, rather than discrimination. For example, Amnesty called on Gambia,[129] Sierra Leone[130] and Malawi[131] to decriminalise same-sex sexual behaviours, without explicitly mentioning SOGII discrimination. Similarly, HRW called on Iraq to investigate persecutions based on sexual orientation,[132] and noted with regret that Cameroon had rejected "several common sense recommendations to protect the security and life of LGBTI individuals, and to end arbitrary arrests for same-sex conduct".[133] These are all examples of good practice that show that gatekeeper NGOs are aware of their critical position in the network and avoid misusing their power.

Moreover, one further aspect of difference between the oral and the written statements is that the fourth most advocated issue in the NGOs' oral statements regard the recommendation to states to develop public education campaigns[134] and training for public officials.[135] In line with Adam, Duyvendak and Krouwel's claims, these education campaigns and training promote the domestic political opportunities of LGBTI NGOs and social movements. This is because these initiatives create visibility on LGBTI people and identities. This aspect is well explained by the NGOs, which recommend that states create public education campaigns and training programmes because these initiatives create awareness on LGBTI people's rights, and "promote their integration and combat violence"[136] based on SOGI. Moreover, these initiatives are important "to promote respect for all persons, including on the grounds of [SOGI], and to ensure that lesbian, gay and transgender citizens are treated equally".[137] These types of recommendations also have the advantage to be 'soft' mechanisms that do not need reforms in law and policies, but that along with other institutional 'hard' reforms can produce long-lasting changes in people's hearts and minds.

---

129 A/HRC/28/2, above n 82, at [486].
130 A/HRC/32/2, above n 80, at [1056].
131 A/HRC/30/2, above n 80, at [439].
132 A/HRC/14/37, above n 80, at [575].
133 A/HRC/24/2, above n 80, at [850].
134 A/HRC/12/50, above n 83, at [258], [321], [615]; A/HRC/13/56, above n 83, at [320], [447], [509], [593]; A/HRC/14/37, above n 80, at [293], [358], [485], [576]; A/HRC/15/60, above n 82, at [465]; A/HRC/16/2, above n 80, at [509]; A/HRC/18/2, above n 85, at [247], [420]; A/HRC/19/2, above n 80, at [486]; A/HRC/22/2, above n 80, at [510]; A/HRC/25/2, above n 80, at [832]; A/HRC/31/2, above n 82, at [859], [864].
135 A/HRC/8/52, above n 82, at [229]; A/HRC/11/37, above n 83, at [294], [501], [589], [716]; A/HRC/12/50, above n 83, at [238], [431]; A/HRC/13/56, above n 83, at [320]; A/HRC/14/37, above n 80, at [293]; A/HRC/15/60, above n 82, at [373], [465], [659]; A/HRC/16/2, above n 80, at [509]; A/HRC/18/2, above n 85, at [291]; A/HRC/21/2, above n 85, at [515]; A/HRC/26/2, above n 91, at [641]; A/HRC/27/2, above n 82, at [347], [516]; A/HRC/30/2, above n 80, at [479]; A/HRC/31/2, above n 82, at [987].
136 A/HRC/22/2, above n 80, at [510].
137 A/HRC/18/2, above n 85, at [291].

The advocacy for public education campaign and training for key members of society, like police officers, journalists and teachers, was not present in the NGOs' written statements. Again, because the written statements were addressed to all states, they discussed human rights in general and they are more principle based. Instead, the oral statements are addressed to the individual states and therefore they can be more specific in suggesting practical ways to promote the visibility and the protection of LGBTI people's rights. In other words, when NGOs deliver oral statements during the UPR sessions, they are able to articulate how the protection of LGBTI people's rights is achieved in practice, and they can develop more targeted recommendations to states.

Furthermore, similar to the NGOs' written statements, NGOs' oral statements often advocate for specific transgender people's rights. Transgender people's issues are addressed 31 times in the oral statements, representing 4.5% of the total. In particular, NGOs call upon states to develop comprehensive legislation to regulate gender reassignment procedures,[138] and to abolish compulsory sterilisation of transgender people.[139] Moreover, similar to the NGOs' written statements, intersex people's human rights violations are addressed only four times, and only fairly recently. Indeed, the HR Council's records report that in four occasions NGOs called upon states to stop forced sterilisation and cosmetic surgical operations on children born with intersex condition, only after 2014.[140] Not surprisingly, specific bisexual people's issues are again invisible and never mentioned in the NGOs' oral statements. In this regard, the NGOs' oral statements present the same limitations of the NGOs' written statements. Bisexual and intersex people are rather invisible in the LGBTI advocacy at the UN, at the detriment of a nuanced and multi-layered LGBTI human rights protection.

Finally, a key similarity between the oral and written statements is that NGOs make comments on same-sex couples' legal recognition, and marriage and family equality only in limited occasion, namely in 29 times, representing 4.2% of the total. The significance of the low advocacy for the right to marry is addressed together with the NGOs' written statements and the interviews later in this chapter. Before moving to that, the next section discusses the interview results, in highlighting the similarities and differences with the NGOs' written and oral statements.

---

138 A/HRC/12/50, above n 83, at [321], [656]; A/HRC/13/56, above n 83, at [417], [697]; A/HRC/14/37, above n 80, at [330]; A/HRC/22/2, above n 80, at [770]; A/HRC/23/2, above n 90, at [731]; A/HRC/26/2, above n 91, at [860]; A/HRC/27/2, above n 82, at [714]; A/HRC/30/2, above n 80, at [523], [811]; A/HRC/31/2, above n 82, at [859].

139 A/HRC/17/2, above n 80, at [670]; A/HRC/18/2, above n 85, at [247]; A/HRC/25/2, above n 80, at [832]; A/HRC/27/2, above n 82, at [347]; A/HRC/31/2, above n 82, at [815]; A/HRC/32/2, above n 80, at [755].

140 A/HRC/23/2, above n 90, at [485]; A/HRC/26/2, above n 91, at [354]; A/HRC/27/2, above n 82, at [714]; A/HRC/32/2, above n 80, at [815].

Horizontal networking: consultations and needs-based approach

Activists participating in the LGBTI network have the chance to share their views by delivering presentations during international conferences, and by engaging in informal conversation with other activists. ILGA-Europe's segment on the needs-based approach is a good example of this latter point:[141]

> The needs of our members are at the core of everything ILGA-Europe does. This **needs-based approach** is a fundamental part of ILGA-Europe ethos. Through open and honest conversations, we listen to what our members really need. We will not intervene at national level unless our members clearly express a wish for us to do so. By giving our members the space to self-assess their strengths and weaknesses, we can help them to grow without imposing our own priorities on them. (Emphasis in the original.)

Interviewees highlight the importance of consultations and the interviewees from ILGA and ILGA-Europe stress the importance of conferences. Indeed, during ILGA conferences, activists, academics and various stakeholders can come together and draft recommendations on ILGA's work. Moreover, LGBTI activists who meet during ILGA's conferences gain experience and knowledge from one another in a dynamic that one interviewee from ILGA-Europe calls "cross-fertilisation".[142] In addition, the interviewee from FELGTB (Federación Estatal de Lesbianas, Gais, Transexuales y Bisexuales), a Spanish NGO with ECOSOC consultative status, stresses that they have "regular networking meetings [with ILGA-Europe] to share the information and provide a synchronized response".[143]

Furthermore, peripheral NGOs also value the work with ILGA. They state that collaborating with ILGA allows them to exchange knowledge,[144] and a number of the interviewees participate in regional or global ILGA meetings and conferences to bring their unique local perspectives.[145] In particular, the interviewee from GALANG Philippines highlights that they participate annually in the ILGA Asia's meeting to talk about the intersectionality between poverty and sexuality.[146] Other interviewees say that they participated in conferences and meetings

---

141 ILGA-Europe "What Is Our Approach Supporting the LGBTI Movement?" ILGA-Europe http://ilga-europe.org/what-we-do/our-work-supporting-movement/approach (Retrieved 31 July 2018).
142 Interview ILGA-Europe (Skype call, 21 August 2015).
143 Interview Federación Estatal de Lesbianas, Gais, Transexuales y Bisexuales (FELGTB) (Questionnaire, 2 April 2016).
144 Interview Pink Cross (Questionnaire, 27 July 2016).
145 Interview GALANG Philippines (Skype call, 25 May 2016); Bisexual Alliance Victoria, above n 72; interview Pink Armenia (Skype call, 21 April 2016); interview with an independent activist from Singapore (Skype call, May 2016); interview anonymous NGO from Saint Lucia (Skype call, 17 June 2016).
146 GALANG Philippines, above n 145.

organised by ARC and OutRight, with the same purpose of sharing knowledge and points of views.[147]

Finally, the interviewee from ILGA-Oceania stresses that they consult NGO partners in the Pacific and listen to what such partners consider to be their agenda priorities. In doing so, ILGA-Oceania can help their NGO partners in the Pacific Islands with their specific needs and can assist and encourage the development of advocacy programmes that are suitable for their partners' capabilities.[148]

Considering that the NGO written and oral statements are submitted by NGOs with ECOSOC consultative status (therefore Western and some gate-keeper NGOs), I compare the results of the findings of the written and oral statements with the findings of the interviews. If it is true that gatekeeper NGOs consult with their peripheral partners, the two bodies of findings should pro-vide similar results. The following sub-paragraphs demonstrate that interviewees frame LGBTI issues in a similar way to those of the NGO written and oral state-ments, and I suggest this consistency of results is proof that gatekeeper NGOs do take into consideration the inputs of peripheral NGOs. Before moving to discuss the case study of the right to marry in the advocacy agenda of LGBTI TANs, the ensuing section discusses the interviewees' opinions on LGBTI issues.

Human rights in practice: the interviewees' opinions

I codified interviewees' opinions on LGBTI issues into 90 items (see Figure 5.4). The most often cited concern is violence, harassment and ill-treatment of LGBTI people, being mentioned 15 times (16.7% of the total). Moreover, interviewees refer 12 times to SOGII discrimination (13.3%); 12 times to visibility, freedom of assembly and expression (13.3%); and ten times to the decriminalisation of same-sex sexual behaviour (11.1%). These findings are consistent with the result of the analysis of the NGOs' written statements sent to the HR Council, and the oral statements delivered during the UPR, demonstrating that gatekeeper NGOs do take account of the input from the wider network. However, there are some differences.

I argue that the political opportunities provided by the international system shape the way in which LGBTI TANs strategically present their legal analysis to advance LGBTI people's rights. Therefore, LGBTI gatekeeper NGOs frame LGBTI issues in a way that maximises their political opportunities, and they use mainly a prohibition of discrimination on the grounds of SOGII. This is because the anti-discrimination principle is a well-consolidated human rights principle, which is a framework that international organizations and states can "swallow".[149]

The prohibition of discrimination on the ground of SOGII is an important concern for the interviewees, but they have an intersectional understanding of

---

147 GALANG Philippines, above n 145; interview LGBT Centre Mongolia (Skype call, 9 March 2016).
148 Interview ILGA-Oceania (Skype call, 29 April 2016).
149 Joke Swiebel, above n 1, at 28.

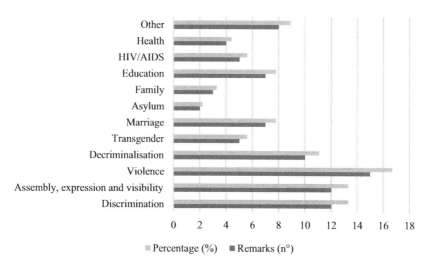

Figure 5.4 Summary of interview findings

LGBTI issues. Indeed, concerns related to discrimination appear as often as criminalisation, violence and visibility. In addition, these frequent concerns are mentioned along with other key words, for example stigma,[150] safety,[151] or homo- and trans-phobia.[152] Hence, the interviewees highlight the interconnectedness of each aspect of the human rights violations with the other. Furthermore, many interviewees highlight the intersectionality between criminalisation, discrimination and violence, with other issues such as poverty,[153] unemployment and homelessness;[154] the spread of HIV/AIDS infection;[155] limitation in the access to religious functions;[156] and limitation to access health services.[157] In particular, the interviewee from Justice for Sisters highlights that adopting an intersectional approach to advocate for the rights of sexually and gender diverse people is an important aspect of their work. The interviewee adds that they collaborate with various human rights groups to work conjointly on harassment and violence.[158]

---

150 Interview Blue Diamond Society (Skype call, 1 March 2016); interview anonymous NGO from Nigeria (Questionnaire, 2 June 2016); anonymous NGO from Saint Lucia, above n 145.

151 Interview Unitarian Universalist Association (UUA) (Skype call, 5 April 2016).

152 Interview Stop AIDS Liberia (Questionnaire, 30 May 2016); interview Australian Lesbian Medical Association (ALMA) (Skype call, 23 March 2016); interview Bisdak Pride (Skype call, 20 May 2016).

153 GALANG Philippines, above n 145; anonymous NGO from Nigeria, above n 150.

154 Interview Rainbow Sunrise Mapambazuko (Questionnaire, 5 April 2016); Unitarian Universalist Association (UUA), above n 151.

155 Stop AIDS Liberia, above n 152.

156 Interview Youth Interfaith Forum on Sexuality (YIFoS) (Skype call, 25 May 2016).

157 Interview Malta LGBT Movement (Skype call, 5 May 2016); LGBT Centre Mongolia, above n 147.

158 Interview Justice for Sisters (Skype call, 16 May 2016).

Moreover, some interviewees comment that education, visibility and movement building – rather than legal protection from discrimination – are instrumental to protecting the right of sexually and gender diverse people and to promote equality. Some interviewees maintain that lack of visibility of LGBTI identities, both on the national and international level, is a concern for their organizations[159] and report that they collaborate with civil societies,[160] schools[161] and police departments[162] to engage with the public and to educate both young people and state authorities on LGBTI issues. This is because education and awareness on SOGII issues are practical tools to fight discrimination and intolerance.[163]

A final point is related to tactics. Chapter 2 reports that in the opinion of some authors, LGBTI NGOs working in non-Western states might prefer to focus on health concerns[164] and providing social services for sexually and gender diverse communities[165] as opposed to engaging in legal strategies, which are typically Western tactics. On the contrary, interviewees, from both Western and non-Western states, say that they do use legal tactics. For example, they often engage in litigation both nationally and internationally,[166] and lobby their national governments and parliaments to change law and policies related to sexually and gender diverse people.[167] I found that many interviewees from non-Western countries use legal

---

159 Bisexual Alliance Victoria, above n 72; Justice for Sisters, above n 158; interview Swedish Federation for LGBTQ Rights (RFSL) (Skype call, 3 May 2016); independent activist from Singapore, above n 145; interview an anonymous NGO (Skype call, 1 April 2016).

160 Anonymous NGO from Nigeria, above n 150; anonymous NGO from Saint Lucia, above n 145.

161 GALANG Philippines, above n 145; Malta LGBT Movement, above n 157; Youth Interfaith Forum on Sexuality (YIFoS), above n 156.

162 Interview Rete Lenford (Skype call, 25 February 2016).

163 Interview ILGA-World (Skype call, 3 April 2016).

164 Marc Epprecht "Sexual Minorities, Human Rights and Public Health Strategies in Africa" (2012) 111 *African Affairs* 223 at 236.

165 Ashley Currier "Deferral of Legal Theory, a Global LGBT Social Movement Organization's Perspective" in Mary Bernstein, Scott Barclay, and Anna-Maria Marshall (eds) *Queer Mobilizations: LGBT Activists Confront the Law* (New York University Press, New York, 2009) 21 at 32–37. See also, Ashley Currier and Joëlle M Cruz "Civil Society and Sexual Struggles in Africa" in Ebenezer Obadare (ed) *The Handbook of Civil Society in Africa* (Springer New York, 2014) 337 at 344.

166 Interview Campaign Against Homophobia (Skype call, 13 May 2016); interview Associazione Radicale Certi Diritti (ARCD) (Phone call, November 2015); interview Hungarian LGBT Alliance (Skype call, 29 April 2016); Justice for Sisters, above n 158; interview with an independent activist in New Zealand (Face-to-face, 20 March 2015); Pink Armenia, above n 145; Rete Lenford, above n 161.

167 Stop AIDS Liberia, above n 152; interview Arcigay (Phone call, 23 November 2015); interview Bilitis Resource Center (Questionnaire, 14 May 2016); Bisdak Pride, above n 152; Blue Diamond Society, above n 150; Campaign Against Homophobia, above n 166; anonymous NGO from Nigeria, above n 150; GALANG Philippines, above n 145; Justice for Sisters, above n 158; Malta LGBT Movement, above n 157; independent activist in New Zealand, above n 166; Pink Cross, above n 144; Rainbow Sunrise Mapambazuko, above n 154; anonymous NGO from Saint Lucia, above n 145.

tactics because of the way I selected my sample. As I selected NGOs that conduct transnational advocacy they already use some form of legal tactics because that is a pre-requisite that facilitates the participation in TANs.[168] Nevertheless, some of the interviewees who do use legal tactics added that they also use non-legal ones. For example, they provide support for individuals with HIV;[169] they bridge the gap between LGBTI people in need and public services by, for example, referring individuals to "friend" health care centres[170] and other public services;[171] they provide counselling[172] and spaces for discussions.[173] The interview findings have some similarities and differences with the written and oral statements. These similarities and differences are explained next.

Similarities and differences between the NGOs' written and oral statements, and the interviews

Interviewees have similar concerns to those expressed in the NGOs' written and oral statements, with some necessary specifications. The interviewees, most of whom are from peripheral NGOs, have a more intersectional and practical perception of LGBTI issues, as opposed to the NGO written statements. Indeed, NGOs' written statements focus mostly on the prohibition of discrimination; while interviewees have a more multi-layered understanding of SOGII discrimination and LGBTI people issues.

Conversely, in the NGOs' oral statements, the prohibition of discrimination framework is still the most often used, but proportionally less often than the NGOs' written statements. This finding is a point of similarity between the NGOs' statements and the interviewees' opinions. Even though in the NGOs' oral statements the prohibition of discrimination on the grounds of SOGII remains the prominent framework, NGOs' oral statements provide a large space to other important concerns related to LGBTI people's safety, such as violence based on SOGII and criminalisation of same-sex sexual behaviours. This is an example of good practice because it shows that still focusing on prohibition of discrimination issues, NGO's oral statements invoke those rights that protect the life and freedom of LGBTI people and at the same time are less controversial for some non-Western states. Moreover, it is a further proof that gatekeeper NGOs listen to and take into consideration peripheral NGOs' concerns and perspectives.

A possible explanation for the similarity between the NGOs' oral statements with the interviews is that when NGOs are able to voice their concerns orally during the interviews, and when they comment upon specific states' human rights records, like during the UPR, they can do so by talking about human rights issues

---

168 Clifford Bob *The Marketing of Rebellion: Insurgents, Media, and International Activism* (Cambridge University Press, Cambridge, New York, 2005) at 34–35.
169 Bisdak Pride, above n 152.
170 LGBT Centre Mongolia, above n 147.
171 GALANG Philippines, above n 145.
172 Malta LGBT Movement, above n 157; anonymous NGO from Saint Lucia, above n 145.
173 Bisexual Alliance Victoria, above n 72.

in practice. The prohibition of discrimination on the grounds of SOGII remains the primary framework, both in the NGOs' oral statements and the interviews, but it is proportionally less prominent when compared with the NGOs' written statements. In this way, the NGOs' oral statements show that even NGOs with ECOSOC consultative status, many of which are recognised as gatekeeper NGOs in this book, have an intersectional and practical understanding of LGBTI issues, in which discrimination is the prominent principle framework but intersected with many other issues.

A key similarity between the interviewees' opinions with both the NGO written and oral statements is that gatekeeper NGOs and peripheral NGOs present similar advocacy agendas, where marriage equality does not appear to have high priority. This comment leads finally to a discussion of the case study of marriage equality as a controversial issue for LGBTI advocates. In the ensuing section I analyse the written and oral statements and the interviewees to discover how important the advocacy for the right to marry is for the LGBTI networks.

Issue framing: prohibition of discrimination and marriage (in)equality

The prohibition of discrimination on grounds of SOGII can lead conservative/ religious states to use a slippery slope argument to oppose LGBTI rights. For example, Pakistan and the Holy See strongly oppose the Brazilian resolution, highlighting that it would have led to a gender-neutral definition of the right to marry. Moreover, marriage and family equality are a controversial topic also among LGBTI and human rights activists, and imposing the right to marry in the advocacy agenda of peripheral LGBTI NGOs can be seen as a misuse of power.

To shed further light on these topics, I discuss in depth the case study of marriage equality in the advocacy agenda of the LGBTI TANs working at the UN. I show that marriage equality has little importance in the LGBTI transnational advocacy agenda, and gatekeeper and Western NGOs do not impose the right to marry in the advocacy agenda of the network working at the UN. The ensuing sections analyse the NGOs' written statements, the NGOs' oral statement and the answers of the interviewees.

The advocacy for the right to marry in the NGOs' written statements

Out of the 155 total remarks identified in the written statements, 12 mention same-sex couples, marriage and family rights for LGBTI individuals, to some extent. Three remarks are actually against any form of recognition of LGBTI couples and family rights for LGBTI people, and they were sent by conservative/ religious NGOs.[174] Out of the remaining nine, three were sent in response to the

---

174 A/HRC/19/NGO/43 *Joint Written Statement Submitted by Caritas Internationalis (International Confederation of Catholic Charities), New Humanity, the Association*

resolutions on traditional values, asking the HR Council to consider a more pluralistic definition of family (1.9%).[175] I argue in this book that the broader political context in which LGBTI TANs operate shapes the way in which gatekeeper NGOs name human rights violations and strategically frame their legal analysis to influence the international human rights debate. Therefore, 1.9% of the total remarks address family rights for LGBTI people, but only as a reaction to opposing TANs and governments.

The other six remarks related to the right to marry for LGBTI individuals constitute 3.9% of the total. Two written statements were sent commenting on states' behaviour. One commends Ireland on the commitment to hold a marriage equality referendum,[176] and in the other Amnesty calls upon Australia to end discrimination on grounds of SOGI and, in particular, to allow same-sex couples to marry.[177] Finally, four remarks discuss marriage equality per se;[178] three are from the Transnational Radical Party (TRP) and one from Article 19.

TRP identifies among the different types of discrimination on the grounds of sexual orientation that "gay-marriage still remains illegal in the majority of UN Member States or is not recognized internationally as a civil right".[179] TRP believes that "the time is ripe to promote [marriage equality] debate also within

---

Points-Coeur, the Associazione Comunità Papa Giovanni XXIII, the Company of the Daughters of Charity of St Vincent de Paul, the Dominicans for Justice an d Peace – Order of Preachers, the International Organization for the Right to Education and Freedom of Education (OIDEL), the World Union of Catholic Women's Organizations (HR Council, 2012); A/ HRC/31/NGO/155 *Joint Written Statement Submitted by Global Helping to Advance Women and Children* (HR Council, 2016); A/HRC/NGO/193 *Written Statement Submitted by the Society for the Protection of Unborn Children (SPUC)* (HR Council, 2016).

175 A/HRC/AC/7/NGO/1 *Joint Written Statement Submitted by the Association for Women's Rights, the International Planned Parenthood Federation, Action Canada for Population and Development, the Asian Forum for Human Rights and Development, the Cairo Institute for Human Rights Studies, the Canadian HIV/AIDS Legal Network, the Centre for Reproductive Rights, the Centre for Women's Global Leadership, Development Alternatives with Women for a New Era, Human Rights Watch, the International Commission of Jurists, the International Lesbian Gay Bisexual Transgender Intersex Association, the International Movement Against All Forms of Discrimination and Racism, the International Service for Human Rights, the International Women's Health Coalition, IPAS, Italian Association for Women in Development, the Federation for Women and Family Planning, the Swedish Federation for Lesbian Gay Bisexual Transgender Rights, Women for Women's Human Rights, – New Ways, the Women's International League for Peace and Freedom, Asian Pacific Forum on Women, Law and Development* (HR Council, 2011); A/HRC/AC/8/NGO/4 *Written Statement Submitted by the Canadian HIV/AIDS Legal Network* (HR Council, 2012); A/ HRC/27/NGO/77, above n 73.

176 A/HRC/25/NGO/52, above n 49.

177 A/HRC/17/NGO/51 *Written Statement Submitted by Amnesty International* (HR Council, 2011).

178 A/HRC/1/NGO/33, above n 9; A/HRC/19/NGO/124 *Written Statement Submitted by the International Society for Human Rights* (HR Council, 2012); E/CN.4/2004/ NGO/191, above n 9; E/CN.4/2006/NGO/162, above n 9.

179 A/HRC/1/NGO/33, above n 9, at 2; E/CN.4/2006/NGO/162, above n 9, at 2.

the United Nations system".[180] Moreover, Article 19 postulates a revised International Bill of Rights that at Article 16 reads: "People of full age have the right to marry".[181] Therefore, it is proposed as a gender-neutral definition of marriage. Although these two NGOs are Western NGOs, and especially Article 19 is a prominent human rights NGO, they have not been identified as gatekeepers in the LGBTI TAN.

The advocacy for the right to marry at the UPR

Out of the 689 remarks identified in the NGOs' oral statements, 29 are directed to the right to marry and to form a family of LGBTI people, which represents 4.2% of the total. Among these 29 remarks, some distinctions can be made.

First, the majority of the remarks refer to some forms of legal recognition of same-sex couples' rights, including the legal recognition of family rights. Indeed, ACPD noted that Colombia did not implement its national court decisions to allow same-sex couples the same rights and benefits of different sex couples.[182] ILGA-Europe – sometimes with the support of other NGOs – noted that same-sex couples are discriminated against, and/or called upon states to eliminate such discrimination, during the UPR of the Yugoslav Republic of Macedonia,[183] Switzerland,[184] Romania,[185] Malta,[186] Slovakia,[187] Latvia,[188] Greece,[189] Poland,[190] VietNam[191] and Albania.[192] Similarly, COC encouraged Estonia[193] and Lithuania[194] to allow same-sex couples the same rights and benefits of different sex couples, and ACPD urged Panama to guarantee legal equality to same-sex couples.[195]

I discuss in this book that the advocacy for the right to marry is controversial and often badly received by many states, especially non-Western states. In some occasions, some other advocacy framework, such as the right of same-sex couples to enjoy some forms of legal recognition, can be less threatening for states and can represent a compromise solution. Therefore, NGOs do not invoke the right to marry for LGBTI people; instead they carefully frame same-sex couples' issues

---

180 E/CN.4/2004/NGO/191, above n 9, at 3.
181 A/HRC/19/NGO/124, above n 178, at [4].
182 A/HRC/10/29, above n 82, at [653].
183 A/HRC/12/50, above n 83, at [615].
184 A/HRC/22/2, above n 80, at [615].
185 A/HRC/8/52, above n 82, at [987].
186 A/HRC/12/50, above n 83, at [321].
187 At [656].
188 A/HRC/18/2, above n 85, at [420].
189 At [524].
190 A/HRC/21/2, above n 85, at [730].
191 A/HRC/26/2, above n 91, at [860].
192 A/HRC/27/2, above n 82, at [388].
193 A/HRC/17/2, above n 80, at [670].
194 A/HRC/19/2, above n 80, at [751].
195 A/HRC/30/2, above n 80, at [524].

in a less threatening way. A clear example of an exceptionally narrow advocacy for same-sex couples rights is the oral statement delivered by COC and ILGA, which encouraged China to recognise the victim of same-sex couples' domestic violence.[196] In this way, the two NGOs start to carefully introduce same-sex couples' protection in the Chinese legal system but maintain a fundamental rights framework (protection from violence).

Moreover, the right to form a family is a particularly important right for LGBTI couples because they might not be able to form a family unless through adoption or assisted reproductive treatments. In much domestic legislation, couples need to be married to access these family rights, such as the right to adopt children and the right to access assisted reproductive treatments. Therefore, to advocate for some forms of legal recognition of unmarried same-sex couples, some NGOs urge states to allow same-sex couples to enjoy their right to form a family, without discrimination. For example, ACPD noted significant obstacles for LGBTI people to enjoy reproductive rights in Mexico[197] and urged Portugal to eliminate the legal obstacles that prevent same-sex partners from co-adopting a child.[198] COC urged New Zealand to address inequality in parenting.[199] ILGA-Europe called upon Hungary to take specific action to address discriminatory laws in the field of family law.[200] COC, ILGA-Europe and GLEN[201] called upon Ireland to address the legal recognition of children in LGBTI households.[202] These NGOs invoke the right of same-sex couples to form a family, without explicitly mentioning the right to marry.

In addressing same-sex couples' issues in a non-threatening way, or at least in a less threatening way, gatekeeper NGOs prevent unwanted backlashes. In doing so they minimise their interference in the internal affairs of peripheral NGOs and LGBTI communities living in the states under UPR. Because gatekeeper NGOs minimise their misuse of power when they do not interfere with LGBTI communities and peripheral NGOs,[203] this section show that gatekeeper NGOs strive to act democratically.

Finally, there are eight remarks dealing with marriage equality, which is 1.2% of the 689 remarks identified in this analysis. Gatekeeper NGOs still operate in a non-threatening way because they addressed seven oral remarks to Western states, or to states that usually support LGBTI rights at the UN. ILGA highlighted the lack of law on marriage equality in Chile;[204] noted that the Dominican

---

196 A/HRC/25/2, above n 80, at [832].

197 At [544].

198 A/HRC/27/2, above n 82, at [518].

199 A/HRC/12/50, above n 83, at [348].

200 A/HRC/18/2, above n 85, at [633].

201 I could not identify the full name of the organization "GLEN" in A/HRC/19/2.

202 A/HRC/19/2, above n 80, at [560].

203 See in general, Jennifer C Rubenstein "The Misuse of Power, Not Bad Representation: Why It Is beside the Point That No One Elected Oxfam" (2014) 22(2) *Journal of Political Philosophy* 204 at 219.

204 A/HRC/26/2, above n 91, at [430].

Republic has put in place various measures to explicitly exclude LGBTI people, such as the 2010 Constitution's definition of marriage;[205] and called upon Canada to amend its refugees' legislation to recognise same-sex spouses and LGBTI parents.[206] COC noted that the Italian Parliament has two bills on marriage equality and one bill on civil unions, which are sitting at the Senate with no scheduled discussion.[207] ILGA and Human Rights Law Centre noted that marriage was a key area on inequality in Australia[208] and, similarly, ILGA-Europe and Australian Coalition for Equality called upon Australia to reconsider its position on marriage equality.[209] The British Humanist Association noted that Latvia legislation did not respect the non-discrimination of the right to marry and to form a family.[210]

In sum, among the eight remarks dealing with marriage, seven oral remarks are addressed towards Chile, Dominican Republic, Canada, Italy, Australia and Latvia, which already allow a certain margin of protection of LGBTI people's rights, and which are usually in favour of LGBTI people's rights.[211] However, it should be noted that on one occasion, a gatekeeper NGO, OutRight, called upon Malawi to repeal the discriminatory section in the national marriage law.[212] The gatekeeper NGO does not explicitly call upon Malawi to legalise marriage equality. Instead, OutRight asked Malawi to avoid an explicit ban on marriage equality. This is a slight difference, but still, this gatekeeper NGO should abstain from commenting upon marriage during the UPR of Malawi because this can be seen as highly provocative and trigger unwanted backlash.

Interviewees' opinions on the right to marry

Out of the 90 items coded in the interviews, seven mention the right to marry (7.8%), and three mention the right to form a family, and family rights in general (3.3%). In particular, organizations that consider marriage equality as an important issue for their domestic advocacy are all Western NGOs, as they are based in Italy,[213] Switzerland[214] and Australia.[215] Furthermore, three interviewees mention that they advocate for family rights of LGBTI couples in their states – namely, the right of LGBTI parent-families to be legally recognised in Hungary,[216] the right

---

205 At [826].

206 A/HRC/24/2, above n 80, at [656].

207 A/HRC/28/2, above n 82, at [415].

208 A/HRC/31/2, above n 82, at [815].

209 A/HRC/17/2, above n 80, at [478].

210 A/HRC/32/2, above n 80, at [1006].

211 See Chapter 4 and Appendix 4.

212 A/HRC/30/2, above n 80, at [462].

213 Arcigay, above n 167; Associazione Radicale Certi Diritti (ARCD), above n 166; Rete Lenford, above n 161; interview ILGA-Europe (Phone call, 12 November 2015).

214 Pink Cross, above n 144.

215 ILGA-Oceania, above n 148.

216 Hungarian LGBT Alliance, above n 166.

to access in-vitro fertilisation for lesbian women in Malta[217] and joint adoption rights for LGBTI couples in civil partnership in Switzerland.[218] The next section analyses all the findings on the advocacy for the right to marry and its significance.

Marriage equality has a low priority in the transnational LGBTI advocacy agenda

The central theme of my book is researching how TANs decide the advocacy agenda, name human rights violations and strategically present legal analysis to advance LGBTI. In particular, I argue that the internetwork relations between gatekeeper and peripheral NGOs, and the broader political context in which the TAN operates, shape the advocacy agenda. Therefore, the right to marry should have a low priority in the advocacy agenda of the LGBTI TAN, if LGBTI gatekeeper NGOs wish to not impose perceived Western priorities upon the NGOs working in the periphery of the network, and if they wish to frame LGBTI issues in a way that maximises their advocacy. In other words, I use the marriage equality analysis as a litmus test of my argument because I claim LGBTI gatekeeper NGOs operate democratically by building the LGBTI TAN from below, and they avoid controversial advocacy framework. The findings of Chapters 3 and 4 showed that LGBTI gatekeeper NGOs avoid advocating for the right to marry because they fear conservative/religious backlash. Moreover, the findings of the NGOs' written and oral statements and the interviews addressed in this chapter further confirm my litmus test.

Marriage and family issues are raised on a number of limited occasions by LGBTI and human rights NGOs submitting written statements to the HR Council. First, the written statements sent to address family rights for LGBTI people are sent as a reaction to the attempt of conservative/religious TANs to limit the rights of LGBTI people. Second, the NGOs' written statements that address directly marriage equality are submitted by NGOs that are not gatekeepers within the LGBTI networks. Third, the only gatekeeper NGO that comments on marriage equality is Amnesty, but it criticises Australia's human rights record, which cannot be considered as a misuse of power because Australia is a Western state that already provides some basic human rights for LGBTI communities.

Moreover, marriage and family issues are seldom raised during the UPR process. In particular, when these issues are mentioned, these are framed in the least threatening way possible. In most of the oral statements delivered during the UPR process that deals with same-sex couples' rights, NGOs invoke some form of legal recognition of same-sex couples' rights, including family rights. This is a much less threatening advocacy framework when compared to marriage equality, and it is a compromise solution between LGBTI people's rights and states' interests. In addition, only 1.25% of the oral remarks advocate for marriage equality.

---

217 Malta LGBT Movement, above n 157.
218 Pink Cross, above n 144.

In general, all these remarks are addressed to states like Canada, Australia and New Zealand, which already provide a large margin of protection of LGBTI people's rights and are part of the pro-LGBTI rights bloc at the UN.

Still, I could detect one case of misuse of power with OutRight's call upon Malawi to repeal the discriminatory section in their national marriage law. Even though this is not an open advocacy for marriage equality, this is a misuse of power and an interference that could be avoided. It should be noted that sometimes national NGOs and associations ask gatekeeper NGOs to bring their grievances before the HR Council because they do not have the ECOSOC consultative status to do so on their own behalf. If this is the case, OutRight would have not misused their power and interfered in peripheral NGOs' affairs, but they would have just complied with the requests of local activists. However, there is no evidence in the report of the HR Council that OutRight is delivering these comments on behalf of other domestic and peripheral NGOs and, therefore, this can only remain a speculation.

Finally, a minority of interviewees said that the right to marry was an important priority for their advocacy. In particular, when concerns related to marriage are raised, these are addressed towards Western states, where LGBTI people already have some rights protection. In any case, marriage and family equality are not considered important for the global LGBTI TAN, rather they are domestic goals.[219]

The ensuing section provides some final considerations on the advocacy for the right to marry by further investigating interviewees' opinions on the right to marry. It is discussed that the right to marry has a low priority within the network and that LGBTI gatekeeper NGOs do not want to impose the advocacy for the right to marry upon NGOs working in the periphery of the network.

Marriage, couple recognition and family rights as national concerns: the flexibility of the advocacy for the right to marry

Interviewees representing gatekeeper NGOs respond that they have a flexible advocacy agenda regarding the right to marry for LGBTI people. They said they have one priority in one state and one priority in another because the right to marry and to form a family cannot always be advocated.[220]

In particular, ILGA-Europe's interviewee explains that ILGA-Europe deals with states in the entire European continent and that issues vary largely. Therefore, not all the peripheral NGOs need or wish to have support in regard to the right to marry. Although marriage and family equality are important for the LGBTI communities, these types of claims are advocated for in states where

---

219 ILGA-Europe (Skype call, 21 August 2015), above n 142; interview LGBT Denmark (Skype call, 2 April 2016); Malta LGBT Movement, above n 157.
220 Interview ILGA-Europe (Skype call, 15 July 2015).

LGBTI organizations are well established; i.e. where LGBTI NGOs do not need the support of the network or of gatekeeper NGOs to achieve their goals. Instead, in states where LGBTI activists are not able to set up an NGO or to organise a Pride Parade, and they are not able to be visible as LGBTI people and express themselves, they are not able to fight discrimination on grounds of SOGII effectively.[221] In the interviewee's words:[222]

> Countries where freedoms of assembly are difficult, hate crimes are unpunished, hate speeches are rampant; in my personal view those are the issues that matter. Of course things like same-sex marriage are important, but those countries where these things are possible are the ones where the organizations are advanced and they are pretty keen to do it themselves, they don't need support. There could be a lot of useful work around it, but in other countries where things are not good, until they get freedom of expression, freedom of assembly and things like that, they can't begin to combat discrimination effectively.

Therefore, for ILGA-Europe it is more important to work to enhance the domestic political opportunities of LGBTI NGOs, so that LGBTI activists can advocate freely at home on what they believe to be relevant rather than imposing marriage equality advocacy.[223]

Furthermore, the interviewee from ILGA-Oceania explains that their branch needs to deal with a lot of different issues. For some of the Pacific Islands the priority is decriminalising same-sex sexual behaviours, while in New Zealand the priority is transgender people's rights, and in Australia it is indeed marriage equality.[224] It is therefore important for ILGA-Oceania to ask for the opinions of their partners in the Pacific and act accordingly.[225] On a similar note, ILGA's interviewee stresses that they let their NGO partners decide whether marriage equality is a priority for them or not,[226] and therefore marriage equality is something that is relevant only in some parts of the world.

The fact that the interviewees from the gatekeeper NGOs (ILGA, ILGA-Europe, and ILGA-Oceania as part of ILGA) maintain that they do not seek to impose marriage equality in the advocacy agenda of their peripheral partners is a major finding. Many authors stress that gatekeeper NGOs – because

---

221 Similar views have been confirmed by the interviewee from Malta LGBTIQ Rights Movement who explained that ILGA focuses on the national level and working to build the capacity of national NGOs so that they can lobby their own governments.

222 ILGA-Europe (Skype call, 21 August 2015), above n 142.

223 Ibid. Similar opinions have been expressed by another interviewee from ILGA-Europe. ILGA-Europe (Skype call, 15 July 2015), above n 220.

224 On 9 December 2017, the Parliament of Australia amended the Marriage Act 1961 (Australia) to allow same-sex couples to marry. See, Marriage Amendment (Definition and Religious Freedoms) Act 2017 (Australia).

225 ILGA-Oceania, above n 148.

226 Interview ILGA-World (Skype call, 13 April 2016).

of their social power and their position in the networks – impose marriage equality advocacy in the periphery, and in doing so they misuse their power. Rather, these interviews suggest that gatekeeper NGOs consider marriage equality as a flexible goal, useful to be advocated in some states, not much in others.

Still, it is important to emphasise the fact that while marriage and family equality are not pressing issues for the interviewees this is not due to negative opinions towards marriage per se. The following sub-paragraphs investigate the interviewees' opinions on marriage and family equality, not as an advocacy item, but as a principle.

"In general, we don't advocate for marriage equality, although we support it": interviewees' opinions on marriage

Even though marriage and family equality are of a low priority in the LGBTI TANs' advocacy agenda, my interviewees express positive attitudes towards these goals. For example, ILGA's interviewee stresses that when a state passes legislation favourable to LGBTI couples, the organization always issues press releases to spread the good news and records the positive law change in their yearly reports.[227]

The opinions of many interviewees can be summarised in what the interviewee from Jerusalem Open Society says: "In general, we don't advocate for marriage equality, although we support it".[228] When directly asked about marriage and family equality, 18 interviewees expressed positive attitudes.[229] In particular, some interviewees stressed that LGBTI couples should be allowed the same rights and benefits of heterosexual couples because whether LGBTI couples want to marry or not, they should be treated equally to heterosexual couples.[230] In the words of the interviewee from Bisdak Pride:[231]

> It is necessary that the state provides some legal, civil, and political protections to couples. Because in the first place, they are taxpayers, right? And

---

227 Ibid.

228 Interview Jerusalem Open Society (Skype call, 3 May 2016).

229 Australian Lesbian Medical Association (ALMA), above n 152; Arcigay, above n 167; Bisdak Pride, above n 152; Bisexual Alliance Victoria, above n 72; Blue Diamond Society, above n 150; interview anonymous NGO from Sri Lanka (Questionnaire, 1 April 2016); Federación Estatal de Lesbianas, Gais, Transexuales y Bisexuales (FELGTB), above n 143; GALANG Philippines, above n 145; Hungarian LGBT Alliance, above n 166; ILGA-World (Skype call, 3 April 2016), above n 163; Jerusalem Open Society, above n 228; independent activist in New Zealand, above n 166; Pink Cross, above n 144; independent activist from Singapore, above n 145; ILGA-World (Skype call, 13 April 2016), above n 226; Rete Lenford, above n 161; anonymous NGO from Nigeria, above n 150; anonymous NGO from Saint Lucia, above n 145.

230 Australian Lesbian Medical Association (ALMA), above n 152; ILGA-World (Skype call, 3 April 2016), above n 163; independent activist in New Zealand, above n 166.

231 Bisdak Pride, above n 152.

as taxpayers they deserve to be protected in their civil, legal, and political rights.

Obviously, not all the interviewees expressed only positive comments towards marriage and family equality. Three interviewees from Western states said that there are some people within the LGBTI communities of their states who do not favour marriage particularly as they consider it to be a patriarchal institution; however, LGBTI people who do not want to marry still wish to have the same right to choose as heterosexual people.[232]

Outside Western states the situation is more complicated. The interviewee from Stop AIDS Liberia reports that marriage equality is seen as a "Western ideology" or a "Western lifestyle". The interviewee highlights the influence of anti-LGBTI rhetoric in their advocacy:[233]

> We are not fully ready to advocate these at the moment cause there have been lies created by many that the west is trying to impose marriage equality into our cultural and tradition between same sex couple [sic].

Similarly, the interviewee from Justice for Sisters highlights that marriage equality is a Western notion and a Western type of advocacy agenda. They also believe that the "gay culture" will be affected by marriage equality because sexually and gender diverse communities have always been polyamorous and have seen marriage as a restrictive institution.[234]

If the majority of the interviewees expressed positive opinions with regard to marriage equality, it needs to be understood why the interviewees report that they do not advocate for marriage equality. The ensuing section explains that they choose to do so because marriage equality has a low priority, or it is non-strategic.

Strategy

Whether they support marriage equality, at least in principle, or not, many interviewees say that they do not have a campaign on marriage equality or any specific action planned or made in the past.[235] I identify two reasons why interviewees do not take action on marriage equality. First, the large majority of interviewees (20)

---

232 Australian Lesbian Medical Association (ALMA), above n 152; Arcigay, above n 167; independent activist in New Zealand, above n 166.
233 Stop AIDS Liberia, above n 152.
234 Justice for Sisters, above n 158.
235 Bilitis Resource Center, above n 167; Jerusalem Open Society, above n 228; independent activist from Singapore, above n 145; ILGA-World (Skype call, 13 April 2016), above n 226; Rainbow Sunrise Mapambazuko, above n 154; Unitarian Universalist Association (UUA), above n 151; Swedish Federation for LGBTQ Rights (RFSL) (Skype call, May 2016), above n 159.

state that marriage equality has low priority as opposed to the decriminalisation of same-sex sexual behaviour,[236] visibility,[237] discrimination,[238] violence, unemployment[239] and hate crimes.[240]

Some interviewees from Europe maintain that marriage equality is not a priority for their organization or the LGBTI European TAN. This is because, among Council of Europe member states, there are basic struggles of discrimination and violence towards the LGBTI populations. Marriage equality is a step even further, which the Council of Europe is not yet ready to take.[241] The interviewee from Malta adds that the EU is investing much of its resources in dealing with the economic crisis, the high rate of unemployment in the continent and the refugee crisis; therefore, the attention on LGBTI issues that was given in the past is no longer possible.[242]

Second, interviewees express considerations about strategy. Some interviewees maintain that marriage and family equality is "impossible",[243] or "non-realistic",[244] and "unachievable"[245] in their states. Even when they believe marriage equality would be achieved at some point, they foresee that would not happen for another 30 to 50 years.[246] Moreover, the interviewee from FELGTB considers that the "European system has not the proper competences to legislate about family or social affairs".[247] The interviewee from Hungarian Rainbow Alliance believes that marriage equality may have a better chance at the Council of Europe when Germany rules in favour of marriage equality;[248] this is because of the crucial role played by Germany in European politics.[249]

Furthermore, at the UN level, both the interviewees from United Unionist Association and RFSL respond that advocating for the right to marry at the UN

---

236 Australian Lesbian Medical Association (ALMA), above n 152; independent activist from Singapore, above n 145; anonymous NGO from Saint Lucia, above n 145; anonymous NGO from Sri Lanka, above n 229.

237 Bisexual Alliance Victoria, above n 72.

238 GALANG Philippines, above n 145; Jerusalem Open Society, above n 228; LGBT Centre Mongolia, above n 147; Rainbow Sunrise Mapambazuko, above n 145; Youth Interfaith Forum on Sexuality (YIFoS), above n 156; anonymous NGO from Sri Lanka, above n 229.

239 Justice for Sisters, above n 158.

240 Pink Armenia, above n 145.

241 ILGA-Europe (Skype call, 15 July 2015), above n 220.

242 Malta LGBT Movement, above n 157.

243 Bilitis Resource Center, above n 167.

244 Hungarian LGBT Alliance, above n 166.

245 Rainbow Sunrise Mapambazuko, above n 145.

246 Rete Lenford, above n 161; independent activist from Singapore, above n 145.

247 Federación Estatal de Lesbianas, Gais, Transexuales y Bisexuales (FELGTB), above n 143.

248 Eventually, Germany ruled in favour marriage equality. Andrea Woelke "At Long Last, Germany's Bells Are Ringing for Same-Sex Marriage" *The Guardian* (30 June 2017) www.theguardian.com/commentisfree/2017/jun/30/same-sex-marriage-bill-passed-germany-equal-family-rights (Retrieved 15 July 2017).

249 Hungarian LGBT Alliance, above n 166.

results in activists losing support from states.[250] Advocating for the right to marry "would be very non-strategic and wouldn't get anywhere".[251]

An interesting aspect regarding strategy was raised by the ILGA's interviewee, who explains that the Yogyakarta Principles (YPs) are crucial for setting the advocacy agenda of the LGBTI network working at the UN. Because the YPs do not mention the right to marry for LGBTI people, the interviewee does not believe that they have the legal basis to advocate for the right to marry at the UN.[252] In other words, marriage equality does not make a good strategic argument because the LGBTI TAN is not supported by the YPs, which have largely been accepted by many states.[253]

In sum, the right to marry has a low priority in the advocacy agenda of the global LGBTI network. Gatekeeper NGOs do not impose marriage and family upon their less powerful allies; rather, they prefer a flexible, needs-based approach to tackle human rights violations for those in a sexually and gender diverse community in an effective way. Moreover, the interviewees are not particularly against marriage equality for ideological reasons, rather they consider it has a low priority for the sexually and gender diverse communities they represent, and it is often non-strategic.

Conclusion

To investigate the LGBTI advocacy agenda, first, Chapter 3 analyses the internetwork relations between gatekeeper and peripheral NGOs. Second, Chapter 4 analyses the political opportunities and constraints provided by international organizations, states and other NGOs outside the network (the broader political context). This chapter brings together the dynamics highlighted in Chapter 3 and 4 to identify finally, and in detail, the LGBTI advocacy agenda at the UN.

First, about the internetwork relations between gatekeeper and peripheral NGOs, I argue that to ensure the success of the LGBTI transnational advocacy, LGBTI gatekeeper NGOs work to build the capacity of peripheral NGOs. Chapter 3 demonstrated that gatekeeper NGOs work to strengthen the network horizontally to decentralise their position in the network, partially relinquish their power and build a more efficient network. These dynamics have consequences in the advocacy agenda. Through a combination of quantitative and thematic qualitative analysis of the NGOs' written statements, this chapter (Chapter 5) shows that among the most advocated issues, LGBTI gatekeeper NGOs advocate for those rights that enhance the domestic political opportunities of LGBTI groups and human rights defenders, with the aim of further building the capacity of the domestic NGOs working at the periphery of the network. The strengthening of the peripheral NGOs is beneficial for the overall network because when

---

250 Unitarian Universalist Association (UUA), above n 151.
251 Swedish Federation for LGBTQ Rights (RFSL) (Skype call, 3 May 2016), above n 159.
252 ILGA-World (Skype call, 13 April 2016), above n 226.
253 Mindy Jane Roseman and Alice M Miller, above n 23, at 377.

peripheral NGOs are weak or non-existent they are not sufficiently able to pressure their governments to vote upon resolutions, recommendations and amendments in favour of LGBTI rights.

Second, I argue that LGBTI gatekeeper NGOs use an advocacy framework that maximises their political opportunities and minimises resistance by conservative/religious NGOs. This chapter provides empirical evidence that LGBTI gatekeeper NGOs frame LGBTI rights as an anti-discrimination claim, to maximise the impact of their advocacy. It is shown that because the prohibition of discrimination is a crucial aspect of the international human rights law, NGOs advocate for the prohibition of discrimination on the grounds of SOGII to allow LGBTI people to fully enjoy all the other human rights.

The current chapter highlights that on some occasions LGBTI gatekeeper NGOs should refrain from using that framework. Despite the best efforts of the LGBTI TANs, the prohibition of discrimination framework can still be considered provocative by some conservative/religious states and NGOs. Therefore, it would be good practice for gatekeeper NGOs to focus more on the prohibition of violence against LGBTI people when they comment upon the human rights violations in states like Iran and Nigeria. Unlike the written statements – most of which are sent in general to all UN members – the oral statements delivered during specific states' UPRs refer proportionally less often to SOGII discrimination, making the decriminalisation of same-sex sexual behaviours and prohibition of violence more relevant. Even though the anti-discrimination framework is still predominant in the NGO oral statements, this slight difference highlights that gatekeeper/Western NGOs are careful to not provoke unwanted reactions when they discuss specific states' behaviours, especially some states like Gambia, Sierra Leone, Malawi, Iraq and Cameroon.

Another key finding related to the broader political context in which LGBTI TANs operate is that gatekeeper NGOs' oral statements delivered during the UPR influence, and are influenced by, states' speeches. Some social movement theorists explain that when states repeat NGOs' claims, they amplify and legitimise NGOs' advocacy frameworks. Indeed, some scholars find that states are more likely to raise SOGII issues when these are previously raised by NGOs. This chapter adds to these considerations that NGOs are also influenced by states' claims because they echo states' recommendations. Therefore, NGOs' issue emergence and framing on LGBTI rights at the UN is not only a one-way dynamic in which NGOs influence states' human rights debate, but it is a ricochet effect in which NGOs and states influence each other.

Third, I compared the results of the NGOs' oral and written statements and the interviews. Regarding the comparison between NGOs' written statements and the interviews, it appears that the peripheral NGOs and gatekeeper NGOs share the same priorities, which is further evidence that LGBTI gatekeeper NGOs operate democratically by consulting with the NGOs working in the periphery of the network. However, the interviewees have a more intersectional and multi-layered understanding of discrimination as opposed to the NGOs that write statements to the HR Council. The interviewees have a broader perspective on sexual and gender diversity, and they aim to fight discrimination suffered by LGBTI people in combination with unemployment, poverty, violence, HIV infection and so on. The integration of the intersectional approach proposed by the peripheral NGOs into the advocacy of the gatekeeper NGOs would further strengthen the democratic legitimacy of the gatekeeper NGOs and ensure that the voices of the NGOs working in the periphery of the network are properly represented.

Regarding the comparison between the oral statements and the interviews, there is a point of similarities between the two. Indeed, the analysis of both the oral statements and the interviews shows that NGOs, peripheral and gatekeeper, address LGBTI issues in a practical way that focuses primarily on discrimination but also allows a large discussion of issues related to LGBTI people's security. I explain that the format of the UPR in which NGOs comment upon specific states' human rights records allows NGOs to make practical and targeted recommendations on ways to protect LGBTI people's rights. This is an important finding because it further shows that gatekeeper NGOs listen to and take into consideration peripheral NGOs' views and perspectives. One key similarity between all the findings, oral and written statements and the interviews is the low priority of marriage equality advocacy.

Finally, I investigate whether Western/gatekeeper NGOs – two categories that often overlap – impose perceived Western priorities upon the NGOs working in the periphery of the network. I use the advocacy for the right to marry for LGBTI people as a litmus test of my overall arguments. In other words, if it is true that gatekeeper NGOs operate democratically and frame LGBTI issues in a way that maximise their political opportunities, I should find that they do not impose the advocacy for the right to marry upon the NGOs at the periphery of the network. Through a combination of quantitative and thematic qualitative analysis of the NGOs' written and oral statements, and interviews, this chapter demonstrates that marriage equality is a low priority among the LGBTI NGOs working at the UN. The right to marry is rarely invoked by gatekeeper NGOs and NGOs with ECOSOC consultative status. In addition, the results of the interviews with LGBTI NGO staff members and activists further support such findings by highlighting that even though the majority of the interviewees view marriage rights positively, they prioritise other issues. This finding helps to explain why the right to marry for LGBTI people is not gaining salience in the international human rights debate, despite NGOs' advocacy for the right to equality and non-discrimination for LGBTI people more generally.

In general, LGBTI gatekeeper NGOs act democratically in consultation with their less powerful peripheral partners. They strive to build the network from below, and they do not impose perceived Western values on the wider network, which is an interference and a misuse of their power. In addition, LGBTI gatekeeper NGOs use a prohibition of discrimination framework that usually maximises their opportunities and minimises resistance to their advocacy. Therefore, LGBTI gatekeeper NGOs use mainly, although not exclusively, a prohibition of discrimination framework and avoid invoking the right to marry.

6 Conclusion

Introduction

Article 1 of the Universal Declaration of Human Rights sets forth: "All human beings are born free and equal in dignity and rights".[1] Not by chance "UN Free & Equal" is the title chosen by the former High Commissioner for Human Rights to launch a "global UN public information campaign aimed at promoting equal rights and fair treatment of LGBTI people".[2] However, the idea that LGBTI people are born free and equal just like anybody else is yet contested by some. Many states still violate the human rights of LGBTI people,[3] and many governments even refuse to discuss SOGII as they claim these are "new" concepts that have no space in the international human rights debate.[4] This book researched how NGOs working in TANs name and conceptualise human rights violations, and strategically present legal analysis to decide the advocacy agenda to push the boundaries of international human rights law to cover LGBTI people's rights.

This chapter provides conclusions, highlights the limits of this research and suggests recommendations. It opens with a summary of the chapters, and it highlights the major findings. Moreover, the chapter clarifies some specific aspects in which this study differs from previous studies on the theme. Finally, the chapter provides recommendations to LGBTI activists on how to enforce a more efficient advocacy, and to researchers on how to progress on the study of LGBTI rights advocacy.

---

1 The Universal Declaration of Human Rights, United Nations (adopted 10 December 1948), Article 1.
2 UN Free & Equal "About" (2013) UN Free & Equal www.unfe.org/about/ (Retrieved 31 July 2018).
3 Aengus Carroll and Lucas Ramón Mendos *State-Sponsored Homophobia: A World Survey of Sexual Orientation Laws: Criminalisation, Protection and Recognition* (12th ed, ILGA, Geneva, 2017).
4 See for example, A/70/738 *Letter Dated 3 February 2016 from the Permanent Representative of Swaziland to the United Nations Addressed to the Secretary-General* (2016) at 1; A/C3/65/SR46 *Summary Record of the 46th Meeting (16 November 2010)* (General Assembly, 2011) at [26].

Summary

Chapter 1 introduces the book, and it spells out the research questions and the central arguments of the book. It presents some clarification and context on the topics addressed. Chapter 2 presents the theoretical framework that underpins the arguments of this book. It is argued that the internetwork relations between gatekeeper and peripheral NGOs, and the broad political context in which LGBTI TANs operate, shape the strategic choices of the LGBTI TANs. First, LGBTI gatekeeper NGOs are aware of the complexity of internetwork relations and, therefore, they strive to decentralise their position in the network and partially relinquish their power. To do so, they build the network horizontally and they advocate for those rights that enhance the domestic political opportunities of peripheral NGOs. Second, LGBTI gatekeeper NGOs maximise opportunities and minimise resistance by using a prohibition of discrimination framework because it matches existing human rights treaties, and therefore it is a politically palatable and pragmatic framework. However, the prohibition of discrimination is sometimes a risky strategy because it is still perceived as provocative by some conservative/religious states and NGOs, who interpret the right to equality as a potential threat to their domestic family law. Third, I provide a litmus test to my study, and I claim that, if the first and second arguments are true, then I should find that LGBTI gatekeeper NGOs do not impose the advocacy for the right to marry upon NGOs working at the periphery of the network.

Chapter 3 shows that LGBTI gatekeeper NGOs engage in consultation with peripheral NGOs and create spaces where LGBTI activists from all over the world can network, exchange points of view and get in touch with potential donors. Gatekeeper NGOs can do so by investing part of their resources in sponsoring conferences and workshops, and by providing travel grants for some activists and NGO staff members. Chapter 3 also provides empirical evidence – from the advocacy around the Brazilian resolution, the Argentinian statement and HR Council resolutions on human rights and SOGII – that LGBTI gatekeeper NGOs are coordinating the work of peripheral NGOs and empowering peripheral NGOs to pressure their own governments from below. Because Western/gatekeeper NGOs are often perceived as foreign agents by some conservative/religious states, and their direct interference can be counterproductive, this strategy is useful to demonstrate that LGBTI issues are not only Western rights and they have a large base of supporters in all the regions of the world.

In rebutting the common assumption that NGOs and TANs work non-democratically, Chapter 3 documented a case study of good practice, which can be of example to other human rights networks. Indeed, both interview findings and empirical examples show that LGBTI gatekeeper NGOs invest in building the network from below, on the one hand, by promoting consultation with peripheral NGOs and enforcing a need-based approach, and on the other hand, by strengthening the network horizontally. Through both dynamics, gatekeeper NGOs decentralise their position in the network and consequently they also slowly relinquish their social power. Potentially all human rights, environmental or other types of TANs would benefit from gatekeeper NGOs decentralising their position in the network by handing over part of their social power to the periphery.

In addition to enhancing the democratic accountability of LGBTI TANs, the strategy of developing the network horizontally that is described in Chapter 3 improves the efficiency of the TANs' advocacy. This is because, as is demonstrated in Chapter 3, the peripheral NGOs' role to pressure their own governments from below is crucial to advance the debate on LGBTI rights. Moreover, the horizontal development of LGBTI TANs has two consequences in the advocacy agenda setting. On the one hand, stronger and empowered peripheral NGOs that work in consultation with gatekeeper NGOs can influence the advocacy agenda decision-making with their specific 'peripheral' perspectives. On the other hand, gatekeeper NGOs advocate for those rights that enhance the domestic political opportunities of the peripheral NGOs.

However, TANs do not work in a vacuum; rather their advocacy is influenced by other NGOs and states, for better or for worse (the broader political context). Chapter 4 discusses the themes of alliance and political alignment and demonstrates that LGBTI gatekeeper NGOs frame LGBTI issues in a way that maximises their political opportunities and minimises resistance. To gather enough consensus among states and to convince non-aligned states to support LGBTI rights, LGBTI gatekeeper NGOs look for a 'minimum common denominator' and often frame LGBTI issues as fundamental human rights protection and prohibition of discrimination. Moreover, Chapter 4 shows that despite LGBTI TANs' best efforts to minimise opposition, conservative/religious NGOs and states still use a 'slippery slope' argument to prevent the advancement of LGBTI people's rights. As a consequence, even though there are some states and international organizations allied to LGBTI TANs, to be able to find a compromise between opposing views they also need to use cautionary tactics and avoid invoking the right to marry. Furthermore, the analysis of the HR Council's resolutions on traditional values and on the protection of the family documents that coalitions of conservative NGOs and states mobilise against LGBTI rights by juxtaposing the right to marry to the anti-discrimination principle. In other words, LGBTI TANs are still facing a difficult battle for equality before the UN, even with the existing legal tool available, like the three HR Council resolutions on human rights and SOGI.

Finally, these dynamics discussed in Chapters 3 and 4 are used as interpretative lenses to finally dissect the LGBTI TANs' advocacy agenda at the UN. This is discussed in detail in Chapter 5.

Chapter 5 tackles the core question of this research by spelling out how LGBTI TANs frame LGBTI issues before the HR Council. First, LGBTI gatekeeper NGOs strategically frame LGBTI rights mainly as an anti-discrimination claim, with some exceptions. Often gatekeeper NGOs use elimination of violence or decriminalisation of same-sex sexual behaviour frameworks when they comment upon some non-Western states' human rights record. This is because in some cases the anti-discrimination framework is considered provocative and other rights are more appropriate. Second, among the NGOs' written and oral statements and the interview findings, the right to marry is a low priority. The interviewees explain that they consider marriage to be a national goal rather than a transnational one. They highlight that at the international level they have more pressing issues to deal with and they consider marriage equality to be non-strategic. Furthermore, Chapter 5 shows that the advocacy agenda identified in the written and oral statements submitted to the HR Council is similar to the interview findings. This consistency in findings confirms that, in general, gatekeeper NGOs do engage in consultations with peripheral NGOs and take into consideration peripheral NGOs' needs.

Because imposing marriage equality in the advocacy agenda of peripheral NGOs can be an interference and a misuse of power, Chapter 5 shows that LGBTI gatekeeper NGOs do not actually impose marriage equality on their less powerful partners working at the UN, and therefore they do not act hegemonically. Chapter 5 documents another example of good practice. Minimising the misuse of power should be the aim of gatekeeper NGOs in any human rights, environmental or other types of TANs, and researchers in the field of TAN theories should identify misuses of powers and recommend ways to overcome such misuses. The next section notes some specific aspects in which this study differs from previous studies on LGBTI advocacy.

Differences with other studies

In general, my study produces different outcomes in comparison to other studies because I use a combined approach of TAN theories and social movement theories, while many studies into LGBTI advocacy have a primary focus either on the domestic or on the international level. The way in which I collected my sample, interpreted my findings and ultimately drew my conclusions has been driven by the fact that I have developed a merged use of these two approaches. More studies, such as my study, which take into consideration domestic factors along with international and transnational factors, would deepen the understanding of LGBTI and human rights advocacy.

Some differences between my book and other studies relate to identity, legal tactics and NGOs' legal status. First, a number of authors criticise Western NGOs for imposing the LGBTI label, which is based on typically Western LGBTI identities, upon non-Western sexually and gender diverse communities.[5] On the contrary, because of the internetwork relation approach used in this research, I find that some of the interviewees from gatekeeper NGOs understand that the LGBTI label is not always recognised by non-Western advocates and therefore they work with peripheral NGOs to better understand sexually and gender diverse identities and to make sure that really no one is left behind.

---

5   See for example Leila J Rupp "The European Origins of Transnational Organizing: The International Committee for Sexual Equality" in Phillip Ayoub and David Paternotte (eds) *LGBT Activism and the Making of Europe: A Rainbow Europe* (Palgrave Macmillan, Basingstoke, 2014) 29 at 44.

Second, a number of authors discuss how LGBTI NGOs working in non-Western states might prefer non-legal tactics, such as support and education towards sexually and gender diverse communities.[6] Although many of the interviewees highlight that they do engage in non-legal tactics – such as support for sexually and gender diverse vulnerable populations, education on LGBTI issues in schools, and HIV/AIDS prevention – many interviewees from non-Western NGOs report that they also engage in legal tactics both domestically and internationally.[7] This result is a direct consequence of the use of transnational advocacy approaches. As I selected my sample from the NGOs that are part of LGBTI TANs, inevitably I found that my interviewees strongly believe that legal tactics are indeed important to advance the rights of sexually and gender diverse people.

Third, in drawing from some authors' studies, Chapter 2 claims that the legal status of peripheral NGOs is important for the development of the LGBTI TANs because without legal status activists are limited in their advocacy. In fact, when groups do not have domestic legal status they can be prevented from obtaining funding and they have limited chances to be heard by international organizations. However, from the interviews it emerges that the lack of legal status is not an obstacle to participate in the LGBTI TANs per se. Some of the interviewees from gatekeeper NGOs have a good understanding of the limits of LGBTI advocacy in many parts of the world, and indeed they maintain that activists can be part of the LGBTI TAN even when they are not legal entities as long as they have some form of accountability, such as a webpage or a Facebook group.

Finally, the crucial difference between my research and other studies regards advocacy for the right to marry. Many studies comment that marriage equality is at the centre of Western LGBTI advocacy, and it is often imposed on the advocacy agenda at the periphery of the network. In particular, Osterbur and Kiel use a mixed methodology based on hyperlink and content analysis, and they identify COC as a gatekeeper NGO within the European LGBTI TAN. They find some tentative evidence that COC influences the advocacy agenda of their less powerful partners by imposing marriage equality claims. My book reaches an opposite conclusion because of the different methodology used. Osterbur and

---

6　Marc Epprecht "Sexual Minorities, Human Rights and Public Health Strategies in Africa" (2012) 111 *African Affairs* 223 at 236; Ashley Currier "Deferral of Legal Theory, a Global LGBT Social Movement Organization's Perspective" in Mary Bernstein, Scott Barclay, and Anna-Maria Marshall (eds) *Queer Mobilizations: LGBT Activists Confront the Law* (New York University Press, New York, 2009) 21 at 32–37.

7　Interview Stop AIDS Liberia (Questionnaire, 30 May 2016); interview Bilitis Resource Center (Questionnaire, 14 May 2016); interview Bisdak Pride (Skype call, 20 May 2016); interview Blue Diamond Society (Skype call, 1 March 2016); interview Campaign Against Homophobia (Skype call, 13 May 2016); interview anonymous NGO from Sri Lanka (Questionnaire, 1 April 2016); interview GALANG Philippines (Skype call, 25 May 2016); interview Justice for Sisters (Skype call, 16 May 2016); interview LGBT Centre Mongolia (Skype call, 9 March 2016); interview Rainbow Sunrise Mapambazuko (Questionnaire, 5 April 2016); interview anonymous NGO from Saint Lucia (Skype call, 17 June 2016); interview anonymous NGO from Nigeria (Questionnaire, 2 June 2016); interview Pink Armenia (Skype call, 21 April 2016); interview Hungarian LGBT Alliance (Skype call, 29 April 2016).

Kiel highlight among the limits of their study that hyperlink analysis might not be able to detect collaborations between NGOs that happened "behind the scene",[8] in other words, that do not leave internet footprints.

On the contrary, my study uses a triangulation of three data sets to provide a holistic picture of the complex dynamics analysed. In addition to NGOs' web-pages, blog posts and other internet material, I have also used archival UN legal and official documents, and semi-structured interviews to investigate my research questions. Therefore, I discovered that marriage equality has low importance for LGBTI NGOs, both gatekeeper and peripherals. In sum, and different to other researchers, I demonstrate that gatekeeper NGOs do not use their social power to impose a perceived Western advocacy agenda – in particular the right to marry – on the periphery of the network.

Despite activists' best intentions, the prohibition of discrimination framework can be used against LGBTI people in a slippery slope argument tailored by con-servative/religious NGOs and states. In other words, the prohibition of discrimi-nation framework can still be a risky strategy and it might create an impasse in the advancement of LGBTI human rights debate. The ensuing section provides some ideas on how to avoid conservative/religious NGOs and states' backlash, and advance LBGTI people's rights.

Recommendations for LGBTI activists and human rights practitioners

My research identifies a problem with the use of the anti-discrimination frame-work in relation to SOGII status. This is because conservative/religious NGOs and governments use a slippery slope argument to block any advancement of the rights of LGBTI people, alleging concerns related to their domestic family laws. One can advance the argument that the LGBTI TAN might frame their issues differently in order to avoid such reaction, and Chapter 2 flags some tentative suggestions for alternative frameworks – for example, a prohibition of violence framework, the concept of sexual rights or other concepts such as justice, libera-tion or self-determination.

The book argues that LGBTI gatekeeper NGOs prefer an anti-discrimination framework because it enhances TANs' ability to be heard by international organi-zations. The prohibition of discrimination on the grounds of SOGII allows for conservative/religious NGOs to use a slippery slope argument, and indeed gate-keeper NGOs do sometimes refrain from invoking the right to equality. How-ever, the prohibition of discrimination framework is the way to go. I suggest two possible ways in which LGBTI TANs might consider tweaking their anti-discrim-ination claims, and one recommendation for gatekeeper NGOs.

First, Chapter 3 discusses an example in which the views of one peripheral NGO were different from the gatekeeper NGOs' mainstream opinion. In 2016,

---

8   Megan Osterbur and Christina Kiel "A Hegemon Fighting for Equal Rights: The Dominant Role of COC Nederland in the LGBT Transnational Advocacy Network" (2016) 17(2) *Global Networks* 234 at 250.

the Coalition of African Lesbians (CAL) distanced themselves from the advocacy for a Special Rapporteur on SOGI human rights violations. CAL's point of view was marginalised and the LGBTI TAN, led by ILGA, kept lobbying for and obtained the long-waited appointment of a Special Rapporteur on SOGI issues.[9] CAL's view was that the mandate of the Special Rapporteur focusing on SOGI issues would have excluded many vulnerable communities who are persecuted because of their sexuality and gender. In other words, CAL called for broader understanding of the human rights violations suffered by people because of their sexuality and gender, such as intersex people, sex workers and people living with HIV. CAL's approach allows a deeper understanding of the multi-layered discrimination deriving from sexuality, gender, health, poverty, unemployment and so on. CAL is not alone in advancing this approach, which, however, is not yet the mainstream. In fact, some of the interviewees who participated in this study said that they take an intersectional approach to tackle multi-layered discrimination suffered by the vulnerable communities they work with.

Evidence reported in Chapter 5 shows that peripheral NGOs, big and small, are aware of the intersectional nature of multi-layered discrimination and the interconnection of discrimination with issues related to poverty, unemployment, violence and so on. Gatekeeper NGOs could do more to develop an advocacy strategy that would take these aspects into account even more. There are driving forces within the LGBTI TAN that are already seeking solutions that account for a more comprehensive advocacy; it is up to LGBTI gatekeeper NGOs to take on board these approaches.

A second possible tweak to the anti-discrimination approach regards the possibility of allowing states to maintain a type of margin of appreciation on the prohibition of discrimination, at least as a temporary measure. The LGBTI TAN could keep advocating for a prohibition of discrimination on the grounds of SOGII but encompass a clause that excludes the right to marry. This margin of appreciation would encourage states to stop discriminating against LGBTI individuals and at the same time would allow them to maintain some discriminatory behaviours, namely regarding the right to marry.[10] Such an approach should prevent conservative/religious NGOs and states from attempting to perpetuate the slippery slope argument. In this way, LGBTI TANs could slowly create consensus among states about LGBTI people's rights and possibly advocate more strongly for complete human rights protections in the future.

A third recommendation is for the two major gatekeeper NGOs of the human rights advocacy network, Amnesty and HRW. These two major gatekeeper NGOs do not often advocate for LGBTI rights during the UPR process. Indeed, out of the 301 paragraphs in which NGOs made references to LGBTI issues, Amnesty appears in 23 of them, and HRW in only nine. Even when they comment upon

---

9 A/HRC/RES/32/2 *Protection Against Violence and Discrimination Based on Sexual Orientation and Gender Identity* (HR Council, 2016) at [4].

10 One similar approach, see also, Dominic McGoldrick "The Development and Status of Sexual Orientation Discrimination under International Human Rights Law" (2016) 16(4) *Human Rights Law Review* 613 at 660.

LGBTI rights, they do so in a rather superficial way. Even though this lack can be justified with the broad range of human rights issues that these two gatekeeper NGOs cover in their mandate, it also might contribute to the scarce visibility of SOGII issues during the UPR process. Because of their central position in the network, and because of their major influence in the human rights debate, more interventions from Amnesty and HRW would go a long way to support LGBTI people's human rights. Finally, my remaining recommendations are addressed to scholars.

Limitations of the study and recommendations for future research

Studying the official documents of the UN was challenging. As much as the UN provides public records of intergovernmental meetings, much of the NGO advocacy happens behind the scenes. Findings from interviews and some NGOs' webpages filled up some of the gaps left by these public records, but that was not always possible.

Approaching suitable interviewee partners was challenging as well. I am grateful to the 36 individuals who agreed to take part in this study, but I approached many more potential interviewees who did not reply to my emails or declined to answer my questions. In particular, well-established NGOs, such as Amnesty and HRW, declined to participate in the study. On a similar point, the majority of the interviewees work for general LGBTI organizations; some of the interviewees focus on transgender issues, one is part of a dedicated bisexual organization, and none work specifically on intersex people's issues. Repeating a similar study with more time, more experience and more resources would result in a larger and more variegated interviewee pool, arguably allowing a better understanding of the impact of NGOs in the work of the UN.

Furthermore, I was only able to access NGOs' websites written in English, French or Italian. Therefore, I may have missed out on a greater range of valuable information, which would have helped to fill some of the gaps highlighted above. These limitations, and the fact that when my data collection was concluded I realised that some questions had gone unanswered, are the basis of my recommendations for future academic research on LGBTI activism.

First, regarding the archival material, the book focuses mainly, although not exclusively, on the HR Council because the research needed to be narrowed to a manageable and still meaningful data collection. The HR Council is considered to be a promising avenue by the activists working with the UN. However, when gathering NGOs' written statements sent to the HR Council, I found numerous NGOs' written statements dealing with SOGII issues addressed to other UN commissions and councils.[11] A textual analysis of NGOs' written statements

---

11 For example, E/CN.15/2015/NGO/3 *Joint Statement Submitted by the Academic Council on the United Nations System* (Commission on Crime Prevention and Criminal Justice, 2015); E/CN.5/2017/NGO/10 *Statement Submitted by International Federation on Ageing* (Commission for Social Development, 2016).

on SOGII issues addressed to, for example, the UN Commission on the Status of Women, or the UN Commission for Social Development, would further the understanding of the advocacy agenda of the LGBTI TAN working at the UN.

Second, I tried to interview activists from all world regions. However, Western European NGOs and Asian-Pacific NGOs are overrepresented compared to any other region. It is easy to imagine that Western European NGOs are overrepresented because the LGBTI advocacy has deep roots in Western Europe, but I cannot explain why so many Asian-Pacific NGOs responded to my interview call. I can only make one hypothesis. While I was conducting the interviews, I noted that many of the interviewees from Asian-Pacific NGOs were happy to be part of the study, and I think they saw the occasion to be part of it as a chance for gaining visibility. In particular, some interviewees were particularly keen to tell me stories of abuses suffered by their friends and fellow activists. Unfortunately, these stories did not find a place in this research because of the nature of the research questions, but the interactions with Asian-Pacific LGBTI activists, and especially their stories and their willingness to be part of the study, made me realise that it would be useful to design a case study on the Asian-Pacific LGBTI TAN.

Third, one of the focuses of this research is on the internetwork relations between gatekeeper NGOs and peripheral NGOs; however, some of the interviewees stressed that part of their goals is decided in a way that accommodates the agenda of their funding agencies. It emerged from my interviews that the theme of funding is a relevant one because numerous interviewees reported that they have limited resources, do not have permanent staff and survive thanks to volunteers.[12] However, funding issues are not addressed in detail, and there is room to develop future research that investigates how funding agencies can shape the advocacy agenda of the LGBTI TANs. In particular, two aspects have emerged from the interviews and would require further investigation; one is the relations between domestic NGOs and international donors, and the other is between domestic NGOs and domestic donors.

On the one hand, some states, like China and India, are not necessarily against LGBTI advocacy within their borders as long as foreign agents do not interfere.[13] This is to say that some states do not want foreign NGOs and foreign donors to finance domestic LGBTI NGOs. With these limitations the work of domestic LGBTI NGOs is particularly difficult, considering, for example, that many of the interviewees reported they receive the majority of their funding from international donors.[14]

---

12 Interview Australian Lesbian Medical Association (ALMA) (Skype call, 23 March 2016); Bisdak Pride, above n 7; interview Bisexual Alliance Victoria (Skype call, 27 May 2016); interview Unitarian Universalist Association (UUA) (Skype call, 5 April 2016); Hungarian LGBT Alliance, above n 7; LGBT Centre Mongolia, above n 7.

13 Unitarian Universalist Association (UUA), above n 12.

14 Stop AIDS Liberia, above n 7; Hungarian LGBT Alliance, above n 7; Bilitis Resource Center, above n 7; Blue Diamond Society, above n 7; GALANG Philippines, above n 7; Pink Armenia, above n 7.

On the other hand, the decision to seek domestic donations can be a political choice of the NGO. For example, the interviewee from Campaign Against Homophobia explained that they do not want to have funding from the Polish government because they want to be independent from the central state.[15] Conversely, the interviewee from Jerusalem Open House (JOH) explained that they have been traditionally supported by Jewish communities in the United States, but they strive to access public funding in Israel because it is 'a point of principle' for them to be recognised as deserving funding like every other NGO.[16]

Some authors have argued that donors do impact LGBTI and human rights advocacy and that donors' influence is one aspect of the broader political context in which TANs operate.[17] On the contrary, the interviewee from LGBT Centre Mongolia wrote to me in an email that followed up on our interview that:[18]

> The idea that LGBTI NGOs are donor-driven is something that has been claimed again and again, but I have often found this to be untrue, especially if the local LGBTI NGOs are governed by the principle of community-ownership and rights-based advocacy, which lead[s] to the articulation of the most pertinent issues by the very community, and not outside donors/organizations. In fact, this legitimation and community-ownership as opposed to being driven by donors is crucial to understanding why some NGOs, while little supported by donors/external global organizations are able to achieve the results not often/at all achieved by donor-agenda-driven organizations.

In sum, this research did not address in detail the topic of how, and to what extent, donors influence the activists' choices in the agenda setting of LGBTI TANs, and future research should address such an angle.

Finally, the scholarship on collective action explores both the themes of progressive TANs and, to a lesser extent, of conservative TANs.[19] Future research could focus on NGOs that are both progressive/LGBTI NGOs and religious NGOs. I started reflecting on the theme of progressive/religious NGOs because of the answers of some of the interviewees. Four of the interviewees are part of NGOs that have both a sexuality and gender mandate and a religious one. The interviewee from the Bisdak Pride maintained that one of their programmes is called 'Queer Theology', in which they organise group discussions and seminars

---

15 Campaign Against Homophobia, above n 7.

16 Interview Jerusalem Open Society (Skype call, 3 May 2016).

17 See especially Lynette J Chua and Timothy Hildebrandt "From Health Crisis to Rights Advocacy? HIV/AIDS and Gay Activism in China and Singapore" (2014) 25(6) *VOLUNTAS: International Journal of Voluntary and Nonprofit Organizations* 1583.

18 Email from interviewee from LGBT Centre Mongolia (1 September 2017).

19 See for example, Graham Macklin "Transnational Networking on the Far Right: The Case of Britain and Germany" (2013) 36(1) *West European Politics* 176; Jennifer Butler "For Faith and Family: Christian Right Advocacy at the United Nations" (2000) 9(2) *The Public Eye* 1; Jennifer Butler "The Christian Right Coalition and the UN Special Session on Children: Prospects and Strategies" (2000) 8(4) *The International Journal of Children's Rights* 351.

on theology in relation to gender and sexuality.[20] Similarly, the interviewee from Youth Interfaith Forum on Sexuality believes that LGBTI individuals suffer limitations in the enjoyment of their right to freedom of religion, and they organise spaces to discuss sexuality, faith and SOGII.[21]

In particular, two interviewees highlighted that their strategic position as a LGBTI/religious NGO can help them to function as a bridge between religious communities and LGBTI communities. The interviewee from JOH maintained that they have transnational connections and collaborations with other Jewish or Christian NGOs, not necessarily LGBTI NGOs.[22] Moreover, the interviewee from Unitarian Universalist Association maintained that when the Ugandan Parliament was discussing the then called 'Kill the Gays Bill' in 2009, HRW contacted them because it recognised that the Bill was prompted by religious NGOs and therefore HRW believed that a religious response would have been appropriate. The interviewee comments:[23]

> We have been very successful in the religious realm to get people from different religions to advocate for LGBT rights. We say [that] it is actually part of your religious duty to make sure that everybody is treated with decency and compassion. If you have a religion, you should act with compassion and not with violence and discrimination.

In sum, the debate on LGBTI rights is polarised between states that are against LGBTI rights for religious and traditional reasons and states that are in favour of LGBTI rights. As Joachim explains, NGOs can benefit from such conflicts among states' blocs if activists are able to create frameworks that provide a bridge to promote consensus among states.[24] So far, the LGBTI TANs have struggled to create such a bridge, while religious/LGBTI NGOs have a lot of potential to function as a link between the religious coalitions and the LGBTI people's rights supporters. Further research on the role of religious/LGBTI NGOs in the transnational advocacy would help, making better recommendations on how to promote the international human rights debate on LGBTI people's rights.

Conclusion

This chapter concludes the book by providing summaries of the findings of the chapters and by advancing recommendations for LGBTI and human rights advocates and scholars. The book demonstrates that LGBTI gatekeeper NGOs work to promote the horizontal development of the network and to do so they

---

20 Bisdak Pride, above n 7.
21 Interview Youth Interfaith Forum on Sexuality (YIFoS) (Skype call, 25 May 2016).
22 Jerusalem Open Society, above n 16.
23 Unitarian Universalist Association (UUA), above n 12.
24 Jutta Joachim *Agenda Setting, the UN, and NGOs: Gender Violence and Reproductive Rights* (Georgetown University Press, Washington, 2007) at 30.

advocate for the rights that develop the political opportunities of domestic NGOs, especially using a prohibition of discrimination framework. The book further shows that the right to marry is highly controversial and is deemed non-strategic, and gatekeeper NGOs do not impose it in the advocacy agenda of the network. These findings contribute to explain that the prohibition of discrimination on the grounds of SOGII is a hot topic in the international human rights debate, while the rights to marry and to form a family are not.

Appendices

Appendix 1
Methodology

Theories: interactive approach to study collective actions

This book develops a syncretic use of TAN and social movement theories to research the LGBTI advocacy at the UN. Sikkink points out that some theories allocate primary relevance to the international level and some others to the domestic level but, for the study of transnational activism, "an interactive approach is necessary to understand the potential for change and innovation in the international system".[1] The combined use of TANs and social movement theories developed here is an example of such an interactive approach because it brings together elements of both international and domestic affairs.[2]

On the one hand, social movement theories can be summarised in three approaches: framing/identity, resource mobilisation and the political opportunity structures.[3] First, the identity/framing approach studies how social movements use collective identities to influence policies and legislation.[4] Second, the resource mobilisation approach analyses the mobilising structures used by individuals to organise collective actions,[5] for example, money, labour and leadership,

1   Kathryn Sikkink "Patterns of Dynamic Multilevel Governance and the Insider-Outsider Coalition" in Donatella Della Porta and Sidney G Tarrow (eds) *Transnational Protest and Global Activism: People, Passions and Power* (Rowman and Littlefield Publishers, Lanham, 2004) 151 at 153.
2   See also, Charles Tilly and Sidney G Tarrow *Contentious Politics* (Paradigm Publishers, Boulder (United States), 2007); Sanjeev Khagram, James Riker, and Kathryn Sikkink "From Santiago to Seattle: Transnational Advocacy Groups Reconstructing World Politics" in Sanjeev Khagram, James Riker, and Kathryn Sikkink (eds) *Reconstructing World Politics: Transnational Social Movements and Norms* (University of Minnesota Press, Minneapolis, 2001) 3.
3   Kelly Kollman *The Same-Sex Unions Revolution in Western Democracies: International Norms and Domestic Policy Change* (Manchester University Press, Manchester, New York, 2013) at 34.
4   See for example, Mary Bernstein "Identities and Politics: Toward a Historical Understanding of the Lesbian and Gay Movement" (2002) 26(3) *Social Science History* 531; Mary Bernstein "LGBT Identity and the Displacement of Sexual Liberation: New York City (1969–1986)" in David Paternotte and Manon Tremblay (eds) *The Ashgate Research Companion to Lesbian and Gay Activism* (Ashgate, Burlington, 2015) 89.
5   Doug McAdam, John D McCarthy, and Mayer Zald "Introduction: Opportunities, Mobilizing Structures, and Framing Processes – Toward a Synthetic, Comparative Perspective

and advocacy tactics.[6] Finally, the political opportunity approach looks at the interactions between states and individuals participating in social movements,[7] and the book discusses three features of political opportunities: access, alliance and political alignment.[8]

And on the other hand, TAN theories draw from international relations and comparative politics traditions and look at international and transnational phenomena.[9] TANs are defined as groups of people or individuals who mobilise domestically or internationally "to advance claims on behalf of external actors, against external opponents, or in favour of goals they hold in common with transnational allies".[10]

Social movements have been passing through a process of NGOisation, which is the process of institutionalisation, professionalisation and bureaucratisation of social movements in becoming an NGO,[11] meaning that the gap between NGOs and social movement is becoming smaller and smaller. Moreover, TAN is an umbrella term that includes "domestic and international NGOs and social movements",[12] as well as activists, academics, media, corporations and domestic interest groups.[13] Finally, TANs,[14] NGOs and social movements[15] do not have simple and unique meanings, and they might intersect and overlap sometimes.[16]

In this overlapping of theories and concepts, I focus on NGOs to study the international human rights debate. The next section explains the focus on NGOs, with advantages and limitations.

---

on Social Movements" in Doug McAdam, John D McCarthy, and Mayer Zald (eds) *Comparative Perspectives on Social Movements: Political Opportunities, Mobilizing Structures, and Cultural Framings* (Cambridge University Press, Cambridge, New York, 1996) 1 at 3.

6 Melinda D Kane "Social Movement Policy Success: Decriminalizing State Sodomy Laws, 1969–1998" (2003) 8(3) *Mobilization: An International Journal* 313 at 317.

7 Stephen M Engel *The Unfinished Revolution: Social Movement Theory and the Gay and Lesbian Movement* (Cambridge University Press, Cambridge, 2001) at 13.

8 Doug McAdam "Conceptual Origins, Current Problems, Future Directions" in Doug McAdam, John D McCarthy, and Mayer Zald (eds) *Comparative Perspectives on Social Movements: Political Opportunities, Mobilizing Structures, and Cultural Framings* (Cambridge University Press, Cambridge, New York, 1996) 1.

9 Margaret E Keck and Kathryn Sikkink *Activists beyond Borders: Advocacy Networks in International Politics* (Cornell University Press, Ithaca, 1998) at 4.

10 Sidney G Tarrow *The New Transnational Activism* (Cambridge University Press, New York, 2005) at 43.

11 Sabine Lang *NGOs, Civil Society, and the Public Sphere* (Cambridge University Press, Cambridge, New York, 2013) at 63–66.

12 Sanjeev Khagram, James Riker, and Kathryn Sikkink, above n 2, at 9.

13 Eduard Grebe "The Treatment Action Campaign's Struggle for AIDS Treatment in South Africa: Coalition-Building through Networks" (2011) 37(4) *Journal of Southern African Studies* 849 at 855.

14 Charli Carpenter and others "Explaining the Advocacy Agenda: Insights from the Human Security Network" (2014) 68(2) *International Organization* 449 at 467.

15 Ana Margarida Esteves, Sara Motta, and Laurence Cox "Civil Society versus Social Movements" (2009) 1(2) *Interface* 1 at 4.

16 See for example, Sidney G Tarrow *Power in Movement Social Movements and Contentious Politics* (3rd ed, Cambridge University Press, Cambridge, New York, 2011) at 242–243.

The focus on nongovernmental organizations: advantages and limitations

The reason for the focus on NGOs is twofold. First, this book aims to tackle legal questions and NGOs are legally recognised entities and institutionalised actors in the international human rights arena,[17] while social movements and transnational advocacy networks are not. Second, NGOs are practical and measurable units to study collective actions.

Nevertheless, studying collective action through the NGO lens has two major limitations. First, NGOs are neither social movements nor TANs exactly. Some social movement theories would disagree with putting NGOs and social movements together as some of them are critical towards NGOs,[18] which are deemed to seldom implement "democratic modes".[19] Moreover, some TAN theorists would disagree with analysing collective actions through the lens of NGOs' work. For example, Paternotte and Kollman criticise TAN theorists' focus on the role of NGOs because "the lines between NGOs, domestic policymakers, transnational activist . . . EU officials, and legal expert are often blurred",[20] as governmental or nongovernmental actors can "wear multiple hats".[21]

Second, the very process of NGOisation of collective actions can impact upon the capacity of activists to promote radical change in the society. This is because the process by which social movements professionalise, bureaucratise and institutionalise to become NGOs "holds both opportunities and costs".[22] The process of NGOisation of social movements helps activists to obtain legal status, funding and credibility, but also "this very process turns down the volume of public advocacy".[23] In other words, activists are faced with the dilemma of choosing between being outside the formal political process so that they can remain radical in their claims, but are less effective, or being institutionalised actors of the political process, as NGOs, which in turn means they can be more effective but less radical in their claims.[24]

---

17 Bas Arts "International Policy Arrangements of State and Non-State Actors" in Bas Arts, Math Noortmann, and Bob Reinalda (eds) *Non-State Actors in International Relations* (Ashgate, Aldershot, Burlington, 2001) at 56.
18 James Petras "Imperialism and NGOs in Latin America" (1997) 49(7) *Monthly Review* 10; Lopes de Souza, "NGOs and Social Movements: Convergences and Divergences" (2013) 17(2) *City* 258.
19 Lopes de Souza, above n 18, at 258.
20 David Paternotte and Kelly Kollman "Regulating Intimate Relationships in the European Polity: Same-Sex Unions and Policy Convergence" (2013) 20(4) *Social Politics: International Studies in Gender, State & Society* 510 at 513.
21 At 4.
22 Sabine Lang, above n 11, at 205.
23 At 205. See also, Aziz Choudry "Global Justice? Contesting NGOization: Knowledge Politics and Containment in Antiglobalization Networks" in Choudry, Aziz, and Kapoor, Dip (eds) *Learning from the Ground Up* (Palgrave Macmillan, New York, 2010) 17.
24 David J Norman "Building Democratic Public Spheres? Transnational Advocacy Networks and the Social Forum Process" (2017) 17(2) *Global Networks* 300 at 2; Thomas Risse "Transnational Actors and World Politics" in Walter Carlsnaes, Thomas Risse, and A Beth

How activists frame pre-existing grievances as human rights claims is a central theme in this book, and therefore Lang's considerations are relevant. However, I have been unable to assess how the process of NGOisation of collective action impacts TANs' agenda setting because the building blocks of my empirical work are NGOs, which by definition are already institutionalised.

NGO advocacy is a complex and multi-faced phenomenon. Therefore, this book uses a triangulation method to capture the complexity of these dynamics. The next sections discuss the triangulation method adopted and spell out how the data have been selected and the limitation of the study.

Triangulation

This book uses a triangulation method, as it uses multiple data sources and collection methods to "paint a more holistic picture of the complex phenomena" researched.[25] Three bodies of documents are analysed: NGO written statements submitted to the HR Council, NGO oral statements delivered during the UPR process and interviews with NGO staff members. Preference is given to the UN HR Council's records because these are arguably more reliable than NGO staff's recollections.[26] These documents are supplemented by 36 semi-structured interviews I personally conducted with NGO staff members and activists, to include the point of view of the insiders.[27] These three bodies of data are thematically analysed with a mix of qualitative and quantitative methods.[28]

United Nations: why the focus on the Human Rights Council?

This book focuses on the HR Council and, for the LGBTI advocacy before 2006, on the Commission on HR. The former Commission on HR used to be composed of 53 states and used to make recommendations and draft human rights conventions and declarations. The Commission on HR was a subsidiary organ of the ECOSOC,[29] and therefore NGOs could submit written and oral statements according to resolution 1996/31.[30]

Simmons (eds) *Handbook of International Relations* (SAGE, London, 2013) 427 at 433; Timothy Hildebrandt *Social Organizations and the Authoritarian State in China* (Cambridge University Press, New York, 2013) at 61.

25 Phillip M Ayoub, Sophia J Wallace, and Chris Zepeda-Millán "Triangulation in Social Movement Research" in Donatella Della Porta (ed) *Methodological Practices in Social Movement Research* (Oxford University Press, Oxford, 2014) 67 at 68.

26 David Paternotte "The NGOization of LGBT Activism: ILGA-Europe and the Treaty of Amsterdam" (2015) 15(4) *Social Movement Studies* 1 at 4.

27 Ibid.

28 Virginia Braun and Victoria Clarke "Using Thematic Analysis in Psychology" (2006) 3(2) *Qualitative Research in Psychology* 77.

29 Office of the United Nations High Commissioner for Human Rights *Working with the United Nations Human Rights Programme: A Handbook for Civil Society* (UN, Online, 2008) at 78.

30 E/RES/1996/31 *Consultative Relationship between the United Nations and Non-Governmental Organizations* (1996).

Since 2006, the Commission on HR was replaced by the HR Council, which is a subsidiary organ of the General Assembly,[31] and it is the principal UN intergovernmental body regarding human rights.[32] The HR Council is composed of 47 state representatives[33] who are elected by the majority of the members of the General Assembly. The seats have a geographical distribution: 13 Africa, 13 Asia and Pacific, eight Latin America and Caribbean, seven Western Europe and other states, and six Eastern Europe. Such geographic distribution of the members has sometimes limited the scope of the LGBTI advocacy at the HR Council. Indeed, Asian and African states, which are 26 out of 47 members, have used "their numerical weight to push for a more state-oriented approach".[34] Still, LGBTI gatekeeper NGOs have been able to seize favourable opportunities and to coordinate the advocacy from LGBTI peripheral NGOs to promote HR Council's resolutions on the prohibition of discrimination and violence against individuals because of their SOGI.

In general, the arrangement regarding NGOs' participation as observers has been transferred from the Commission on HR to the HR Council.[35] NGOs with ECOSOC consultative status can participate in special and regular sessions of the HR Council, and they can submit oral or written statements.[36] In addition to the UPR process analysed in this book, the HR Council established Special Procedures, which monitor the implementation of human rights, and their mandates can be given to independent experts.[37]

The data collection of the LGBTI advocacy at the UN focuses mainly, although not exclusively, on the HR Council. In particular, I analyse written and oral statements submitted by NGOs with consultative status to the HR Council. First, I found the written statements with key word searches in the UN Official Documents System Search. I made a number of separate searches to ensure I reached all the relevant documents. I searched the words 'sexual orientation', 'gender identity', 'same-sex couple', 'intersex', 'lesbian', 'gay', 'bisexual', 'transgender', 'LGBTI' and 'LGBT'. I identified 92 NGOs' written statements, submitted from 1997 to February 2016. Second, I analysed the oral statements delivered by NGOs during the UPR process. To find these oral statements I downloaded the 32 reports on the HR Council meetings from the UN website. However, nine of these documents have been excluded from the analysis because seven do

---

31 Office of the United Nations High Commissioner for Human Rights, above n 29, at 78.
32 Ibid.
33 A/RES/60/251 *Human Rights Council* (General Assembly, 2006) at [7].
34 Theodor Rathgeber *Performance and Challenges of the UN Human Rights Council: An NGOs' View* (Friedrich Erbert Stifgung, 2013) at 4.
35 Office of the United Nations High Commissioner for Human Rights, above n 29, at 90. See also, A/HRC/RES/5/1 *Institution-Building of the United Nations Human Rights Council* (2006) at Rule 7(a).
36 At 91.
37 A/HRC/RES/5/2 *Code of Conduct for Special Procedures Mandate-Holders of the Human Rights Council* (2007). See especially, A/HRC/35/36 *Report of the Independent Expert on Protection Against Violence and Discrimination Based on Sexual Orientation and Gender Identity* (HR Council, 2017).

not record the UPR process,[38] and in two there is no sign of any discussion on LGBTI issues.[39] These data are updated to November 2016. Both the NGOs' written statements and the HR Council's records of the meetings were coded with NVivo 11. In doing so, I was able to identify both the frequency in which some issues where addressed (quantitative research), and how these issues where framed (qualitative research).

NGOs can also submit statements and reports to other UN institutions. However, I analysed the NGOs' advocacy in relation to the HR Council because the HR Council is a central forum to discuss LGBTI rights.[40] Indeed, the HR Council is the major UN intergovernmental organ dealing with human rights and, as a consequence, the resolutions of the HR Council are significant because they signal at least some agreement among the countries. On the contrary, other organs, such as the OHCHR and HR Comm, are composed of experts rather than governmental delegates, and it cannot be claimed that they represent the consensus among UN member states. Moreover, Rathgeber observes that states participating in the UPR are likely to raise concerns on SOGI issues when these have been previously raised by NGOs.[41] Therefore, it is particularly relevant to analyse NGOs' oral statements during the UPR process.

While conducting my data collection I discovered further reasons to focus on the analysis of the HR Council. First, some of my interviewees reported that they considered the HR Council a more promising venue to lobby for LGBTI rights as opposed to the General Assembly.[42] This is because both the HR Council and the General Assembly deliberate by consensus or by majority vote. Therefore, as the HR Council is composed by 47 members – as opposed to the General Assembly which comprises the 193 UN member states – the majority at the HR Council requires a lower number of states. Second, when analysing NGO written statements sent to the HR Council, I found that NGOs perceive the HR Council

38 A/HRC/1/L.10 *Report to the General Assembly on the First Session of the Human Rights Council* (HR Council, 2006); A/HRC/2/9 *Report to the General Assembly on the Second Session of the Human Rights Council* (HR Council, 2007); A/HRC/3/7 *Report to the General Assembly on the Third Session of The Human Rights Council* (HR Council, 2007); A/HRC/4/123 *Report to the General Assembly on the Fourth Session of the Human Rights Council* (HR Council, 2007); A/HRC/5/21 *Report to the General Assembly on the Fifth Session of the Council* (HR Council, 2007).; A/HRC/6/22 *Report of the Human Rights Council on Its Sixth Session* (HR Council, 2008); A/HRC/7/78 *Report of the Human Rights Council on Its Seventh Session* (HR Council, 2008).
39 A/HRC/9/28 *Report of the Human Rights Council on Its Ninth Session* (HR Council, 2008); A/HRC/20/2 *Report of the Human Rights Council on Its Twentieth Session* (HR Council, 2013).
40 Mindy Jane Roseman and Alice M Miller "Normalizing Sex and Its Discontents: Establishing Sexual Rights in International Law" (2011) 34 *Harvard Journal of Law and Gender* 313 at 361.
41 Theodor Rathgeber, above n 34, at 10–11.
42 Interview Unitarian Universalist Association (UUA) (Skype call, 5 April 2016); interview ILGA-World (Skype call, 13 April 2016).

to have an important role in the standard setting of human rights violations, especially in areas that have gone previously unaddressed, such as SOGII issues.[43]

Interviews

I interviewed 36 human rights and LGBTI NGO staff and activists. Most of the interviews were via Skype, one was face-to-face, and four participants answered questionnaires. The following sub-paragraphs describe the participants' selection and the questions asked.

The NGOs contacted all have a common feature: they do some sort of transnational advocacy on LGBTI and SOGII issues. This means that they have collaborated either with the UN or with international NGOs. I selected them in the following way. First, I contacted the NGOs that are mentioned in the literature around LGBTI transnational advocacy. Second, I contacted the NGOs that sent written statements to the HR Council and delivered speeches during the UPR. Third, I used a 'snow ball' technique, which means that while I was doing the first interviews I asked the participants to name one or more NGOs they collaborate with. Furthermore, I researched within the websites of the NGOs initially selected if they had links to external NGO websites.

Interview questions

The interviews were conducted, and the questionnaires were received between March 2015 and July 2016. The duration of the interviews was between 30 and 45 minutes, and I transcribed the interview recordings word by word. Some interviewees did not agree on having their answers recorded; therefore, I took notes during our interactions. The interviews covered three major topics: how NGOs network with one another, what their opinions were on the most pressing LGBTI issues and their opinions on marriage equality. I did not ask the interview partners about personal characteristics, such as age, gender identity or sexual orientation. Rather, I asked them to share the general 'feeling' of the NGO. On a terminology note, when I refer to an interviewee, I often use the gender neutral 'they' because it is a gender inclusive pronoun, and it helps erase personal identifiers.

The interviews were semi-structured, meaning that some questions were fixed while others where flexible or ad hoc. First, to assess the NGOs' opinions on agenda setting, I asked the interviewees what the most pressing issues are for the LGBTI community both in their country and internationally, and what they

---

43 A/HRC/1/NGO/47 *Joint Written Statement Submitted by Action Canada for Population and Development (ACPD), Canadian HIV/AIDS Legal Network, Centre for Women's Global Leadership (Global Centre, CWGL), Global Rights, International Service for Human Rights (ISHR), International Women's Health Coalition (IWHC), and New Ways: Women for Women's Human Rights* (HR Council, 2006) at 2.

thought about marriage and family equality. Second, I asked how NGOs interact. This second set of questions needed to be flexible because I asked peripheral NGOs about their relations with gatekeeper NGOs, and gatekeeper NGOs about their relations with the periphery of the network. Finally, part of the aim of the interviews was to gain a better understanding of the facts. Therefore, some questions were tailored to investigate the specific roles of the NGOs during transnational advocacy campaigns. In any case, when needed, I asked follow-up questions to clarify concepts or ideas.

I encountered various obstacles when organising the interviews. Many prospective interviewees felt they were not proficient in English and refused to participate in the study. Moreover, because of time zones, setting a time and date was difficult. Finally, a number of NGOs replied that they are understaffed, overworked and often run by volunteers; therefore, they did not have the time or resources to be part of the study. Providing the option to answer a questionnaire helped to solve some of these problems; on other occasions, setting up an interview meeting was impossible. I am extremely thankful to the 36 people who agreed to be a part of this research, overcoming language barriers, time zones and other difficulties.

Description of the interviewees

In some cases, I interviewed more than one staff member of the same NGO because I was referred to a different person in the same organization who was able to better answer my questions. In one case, because one interviewee was working simultaneously in two different NGOs, I was able to ask questions related to both NGOs. Furthermore, I interviewed two activists who are not currently members of any NGOs. This means that, out of the 36 interviews, I gathered information on 30 NGOs and two independent activists. I interviewed five staff members from the NGOs that I identified as gatekeepers, namely ILGA and ILGA-Europe. Seven of these NGOs have consultative status with the ECOSOC. Even though they are not really gatekeeper NGOs, the fact that they have consultative status signals a certain degree of engagement with the UN.

The majority of NGOs (17) that participated in the study have their headquarters in the countries that are part of the Western European and Other Groups, identified in this book as representing the 'West'. The second most represented region was the Asia-Pacific Group with eight NGO participants, then the African Group with three, Eastern European Group with three, and finally Latin America and Caribbean one. Appendix 3 summarises in a table the key features of the NGO participants.

Finally, I tried to talk with the staff involved directly in the advocacy in the UN. I also tried to talk with senior officers to gain a more experienced point of view. When possible, I tried to talk with people who held strategic positions within the NGOs. Among my interviewee partners there were six directors, five presidents and one vice-president; others were coordinators, volunteers or in junior positions. To safeguard the anonymity of the interviewees, their roles are not mentioned in the footnotes or anywhere else in the book.

Online materials

While conducting the research, I read a lot of online materials, such as mainstream media and pink press articles, to keep myself updated on the evolution of events. Reading these materials informed my thinking; however, all the internet material is collected from NGOs and the UN's websites. I collected relevant webpages, press releases and blog posts with repeated Google searches. I accessed and read these webpages between May 2014 and July 2018. Most of the online materials I accessed for this research are in English, Italian and French.

The triangulation of the data sets, combined with TAN theories, helped me identify the gatekeeper NGOs in the LGBTI TAN. The next, and final, section explains how gatekeeper NGOs have been identified for the purposes of this research.

LGBTI gatekeeper NGOs

Gatekeeper NGOs are major human rights NGOs functioning as gatekeepers because they have a considerable influence in the standard setting of new human rights norms.[44] The most important characteristic of gatekeeper NGOs is they are recognised as such. The gatekeeping power is 'awarded' by international organizations, states and other non-state actors to those NGOs that are recognised as important nodes in the network. Therefore, to identify the gatekeeper NGOs, I draw from major TANs' scholarship, from the analysis of the HR Council documents and from the interviews. The gatekeeper NGOs for this book are Amnesty, HRW, ILGA, OutRight, ARC, ILGA-Europe and COC.

Bob first defined the meaning of gatekeeper NGO and identifies Amnesty and HRW as human rights gatekeeper NGOs.[45] In addition to Amnesty and HRW, scholars highlight the central position of five other NGOs in the LGBTI network.[46] Linde highlights that there are other four central nodes in the LGBTI

---

44 Clifford Bob *The International Struggle for New Human Rights* (University of Pennsylvania Press, Philadelphia, 2009) at 4.

45 Ibid.

46 Ryan R Thoreson *Transnational LGBT Activism: Working for Sexual Rights Worldwide* (University of Minnesota Press, Minneapolis, 2014); Douglas Sanders "Getting Lesbian and Gay Issues on the International Human Rights Agenda" (1996) 18 *Human Rights Quarterly* 67; Julie Mertus "The Rejection of Human Rights Framings: The Case of LGBT Advocacy in the US" (2007) 29 *Human Rights Quarterly* 1036; Eduard Jordaan "The Challenge of Adopting Sexual Orientation Resolutions at the UN Human Rights Council" (2016) 8(2) *Journal of Human Rights Practice* 298; Phillip M Ayoub and David Paternotte "L'International Lesbian and Gay Association (ILGA) et L'Expansion du Militantisme LGBT dans une Europe Unifiée" (2016) 70 *Critique Internationale* 55; Loveday Hodson, "Activists and Lawyers in the ECtHR: The Struggle for Gay Rights" in Dia Anagnostou (ed) *Rights and Courts in*

TAN, which are ILGA, OutRight, ARC and ILGA-Europe, that she calls "broker".[47] Broker NGOs intermediate "between international institutions and smaller regional or national organizations",[48] and they have "similar features and functions" to gatekeeper NGOs.[49] Linde uses the terms 'gatekeeper' and 'broker' interchangeably throughout her article. Moreover, commenting on the relationships between human rights gatekeeper NGOs and LGBTI activists in the 1990s, Mertus stated that ILGA not only brought their concerns before international organizations through gatekeeper NGOs, they also "raise their own issues before international bodies".[50] That is further evidence that ILGA operates like a gatekeeper NGO, bypassing Amnesty and HRW. Finally, Osterbur and Kiel use a hyperlink analysis to determine that COC and ILGA-Europe are the central and hegemonic nodes within the LGBTI network, at least in Europe.[51]

The centrality of these seven NGOs in the LGBTI TANs is also supported by this research's findings. Indeed, Amnesty submitted or participated in 12 written statements, and HRW provided five out of the 92 written statements analysed in this book. Moreover, COC, ILGA and ILGA-Europe delivered many of the oral comments on LGBTI issues during the UPR process. COC delivered 51 oral statements on LGBTI issues, while ILGA and ILGA-Europe delivered respectively 43 and 41 oral statements, which is a combined 84 oral remarks on LGBTI rights. Finally, the interviewees identify these NGOs, especially ILGA, ILGA-Europe, COC and OutRight, as being the central hubs of their advocacy network.

Pursuing of Social Change: Legal Mobilisation in the Multi-Level European System (Hart Publishing, Oxford, 2014) 181; Joke Swiebel "Lesbian, Gay, Bisexual and Transgender Human Rights: The Search for an International Strategy" (2009) 15(1) *Contemporary Politics* 19; Ronald Holzhacker "Transnational Strategies of Civil Society Organizations Striving for Equality and Nondiscrimination: Exchanging Information on New EU Directives, Coalition Strategies and Strategic Litigation" in Laszlo Bruszt and Ronald Holzhacker (eds) *Transnationalization of Economies, States, and Civil Societies: New Challenges for Governance in Europe* (Springer, New York, London, 2009) 219.

47 Robyn Linde "Gatekeeper Persuasion and Issue Adoption: Amnesty International and the Transnational LGBTQ Network" (2017) 17(2) *Journal of Human Rights* 245 at 246.

48 At 249.

49 Ibid.

50 Julie Mertus "Applying the Gatekeeper Model of Human Rights Activism: The US-Based Movement for LGBT Rights" in Clifford Bob (ed) *The International Struggle for New Human Rights* (University of Pennsylvania Press, Philadelphia, 2009) 52 at 66.

51 Megan Osterbur and Christina Kiel "A Hegemon Fighting for Equal Rights: The Dominant Role of COC Nederland in the LGBT Transnational Advocacy Network" (2016) 17(2) *Global Networks* 234.

Appendix 2
NGOs' written statements submitted to the Human Rights Council

Under 'Type', the table identifies written statements that focus on LGBTI and SOGII issues, written statements that discuss LGBTI people's rights in combination with other matters (Com), written statements that address LGBTI issues when commenting upon states' human rights records and, finally, written statements that are submitted against LGBTI rights.

Under 'Code', the table highlights how the written statements frame LGBTI rights. They are abbreviated as follows: prohibition of discrimination on the grounds of sexual orientation (SO); sexual orientation and gender identity (SOGI); sexual orientation, gender identity and intersex status (SOGII); call to erase violence, ill-treatment, torture, attack against LGBTI individuals (VIO); call for decriminalisation of same-sex sexual behaviour (CRI), call for freedom of association, peaceful assembly, expression (AAE). Further frameworks are expressed in full.

Code/Year	NGO(s)	Type	Code
E/CN.4/1997/NGO/29 (1997)	International Federation of Jurists	Com: detention and imprisonment	SO
E/CN.4/1998/NGO/3 (1998)	Latin American Committee for the Defence of Women's Rights	Com: gender issues	SO
E/CN.4/2001/NGO/33 (2001)	Human Rights Watch	Com: right of the child	VIO
E/CN.4/2003/NGO/233 (2003)	International Federation of Human Rights Leagues (FIDH)	State: Egypt	SO, VIO, CRI
E/CN.4/2004/NGO/163 (2004)	FIDH	State: Egypt	SO, VIO, CRI
E/CN.4/2004/NGO/187 (2004)	Canadian HIV/AIDS Legal Network	Primary focus	SOGI, specific transgender issues
E/CN.4/2004/NGO/191 (2004)	Transnational Radical Party (TRP)	Primary focus	SOGI, CRI, marriage and family.
E/CN.4/2004/NGO/232 (2004)	Human Rights Watch	Primary focus	SOGI, CRI
E/CN.4/2004/NGO/259 (2004)	American Psychological Association	Primary focus	SO, VIO
E/CN.4/2004/NGO/33 (2004)	Asian Legal Centre	States: Nepal, Myanmar, China	VIO
E/CN.4/2005/NGO/122 (2005)	International Commission of Jurists (ICJ)	Com: protection of human rights while countering terrorism	SO
E/CN.4/2005/NGO/143 (2005)	Canadian HAIV/AIDS Legal Network	Primary focus	SOGI, specific transgender issues
E/CN.4/2005/NGO/154 (2005)	FIDH	State: Bahrain	SOGI, violence
E/CN.4/2005/NGO/156 (2005)	FIDH	State: Egypt	SO
E/CN.4/2005/NGO/255 (2005)	Colombian Commission of Jurists	State: Colombia	SOGI
E/CN.4/2005/NGO/261 (2005)	TRP	States: various	CRI
E/CN.4/2005/NGO/346 (2005)	Coordinating Board of Jewish Organizations	No analysis	–
A/HRC/1/NGO/33 (2006)	TRP	Primary focus	SO, CRI, AAE, asylum, marriage and family

(Continued)

Code/Year	NGO(s)	Type	Code
A/HRC/1/NGO/47 (2006)	Action Canada for Population and Development, Canadian HIV/AIDS Legal network, Centre for Women's Global Leadership (Global Centre, CWGL), Global Rights, International Service for Human Rights, International Women's Health Coalition, and New Ways: Women for Women's Human Rights	Primary focus	SOGI, CRI, VIO, AAE
E/CN.4/2006/NGO/109 (2006)	International NGO Forum on Indonesia Development	State: Indonesia	SOGI
E/CN.4/2006/NGO/112 (2006)	International NGO Forum on Indonesia Development	Com: freedom of expression	AAE
E/CN.4/2006/NGO/162 (2006)	TRP	Primary focus	SO, CRI, VIO, AAE, marriage and family
A/HRC/4/NGO/130 (2007)	Colombian Commission of Jurists	State: Colombia	VIO
A/HRC/4/NGO/81 (2007)	International NGO Forum on Indonesian Development	State: Indonesia (violence against women)	AAE
A/HRC/4/NGO/124 (2007)	World Organization Against Torture	States: Algeria, Morocco, South Africa, Tunisia, Bahrain, India, Indonesia, Philippines, Czech Republic, Poland, Argentina, Ecuador, Finland, Netherlands	VIO
A/HRC/8/NGO/12 (2008)	Amnesty International	No analysis	--
A/HRC/11/NGO/25 (2009)	Federation of Western Thrace Turks in Europe	Com: discrimination on grounds of ethnicity	SO
A/HRC/11/NGO/49 (2009)	Amnesty International	State: Nigeria	SOGI, CRI
A/HRC/13/NGO/106 (2010)	Amnesty International	State: Colombia	VIO, AAE

A/HRC/14/NGO/33 (2010)	International NGO Forum on Indonesian Development	State: Indonesia (women's reproductive health)	SOGI
A/HRC/16/NGO/57 (2011)	Asian Legal Resource Centre	State: Nepal (protection of women human rights defenders)	VIO, AAE
A/HRC/16/NGO/73 (2011)	Organization for Defending Victims of Violence, the Khiam Rehabilitation Center for Victims of Torture, the Charitable Institute for Protecting Social Victims, the Network of Women's Non-governmental Organizations in the Islamic Republic of Iran	State: United States of America	SO
A/HRC/16/NGO/104 (2011)	Front Line International Foundation for the Protection of Human Rights Defenders, the Center for Reproductive Rights, Inc., the BAOBAB for Women's Human Rights	Com: Special Rapporteur on human rights defenders	AAE
A/HRC/16/NGO/126 (2011)	Action Canada for Population and Development, Madre, Inc., the Urban Justice Center	State: United States of America (violence against sex workers)	VIO
A/HRC/17/NGO/38 (2011)	Association for Progressive Communications (APC)	Com: internet	Right to privacy
A/HRC/17/NGO/51 (2011)	Amnesty International	State: Australia	SOGI, marriage and family
A/HRC/AC/7/NGO/1 (2011)	Association for Women's Rights, the International Planned Parenthood Federation, Action Canada for Population and Development, the Asian Forum for Human Rights and Development, the Cairo Institute for Human Rights Studies, the Canadian HIV/AIDS Legal Network, the Centre for	Com: traditional values	SOGI, marriage and family

(Continued)

Code/Year	NGO(s)	Type	Code
A/HRC/AC/7/NGO/2 (2011)	Reproductive Rights, the Centre for Women's Global Leadership, Development Alternatives with Women for a New Era, Human Rights Watch, the ICJ, ILGA, the International Movement Against All Forms of Discrimination and Racism, the International Service for Human Rights, the International Women's Health Coalition, IPAS, Italian Association for Women in Development, the Federation for Women and Family Planning, RFSL, Women for Women's Human Rights – New Ways, the Women's International League for Peace and Freedom, Asian Pacific Forum on Women, Law and Development Association for Women's Rights in Development	Com: traditional values	VIO
A/HRC/AC/7/NGO/3 (2011)	Commission of the Churches on International Affairs of the World Council of Churches	Com: human right to peace	SO
A/HRC/19/NGO/43 (2012)	Caritas Internationalis (International Confederation of Catholic Charities), New Humanity, the Association Points-Coeur, *the Associazione Comunità Papa Giovanni XXIII*, the Company of the Daughters of Charity of St. Vincent de Paul, the Dominicans for Justice and Peace – Order of Preachers, the International Organization for the Right to Education and Freedom of Education, the World Union of Catholic Women's Organizations	Against LGBTI rights	Marriage and family (against)
A/HRC/19/NGO/61 (2012)	Commonwealth Human Rights Initiative	Primary focus	SOGII, CRI
A/HRC/19/NGO/124 (2012)	International Society for Human Rights	Com: International Bill of Rights	SO, marriage and family

Document	Organization	Focus	Keywords
A/HRC/19/NGO/150 (2012)	Canadian HIV/AIDS Legal Network	Primary focus	SOGI, CRI, VIO, asylum, transgender issues
A/HRC/20/NGO/11 (2012)	ICJ	Primary focus	SOGI, AAE
A/HRC/20/NGO/13 (2012)	ICJ	Primary focus	SOGI, AAE
A/HRC/20/NGO/50 (2012)	CIVICUS – The World Alliance for Citizen Participation	Com: disenabling environment for civil society	CRI, AAE
A/HRC/20/NGO/59 (2012)	Commission of the Churches on International Affairs of the World Council of Churches, and others	Com: human right to peace	SO
A/HRC/21/NGO/29 (2012)	ICJ	Com: discrimination and inequality, including the rights to water and sanitation	SOGI, transgender issues, intersex people's issues
A/HRC/21/NGO/62 (2012)	Liberal International (World Liberal Union)	Primary focus	SOGI, CRI, AAE, asylum
A/HRC/21/NGO/68 (2012)	International Movement Against All Forms of Discrimination and Racism	Com: Dalit	Right to water
A/HRC/AC/8/NGO/2 (2012)	Commission of the Churches on International Affairs of the World Council of Churches and others	Com: human right to peace	SO
A/HRC/AC/8/NGO/4 (2012)	Written statement submitted by the Canadian HIV/AIDS Legal Network	Com: traditional values	SOGI, marriage and family
A/HRC/AC/9/NGO/3 (2012)	Joint written statement submitted by the World Council of Churches and others	Com: human right to peace	SO
A/HRC/22/NGO/11 (2013)	International Commission of Jurists	Primary focus	SOGI, AAE
A/HRC/22/NGO/81 (2013)	International Movement Against All Forms of Discrimination and Racism	Com: caste discrimination, violence against women and post-2015 development	SO

(Continued)

Code/Year	NGO(s)	Type	Code
A/HRC/22/NGO/159 (2013)	Human Rights House Foundation	State: Russian Federation (freedom of association, expression and assembly)	AAE
A/HRC/22/NGO/156 (2013)	Commission of the Churches on International Affairs of the World Council of Churches and others	Com: human right to peace	SO
A/HRC/22/NGO/88 (2013)	Plan International, Inc.	Com: children's right to sexual and reproductive health	SOGI
A/HRC/24/NGO/112 (2013)	*Verein Sudwind Entwicklungspolitik*	State: Islamic Republic of Iran (women's rights)	Transgender people's issues
A/HRC/24/NGO/2 (2013)	*Mouvement contre le racisme et pour l'amitié entre les peuples*	State: United States of America (death penalty)	SO
A/HRC/24/NGO/27 (2013) A/HRC/24/NGO/39 (2013)	Human Rights Law Centre International Service for Human Rights, the Action Canada for Population and Development, Amnesty International, the Asian Forum for Human Rights and Development, the Cairo Institute for Human Rights Studies, the Canadian HIV/AIDS Legal Network, *Centro de Estudios Legales y Sociales (CELS) Asociación Civil*, the Commonwealth Human Rights Initiative, *Conectas Direitos Humanos*, the East and Horn of Africa Human Rights Defenders Project, *Groupe des ONG pour la Convention relative aux droits de l'enfant*, the Human Rights House Foundation, ICJ, the International Federation for Human Rights Leagues, the International Rehabilitation Council for Torture Victims, the World Organization Against Torture, CIVICUS – World Alliance for Citizen Participation	State: Australia Com: Special Rapporteur on human rights defenders	CRI

Document	Organization	Com/State	Codes
A/HRC/AC/10/NGO/2 (2013)	Commission of the Churches on International Affairs of the World Council of Churches and others	Com: human right to peace	SO
A/HRC/25/NGO/130 (2014)	CIVICUS – World Alliance for Citizen Participation	Com: civil society	SOGII, CRI, AAE
A/HRC/25/NGO/133 (2014)	International Educational Development, Inc.	No analysis	--
A/HRC/25/NGO/176 (2014)	Asian Legal Resource Centre, Amnesty International, Cairo Institute for Human Rights Studies, the East and Horn of Africa Human Rights Defenders Project, International Service for Human Rights, *Reporters Sans Frontieres International* – Reporters Without Borders International, Article 19 – International Centre Against Censorship	Com: Special Rapporteur on the promotion and protection of the right to freedom of opinion and expression	AAE
A/HRC/25/NGO/36 (2014)	Amnesty International	State: Honduras	SOGII, VIO
A/HRC/25/NGO/52 (2014)	International Federation for Human Rights Leagues	State: Ireland	CRI, marriage and family
A/HRC/26/NGO/112 (2014)	Amnesty International	Com: torture	VIO
A/HRC/26/NGO/20 (2014)	International Educational Development Inc.	Com: freedom of expression	AAE
A/HRC/26/NGO/46 (2014)	Asian Legal Resource Centre	State: India (women's rights)	SO
A/HRC/26/NGO/80 (2014)	Asian Legal Resource Centre, International Association for Religious Freedom and others	Com: human right to peace	SO
A/HRC/26/NGO/81 (2014)	Liberal International (World Liberal Union)	Com: human rights of migration	SO, asylum
A/HRC/27/NGO/18 (2014)	HelpAge International	Com: independent expert on the enjoyment of all human rights by older persons	SOGI

(Continued)

Code/Year	NGO(s)	Type	Code
A/HRC/27/NGO/77 (2014)	International Humanist and Ethical Union	Com: traditional values	SOGII
A/HRC/S-22/NGO/5 (2014)	International Gay and Lesbian Human Rights Commission (IGLHRC – now OutRight)	State: Iraq (focus on LGBT people)	CRI, VIO
A/HRC/28/NGO/102 (2015)	Servas International	Com: hate and intolerance	SO
A/HRC/28/NGO/143 (2015)	OutRight	State: Iran (focus con LGBT people)	SOGI, VIO, CRI, AAE
A/HRC/28/NGO/159 (2015)	Amnesty International	Comp: gender discrimination	SOGI
A/HRC/28/NGO/166 (2015)	International Service for Human Rights	Com: human rights defenders	AAE
A/HRC/28/NGO/170 (2015)	Amnesty International	State: Gambia	VIO, CRI
A/HRC/28/NGO/21 (2015)	Federacion de Asociaciones de Defensa y Promocion de los Derechos Humanos	Com: right to non-discrimination in Western Sahara	SOGI
A/HRC/29/NGO/106 (2015)	Article 19 – International Centre Against Censorship	Primary focus	SOGI, AAE, hate speech, transgender people's issues, right to privacy
A/HRC/29/NGO/109 (2015)	Freemuse – The World Forum on Music and Censorship, International PEN, the Article 19 – International Centre Against Censorship	Com: Special Rapporteur in the field of cultural rights	Cultural rights
A/HRC/29/NGO/114 (2015)	Amnesty International	Com: girls' education	SOGI
A/HRC/29/NGO/118 (2015)	Amnesty International, Human Rights Watch	Primary focus	SOGII, VIO, CRI, AAE, transgender people's issues
A/HRC/30/NGO/126 (2015)	Le Collectif des Femmes Africaines du Hainaut	Com: young people	SOGII

A/HRC/31/NGO/140 (2016)	Human Rights Watch	Com: ending discrimination based on caste and descent	SO
A/HRC/31/NGO/155 (2016)	Global Helping to Advance Women and Children	Against LGBTI rights	Marriage and family (against)
A/HRC/31/NGO/179 (2016)	Association for Progressive Communications (APC)	Com: freedom of expression in the context of religion	SOGI, AAE
A/HRC/31/NGO/181 (2016)	Servas International	Com: refugees	Asylum
A/HRC/31/NGO/193 (2016)	Society for the Protection of Unborn Children	Against LGBTI rights	Marriage and family (against)

Appendix 3

Interviewees

Organization	Consultative status	Country	UN Regional Groups
Stop AIDS Liberia	No	Liberia	African Group
ALMA	Yes	Australia	Western European and Other Groups
Arcigay	No	Italy	Western European and Other Groups
Bilitis Resource Centre	No	Bulgaria	Eastern European Group
Bisdak Pride	No	Philippines	Asia-Pacific Group
Bisexual Alliance Victoria	No	Australia	Western European and Other Groups
Blue Diamond Society	No	Nepal	Asia-Pacific Group
Campaign Against Homophobia	No	Poland	Eastern European Group
ARCD	No	Italy	Western European and Other Groups
FELGTB	Yes	Spain	Western European and Other Groups
GALANG Philippines	No	Philippines	Asia-Pacific Group
Hungarian Rainbow Alliance	No	Hungary	Eastern European Group
ILGA-Europe	Yes	Belgium	Western European and Other Groups
ILGA-Oceania	Yes (as a branch of ILGA)	New Zealand	Western European and Other Groups
ILGA World	Yes	Switzerland	Western European and Other Groups
J4S	No	Malaysia	Asia-Pacific Group
JOH	No	Israel	Western European and Other Groups
LGBT Centre (Mongolia)	No	Mongolia	Asia-Pacific Group
LGBT Denmark	Yes	Denmark	Western European and Other Groups

Organization	Consultative status	Country	UN Regional Groups
Malta Gay Rights Movement	No	Malta	Western European and Other Groups
Pink Armenia	No	Armenia	Eastern European Group
Pink Cross	No	Switzerland	Western European and Other Groups
Rainbow Sunrise Mapambazuko	No	Congo	African Group
Rete Lenford	No	Italy	Western European and Other Groups
RFSL	Yes	Sweden	Western European and Other Groups
UUA	Yes	United States	Western European and Other Groups
YIFoS	No	Thailand	Asia-Pacific Group
Pink Cross	No	Switzerland	Western European and Other Groups
Anonymous	No	Nigeria	African Group
Anonymous	No	Sri Lanka	Asia-Pacific Group
Anonymous	No	Saint Lucia	Latin America and Caribbean Group
No current NGO	N/A	New Zealand	Western European and Other Groups
No current NGO	N/A	Singapore	Asia-Pacific Group

Appendix 4
United Nations vote results

The table indicates votes in favour (f), against (a) and abstained (ab). Some states could not vote at the HR Council (or Commission on HR before 2006) because the HR Council is composed of 47 members at a time; therefore, some slots are left blank.

For the 2008 Argentina Statement and Syrian Counterstatement, I indicate favour (f) for the states signatories of the Argentinian statement, and against (a) for the states signatories of the Syrian counterstatement. Moreover, for the 2010 General Assembly Resolution on Extrajudicial, Summary or Arbitrary Executions, I signal favour (f) for states that supported LGBTI rights, i.e. those states that voted to include explicit reference to 'sexual orientation' in the text of the resolution. I signal against (a) for states that voted to bar such reference.

	Brazilian Resolution (2003) E/CN.4/2003/L.92	New Zealand Statement (2005)	Norway Statement (2006)	Argentina Statement/ Syrian Counterstatement (GA/2008)	Res on ESA Executions (GA/2010)		2011 HR Council Res A/HRC/ RES/17/19	2014 HR Council Res A/HRC/ RES/27/32	2016 HR Council Res A/HRC/ RES/32/2
					Nov vote	Dec vote			
Afghanistan				a	a	ab			
Albania			f	f		f			f
Algeria			f	a	a	f		a	a
Andorra		f	f	f	f	f			
Angola					a	ab	a		
Antigua and Barbuda					ab	f			
Argentina		f	f	f		f	f	f	
Armenia			f	f		f			
Australia		f	f	f		f			
Austria	f	f	f	f		f		f	
Azerbaijan					a	f			
Bahamas					a	f			
Bahrain				a	a	ab	a		
Bangladesh				a	a	ab	a		a
Barbados					ab	f			
Belarus					ab	f			
Belgium	f	f	f	f		f	f		f
Belize					a	f			
Benin				a	a	ab			
Bhutan					f	f			
Bolivia			f	f		f			f
Bosnia and Herzegovina				f		f			
Botswana				a	a	ab		a	ab
Brazil	f	f	f	f	f	f	f	f	
Brunei Darussalam				a	a	ab			

(*Continued*)

	Brazilian Resolution (2003) E/CN.4/2003/L.92	New Zealand Statement (2005)	Norway Statement (2006)	Argentina Statement/Syrian Counterstatement (GA/2008)	Res on ESA Executions (GA/2010)		2011 HR Council Res A/HRC/RES/17/19	2014 HR Council Res A/HRC/RES/27/32	2016 HR Council Res A/HRC/RES/32/2
					Nov vote	Dec vote			
Bulgaria		f	f	f	f	f			
Burkina Faso					a	ab	ab	ab	
Burundi					a	ab			a
Cabo Verde				f	ab	f			
Cambodia					ab	f			
Cameroon				a	a	f	a		
Canada	f	f	f	f	f	f			
Central African Republic				f					
Chad				a					
Chile		f	f	f	f	f	f	f	
China					a	ab	ab	ab	a
Colombia				f	ab	f			
Comoros				a	a	ab			
Congo					a	ab	ab	ab	a
Costa Rica					f	f		f	
Côte d'Ivoire				a	a			a	a
Croatia	f		f	f	f	f	f	f	
Cuba				f	a	f			f
Cyprus	f	f	f	f	f	f			
Czech Republic	f	f	f	f	f	f	f	f	
Democratic People's Republic of Korea				a	a	ab			
Democratic Republic of the Congo						ab			
Denmark	f	f	f	f	f	f			
Djibouti				a	a	ab	a		

Country	1	2	3	4	5	6	7
Dominica							
Dominican Republic							
Ecuador				f		f	f
Egypt					ab	a	
El Salvador				f	f	a	f
Equatorial Guinea							
Eritrea			f	a	f	a	
Estonia	f	f	f	f	f	f	f
Ethiopia			a	a	ab	a	a
Fiji				a	f	f	
Finland	f	f	f	f	f	f	
France	f	f	f	f	f	f	f
Gabon				f	f	a	a
Gambia				a	ab		
Georgia	f	f	f	f	f		
Germany	f	f	f	f	f	f	f
Ghana	f		a	a	ab	a	ab
Greece	f	f	f	f	f		
Grenada				a	a		
Guatemala		f	f	f	f	f	
Guinea					ab		
Guinea-Bissau			f		ab		
Guyana				a	f		
Haiti				a	f		
Honduras					f		
Hungary	f	f	f	f	f	f	
Iceland	f	f	f	f	f	f	
India			f	f	f	ab	ab
Indonesia			a	a	ab	a	a
Iran			a	a	ab		a

(Continued)

	Brazilian Resolution (2003) E/CN.4/2003/L.92	New Zealand Statement (2005)	Norway Statement (2006)	Argentina Statement/ Counterstatement (GA/2008)	Res on ESA Executions (GA/2010) Nov vote	Dec vote	2011 HR Council Res A/HRC/ RES/17/19	2014 HR Council Res A/HRC/ RES/27/32	2016 HR Council Res A/HRC/ RES/32/2
Iraq	f			a		ab			
Ireland		f	f	f		f		f	
Israel	f			f		ab		f	
Italy		f	f	f		f		f	
Jamaica						f			
Japan				f		f	f	f	
Jordan				a		ab	a		
Kazakhstan						f		ab	
Kenya				a		f		a	a
Kiribati									
Kuwait				a		ab		a	
Kyrgyzstan				a		f			a
Lao People's Democratic Republic						f			
Latvia			f	f		f			f
Lebanon				a		ab			
Lesotho						ab			
Liberia						ab			
Libya				a		ab			
Liechtenstein	f		f	f		f			
Lithuania			f	f		f			
Luxembourg	f	f	f	f		f			
Madagascar						ab			
Malawi				a		f			
Malaysia				a		ab	a		

Country								
Maldives				a	a	a	a	a
Mali			a	a	f			a
Malta	f		f	f	f			
Marshall Islands								
Mauritania		f	a	ab	ab	a		
Mauritius	f		f	f	f	f	f	f
Mexico	f	f	f	f	f	f	f	
Micronesia			f	f				
Monaco			f	f				
Mongolia	f		f	ab	ab		f	f
Montenegro			f	f	f		f	
Morocco			a	a	ab		a	a
Mozambique			a	a	f			
Myanmar			a	a	f			
Namibia			a	a	ab		ab	ab
Nauru					ab			
Nepal			f	f	f			f
Netherlands	f	f	f	f	f			
New Zealand	f	f	f	f	f			
Nicaragua			f	f	f			
Niger			a	a	f			
Nigeria	f		a	a	ab	a	a	a
Norway	f	f	f	f	f	f		
Oman			a	a	ab			
Pakistan			a	a	ab	a	a	
Palau					ab			
Panama	f		f	f	f			f
Papua New Guinea				ab	f			f
Paraguay		f	f	f	f			f
Peru	f			f	f		f	
Philippines				ab	f	f	f	ab
Poland	f	f	f	f	f			
Portugal	f	f	f	f	f	f	f	f

(Continued)

	Brazilian Resolution (2003) E/CN.4/2003/L.92	New Zealand Statement (2005)	Norway Statement (2006)	Argentina Statement/ Counterstatement (GA/2008)	Res on ESA Executions (GA/2010) Nov vote	Res on ESA Executions (GA/2010) Dec vote	2011 HR Council Res A/HRC/ RES/17/19	2014 HR Council Res A/HRC/ RES/27/32	2016 HR Council Res A/HRC/ RES/32/2
Qatar				a	a	ab	a		a
Republic of Korea		f	f		f	f	f	f	f
Republic of Moldova		f	f	f	f	f	a	f	
Romania		f	f	f	f	f	a		
Russian Federation				a	a	ab	a	a	a
Rwanda				a	a	f			
Saint Kitts and Navy					a	f			
Saint Lucia				a	a	ab			
Saint Vincent and the Grenadines					a	f			
Samoa					f	f			
San Marino				f	f	f			
Sao Tome and Principe				f	f	f			
Saudi Arabia				a	a	a	a	a	a
Senegal				a	a	ab	a		
Serbia	f		f	f	f	f			
Seychelles									
Sierra Leone				a	a	ab		ab	
Singapore				f	ab	f	f		
Slovakia	f	f	f	f	f	f			
Slovenia			f	f	f	f			f
Solomon Island				a	a	f			
Somalia				a	a	f			
South Africa					a	f		f	
South Sudan									
Spain	f	f	f	f	f	f	f	f	ab

Sri Lanka					ab			
Sudan			a	ab	ab			
Suriname			a	a	f			
Swaziland			a	a	ab			
Sweden	f		f	f	f			
Switzerland	f		f	f	f	f		f
Syria			a	a	ab			
Tajikistan			a	a	ab			
Thailand			f	ab	f	f	f	
The former Yugoslav Republic of Macedonia		f	f	f	f			f
Timor-Leste		f	f	f	f			
Togo			a					a
Tonga					f			
Trinidad and Tobago				ab	f			
Tunisia			a	a	f			
Turkey					ab			
Turkmenistan			a		f			
Tuvalu				ab	ab			
Uganda			a	a	ab	a		
Ukraine		f		f	f	f		
United Arab Emirates	f		a	a	ab			a
United Kingdom	f		f	f	f	f	f	f
United Republic of Tanzania			a	a	ab			
United States of America			f	f	ab	f	f	
Uruguay	f		f	f	f	f		
Uzbekistan			a	a	f			
Vanuatu			f	ab	f			
Venezuela	f		f	f	f			f

(*Continued*)

	Brazilian Resolution (2003) E/CN.4/2003/L.92	New Zealand Statement (2005)	Norway Statement (2006)	Argentina Statement/ Counterstatement (GA/2008)	Syrian Statement (GA/2008)	Res on ESA Executions (GA/2010)		2011 HR Council Res A/HRC/ RES/17/19	2014 HR Council Res A/HRC/ RES/27/32	2016 HR Council Res A/HRC/ RES/32/2
						Nov vote	Dec vote			
Viet Nam						a	f		f	f
Yemen			a			a	ab			
Zambia						a	ab	ab		
Zimbabwe			a			a	ab			

Index